A Hundred Years
in the
HIGHLANDS

A Hundred Years
in the
HIGHLANDS

OSGOOD HANBURY MACKENZIE
OF INVEREWE

*Edited and with an
additional chapter by his daughter*
M.T. SAWYER
OF INVEREWE

Foreword by
THE EARL OF WEMYSS
*President Emeritus,
The National Trust for Scotland*

Birlinn

This edition first published in 1995 by
Birlinn Limited
West Newington House
10 Newington Road
Edinburgh EH9 1QS

www.birlinn.co.uk

First published in 1921 by Edward Arnold and Co.,
revised edition published in 1949

ISBN 1 874744 29 7

British Library Cataloguing-in-Publication Data
A Catalogue record for this book is available from
the British Library

Printed and bound by Antony Rowe Ltd, Chippenham

To my Daughter
Mairi T. Nic Coinnich (Mrs. R.W. Sawyer)
*who loves the Gaelic and keeps our simple Highland
ways, and for whose strong, unchanging love
I am forever grateful*

FOREWORD TO THE TENTH EDITION
by the Earl of Wemyss

THE good fortune which attended Osgood Mackenzie for a lifetime has pursued his book. There have been ten editions and impressions since it was first published in 1921. When it reappeared in 1949, revised and with a new chapter added by Mairi Sawyer on the subject of the garden at Inverewe, it made a vivid impression on a generation to whom life in the Highlands in the nineteenth century was almost unimaginable. And its fame grows as the number of visitors to the garden mounts year by year.

The wonder and affection which Inverewe has aroused in hundreds of thousands of people would have delighted Mrs. Sawyer. I recall very clearly the discussions I had with her before she made a gift of Inverewe to the National Trust for Scotland in 1952. It was her hope that all the world would share her pleasure in the garden which her father had created and she had tended and enlarged with loving care. I think I may say her wish is being fulfilled: the record of 100,000 visitors, first established in 1969, has been exceeded in each succeeding year.

WEMYSS

PRESIDENT EMERITUS
The National Trust for Scotland

AUTHOR'S PREFACE

MY uncle, Dr. John Mackenzie, having left behind him ten manuscript volumes of Highland Memories, covering the period 1803 to 1860, and I, who inherited these manuscripts, having reached the age of seventy-nine, it has occurred to me that I might make a book of reminiscences which would give pleasure to those who reverence ancient customs and love the West Coast Highlands.

I make no pretence to the art of the writing man. The reader must be kind enough to imagine that he is sitting on the opposite side of a peat fire listening to the leisurely memories of one who has lived a great number of years, observant of the customs of his neighbours, attentive to things of the passing moment, and who finds an increasing pleasure, after a life of the open air, in dwelling on the times that are gone.

If my book should give pleasure to its readers, I shall be glad; if it should do anything to deepen affection and give them reverence for the noblest memories of our Scottish past, I shall be humbly grateful.

OSGOOD HANBURY MACKENZIE

TOURNAIG, POOLEWE,
March, 1921

EDITOR'S PREFACE
to the Revised Edition

My father died in 1922 and, as his only child, I inherited his properties, including the gardens here.

This book went out of print some time before 1939 and since then there have been many requests for a new edition to be published. Perhaps, as the old life of the Highlands becomes more and more a thing of the past, the desire to preserve, if not always its delights at any rate its memories, becomes stronger and I should like to feel that my father's contribution to all these things should not be forgotten.

To him, as they still are to me, the gardens at Inverewe were a special joy and pride. But in the original edition of the book he only devoted one short chapter to them. I believe, therefore, that readers would like to hear more about their progress during the past twenty-five years since the original book was issued: for they comprise, in many ways, a living link between the past and the present. To this end I have therefore added a further chapter in the new edition.

Several people have suggested that I might edit some of the text. But, rightly or wrongly, I have preferred to leave it practically in its original state. My father explained in his Preface that he made "no pretence to the art of the writing man," and I think it would only detract from the essential character of his narrative if I were to attempt to interfere with it at all. In certain instances, however, I have effected minor alterations, sometimes of fact, in the light of kind criticisms which have been received from the readers of the earlier editions. Some of these came from the Dominions and Colonies, where there are so many people of Highland blood and from which the garden derives some of its essential beauty.

M. T. SAWYER

INVEREWE,
POOLEWE,
March, 1949

CHAPTERS

I. PARENTAGE   17

*Birth in Brittany—Curious coincidences—My father's death and burial—
An eventful voyage—Highland stage-coach in winter—The Gairloch property—
Annual migrations—Incidents on the journey—The old Inn—Milkers and their
cows—Pandemonium—Tigh Dige, the old home*

II. FAMILY HISTORY   28

*Our Gairloch ancestor—Threat by Lews Macleods—Murder of kins-
man's two boys—Retribution—Slaughter of the Macleods—Treachery to the
Mackenzies—Fight on the ship—An unpopular clan—Personal beauty of the
Macleods—The 'forty-five—The family bard—Search for Prince Charlie—
The secret chamber*

III. CHILDHOOD   37

*Potato blight—Relief work at Gairloch—The Loch Maree road—I cut the
first sod—The first wheeled vehicle—Transport before the days of roads—My
mother's love for Gaelic—Schools in the parish—My mother as parish doctor—
Early recollections—My grandmother as housekeeper—Old-time customs and
habits—Climatic changes—Strawberries in June—Disappearance of wild bee*

IV. BOYHOOD   51

*Amusements—Nesting on Loch Maree—Pine marten and the gulls—
Trout-fishing—My uncle's adventure on the hill—Fox-hunter's eerie experience—Eagles' nests—The shepherd's ruse—Stormy petrels in Longa—Otter-
hunting—Polecats—My education—Successful young man—Highland lairds
and the Gaelic—Family affection—My grand-uncles—Kidnapping recruits for
the Army—Kerrysdale garden*

V. YOUTH   62

*My first gun—Game in the old days—Introduction of rabbits into the
Highlands—Abundance of vermin—Martens as robbers of gardens—The
sheep-killer: a unique experience—Stories of the wild-cat—Simple shooting—
Expeditions to the Shiant Islands—Sea-fishing—Boatloads of puffins—Netting
rock-pigeons—Tour in Normandy—Visit to 1851 Exhibition*

VI. VOYAGE TO ST. KILDA 70

*We set out—Our vessel—At Lochmaddy—The Sound of Harris—
Countess of Dunmore's school—At Rodal—Tossing on the ocean—Arrival at
St. Kilda—Difficulties of landing—Description of the island—Primitive houses
—The church—A healthy people—The fulmar and the puffin—Solan-geese—
Return voyage—Typical South Harris house—What I saw in the "black house"*

VII. THE LEWS 87

*My oldest story—A Stornoway whale-hunt—My first visit to Lews Castle
—Plentiful sport—Salmon-fishing on the Ewe—Netting in my uncle's time—
Kate Archy and her chickens—More expeditions—Lawsuit with Seaforth—
Foolish and expensive litigation*

VIII. EARLY SPORTING DAYS 98

*Trip to Germany—A quick return—Shooting over Inverewe—My first dog
—On the hill—The pointers—Dogs versus badger—Breeding setters—My
friend "Fan"—A wonderful hunter—Shooting experiences—Increased sporting
area—Big bags—A wandering quail—A ptarmigan at sea-level—Late Dr.
Warre's best day's sport—Flock of strange grouse—Some curious shots—
Swan-shooting*

IX. DEER-STALKING 109

*Our guns—Deer asleep—A monster royal stag—In a corrie—A ten-pointer
—A difficult journey—Wounded deer—Gill the lurcher—A "grand beast"—
Fox versus roebuck—The poachers—Cave robber—Modern stalkers—Donald
the gillie—Drowning the deer*

X. DEER-STALKING—continued. 119

*A cheap licence—Start for the forest—The shepherd's bothy—Almost un-
bearable—The two stags—Present to the laird—Ceremony at the big house—
An eccentric laird—His ideas about a kilt—My biggest stag—Cornish tenant's
disgust—Watson and the eagles—Two and a half brace before breakfast—
Vermin-killing—Mystery of the heronry—A handy drug*

XI. THE FIONN LOCH 128

*Description of Loch—A snake story—Eyrie of white-tailed eagles—
Expedition for eggs—The Osprey's Loch—Goosander's nest—Extinct birds—
A hare drive—Ptarmigan and grouse—Wild cats and otters—My tame otter—
Amazing fishing records*

XII. REMINISCENCES   139

*My grandfather—His dress and habits—Highland hospitality—Shooting
with flint-locks—Dinner at Tigh Dige—Training of landlords—Loyalty of the
people—Stories of hard times*

XIII. AGRICULTURE   150

*The runrig system—Caschrom and croman—The modern crofter—
Modes of cultivation—Sea-ware for the land—Cultivating enclosures—Cattle,
sheep, and goats—A hard-working people*

XIV. CHURCH AND STATE   156

*The disruption—Old-time Communion—People gather from all quarters—
—"The Bed of the White Cow"—Congregation of three thousand—Preachers'
warnings—Sabbath observance—The Parish Manse—Minister and his glebe—
Minister's wig in the cream—Funerals—Copious supplies of whisky—Coffin
left behind—A jovial outing—A great funeral—Parliamentary elections—How
votes were secured*

XV. .SMUGGLING AND SHEEP-STEALING   171

*Drinking habits—The Rover's Bride—Justice of the Peace's qualms of
conscience—Attitude of the clergy—The gaugers and the people—Smuggling
stories—Sheep-stealing stories*

XVI. LOCAL SUPERSTITIONS   179

*Lunatics—The Holy Island cure—Heuk Donald at Tain—Inverness judge
and "the calf"—Dingwall's doctor's encounter with Jock—Witches—Curing the
cows—The cure for epilepsy—Apparitions—Fairies and kelpies—Draining the
Beiste Loch—The laird's revenge*

XVII. THE FAMOUS GAIRLOCH PIPERS   190

XVIII. THE INVEREWE POLICIES (1)   195

XIX. THE INVEREWE POLICIES (2) *by the Editor* (M. T. SAWYER)   205

XX. VANISHING BIRDS   210

XXI. PEAT   214

ILLUSTRATIONS

1. Map of Gairloch and surrounding country.

2. John MacKenzie of Eileanach.

3. The Old Gairloch Mansion House, An Tigh Dige, The Moat House.

4. Facsimile Extracts from Dr. John MacKenzie's *'Memories'*.

5. Inverewe House.

6. Inverewe House on fire, 1914.
   Inverewe House, the remains after the fire, 1914.

7. Inverewe Gardens in its impressive West Highland setting.

8. The splendour of Inverewe Gardens in the 1980's.

CHAPTER I

I WAS born on the 13th of May, 1842, at the Château de Tal-houet, not far from the little town of Quimperlé, in the Mor-bihan, Brittany. It seems I was destined from the very beginning to pass through life in the atmosphere of the Gulf Stream and among the Celts, for my dear mother told me the servants in the château all spoke Breton among themselves, and were like west-coast Highlanders in every way, except that they had the fear of wolves added to that of ghosts and goblins when they had to go out at night and pass through the Forest de Barbebleue which surrounded the château.

As I left France when I was only just a year old, I cannot tell much about our life in Brittany, except that the family consisted of my father, Sir Francis Mackenzie, fifth baronet and twelfth laird of Gairloch; my mother, Mary Hanbury, or Mackenzie; and my two half-brothers—Kenneth, who became the sixth baronet and thirteenth laird, and Francis, who was just a year younger, the boys being respectively ten and nine years of age. There were in the household a young French tutor and a Scottish maid, and my father had brought an Aberdeenshire salmon-fisher with him, with the usual appliances, such as nets, etc., for the capture of the salmon in the River Ellé. But though there were, and doubtless are, salmon in that river, I do not think the fishing enterprise proved much of a success.

My mother told me that immediately after my birth I was taken in charge by the *accoucheuse*, a Madame Le Blanc, but during the first night my mother's sharp ears thought they heard some small cries from a distant room. So, not thinking for a moment of her-self and the danger to her life, she sprang out of her bed and made straight for our room, where she found Madame Le Blanc sound asleep and no one attending to her precious son, whom she snatched up in her arms and carried back to her bed; no one else was allowed to have charge of him from that day forward.

Although my father had a big extent of *chasse* to shoot over, there was no game to speak of, and the bags consisted chiefly of squirrels, which it was the fashion there to eat, and of which pies were made until the Breton cook struck against preparing them, declaring they suggested skinned babies to her. The food in those days was very poor in Brittany, and the peasants subsisted chiefly on porridge made of *blé noir* (buck-wheat). Often, to get decent rolls and bread, my father had to drive to the town of L'Orient, a good many miles away.

I was registered in Brittany by the name of Hector, after my paternal grandfather, Sir Hector; but afterwards my father, recollecting that the eldest son of my Uncle John Mackenzie was called Hector, thought two of the same name in the family might be confusing, so, when we reached England and I was christened, the name of Osgood was given me, after my maternal grandfather, Osgood Hanbury, of Holfield Grange, Essex, and also after my cousin, who was my godfather. The eldest sons of these Hanburys were always called Osgood from 1730, when John Hanbury, son of Charles and Grace Hanbury, of Pontymoil and other estates in Monmouthshire, married Anne, daughter and heiress of Henry Osgood, of Holfield Grange, who held 3,392 acres of land in the parish of Coggeshall. I have always rather regretted that my original name of Hector was not adhered to, as our family has, since about 1400, been known as Clan Eachainn Ghearloch (children of Hector of Gairloch), and Eachainn MacCoinnich would have been so much more appropriate when writing my signature in Gaelic.

My readers may wonder at my writing anything about a place which I could not possibly have viewed with intelligent eyes when I left it, but I renewed acquaintance with it many years later. When I was about thirty my mother and I made a tour through Normandy and Brittany, one of the chief aims of which was to visit my birthplace. I remember we arrived at Quimperlé on a Saturday evening, and I soon found out that the following day there was to be a religious festival, what they called in Brittany a "Pardon," finishing up in the evening with unlimited music and dancing in the Grande Place of the town. Thousands of peasants had come in from the surrounding country, many of the older men in the native costume—their nether garments being like the most voluminous of knickerbockers—and the women with their wonderful coiffes. Dancing was in full swing to the music of the biniou, the Breton bagpipes, and the music and dancing were certainly first-cousins to our Highland bagpipe music and reels.

After a struggle I managed to make my way through the crowd to the side of the old piper, and during the short intervals between the dances I carried on a brisk conversation with him in French on the subject of bagpipes. I informed him that we had nearly the same kind of pipes in the North of Scotland, and that we also spoke an ancient language related to the Breton. He suddenly brightened up and became quite excited. Talking of Écosse, he said, reminded him of days long gone by, when he was a lad, and there was a Monsieur Écossais living in the Château de Talhouet not far away, a big gentleman with reddish hair and whiskers. Whilst monsieur was there, a baby son was born and a dance was given, for which he was hired as musician. My mother could well remember that dance being given and the hiring of the piper, and here was the very man who had played all night in honour of my birth.

Another curious coincidence I must mention here in connection with the Château de Talhouet, which was in olden times the seat of a great Breton nobleman, the Marquis de Talhouet. About five years ago, during the late war, when Lochewe was a naval base, a French warship came in, and, as none of the naval officers stationed at Aultbea happened to be very fluent in French and the French officers were said not to be very good at English, I was asked to entertain half a dozen of them at luncheon. It turned out that the mother of one of these officers was then actually owner of the Château de Talhouet and was residing in it.

On the Monday after the gay scene in the Grande Place of Quimperlé, my mother and I drove out to the château that she might show me the very room in which I was born; but though the then owner, whose name was, I think, the Comte de Richemond, was most kind and hospitable, he had so much improved and altered the château that my mother could hardly make sure of the actual room where I first saw the light. One thing, however, she did recognise, which she had often described to me, and that was a magnificent specimen of the tulip-tree which grew on the lawn. How well do I remember the dinner in the inn at Quimperlé, where everything was very old-fashioned, and where the host sat at the head and the hostess at the foot of the table. There was great excitement over something unusual which had occurred that morning—namely, the catching by the gendarmes of a young priest poaching the river, with a fresh-run salmon in his possession. The ladies all took the side of the priest, whilst most of the men supported the authorities. The salmon was to be sold by public auction, and the ladies all swore solemnly that none of them would bid at the sale, as it was monstrous that their Father Confessor should be deprived of the fish which he had captured so cleverly.

When my father and his family left Brittany, we stayed a short time in Jersey, but all I can remember to have heard of the visit to that charming island was that I there first showed a love of music, which has continued all through my life. I was told that when a brass band played I almost jumped out of my mother's arms. A friend of my father, a Colonel Lecouteur, gave a dinner, and the dessert consisted of pears only, there being thirty dishes, each containing a different variety. So it seems that their culture was pretty well advanced even as far back as 1842.

And now my memory of the events that happened for a couple of years is more or less vague, and I can depend only on what I was told by others. Soon after our arrival in England my father became very ill, and, according to the stupid practice of doctors in those days, he was bled in the arm, erysipelas set in, and he died in the course of a few days. His remains were taken north by sea, from London to Invergordon, by my mother and her brother and sister, to be buried in the family burying-place in the old ruined Priory of Beauly. I was just a year old when this calamity happened, and consequently can remember nothing of the voyage north or anything else for some time after. But subsequent voyages of a like kind when I was four or five years old made impressions on me which have never been forgotten. How well I remember, as though it were only yesterday, a horrible voyage from Invergordon to London in a kind of paddle-boat, which lasted nine whole days. We called at every small port along the Banffshire and Aberdeenshire coasts for dead meat for the London market. Stacks of it were piled up on the deck, and consisted chiefly of dead pigs. By way of amusing me, our butler, Sim Eachainn (Simon Hector), cut off many of the black and white tails and presented them to me as toys. Then we were stuck for some days in a dense fog at the mouth of the Thames. It was not, however, so long a voyage as my uncle took as a young man, when he was seventeen days in a smack sailing between London and Inverness; and even then he never reached it, but had to disembark at Findhorn in Morayshire.

On our return journey north my mother wished to go by land, but it was, if possible, even less successful. I cannot remember how we got to Perth, but from there we travelled by the Highland stage-coach. It was mid-winter, and we managed to get as far as Blair Atholl, when a violent snowstorm started, and a few miles beyond the village the coach was suddenly brought to a standstill by trees being blown across the road both in front and behind us. A runner was despatched for a squad of men with saws and axes, but the blizzard was so severe that by the time help came the coach could not be moved on account of the depth of the snow, and we got back to Blair Inn by the help of a very high-wheeled dog-cart. How well I remember being lifted by our faithful Simon and carried in his arms to the trap. After being kept prisoners at Blair for several days, we managed to get back to Perth, whence we got to Aberdeen by the newly opened railway, and from there to Inverness by steamboat. Thus we had to fall back upon the sea after all to get us north.

My father in his will had appointed my mother and Thomas Mackenzie, the laird of Ord, as trustees for the Gairloch property during my elder half-brother's minority, and my father's brother, John Mackenzie, M.D., of Eileanach, was to be factor on the estate. For the first six months or year after my father's death my mother resided at Conon House, near the county town of Dingwall, which was the east-coast residence of the Gairloch family. The Conon property was a comparatively small one, with a small population, whereas Gairloch consisted of some 170,000 acres and a large crofter population of several thousand souls; so my mother felt it her duty to remove there and make it her permanent home. It was not very easy getting from Conon to Gairloch in those days, for, though a road had been made from Dingwall to Kenlochewe, or rather two miles farther on to Rudha n'Fhamhair (the Giant's Point), at the upper end of Loch Maree, there was still no road for some twelve miles along the loch-side, and often it was stormy and the loch difficult to navigate in small rowing-boats.

But Gairloch was far more difficult of access in the days of my grandfather and my uncles. In those days the larger tenants had, if required, to provide several days' labour by men and horses for the journey. My uncle writes:

"My eyes and ears quite deceived me if those called out on these migration duties did not consider it real good fun, considering the amount of food and drink which was always at their command."

A troop of men and some thirty ponies came from Gairloch, and would arrive, say, on a Tuesday night, and all Wednesday a big lot of ponies, hobbled and crook-saddled, were strewn over our lawns at Conon, with a number of men and women helpers hard at work packing. Everything had to go west—flour, groceries, linen, plate, boys and babies, and I have heard that my father was carried to Gairloch on pony-back in a kind of cradle when he was only a few weeks old. The plan usually followed was to start the mob of men and ponies about four o'clock on the Thursday afternoon for the little inn at Scatwell at the foot of Strathconon; and as there was a road of a kind thus far and no farther, the old yellow family coach carried "the quality" (*i.e.*, the gentry) there before dark.

There were several great difficulties in those days. One was the crossing of the various fords over the rivers, and the next was keeping dry all the precious things contained on the pack-saddles, including the babies. The great waterproofer, Mackintosh, was unborn and rubber was still unknown, so they just had to do their best with bits of sheep-skins and deer-skins, which were not very effective in a south-westerly gale, with rain such as one is apt to catch along Druima Dubh Achadh na Sine, the Black Ridge of Storm Field, as Achnasheen is very properly called in Gaelic.

Next morning the start was made at six o'clock right up Strath-conon and across the high *beallach* (pass) into Strath Bran, and on and on till Kenlochewe was reached, which ended the second day at about seven o'clock at night. I have been told that my grand-father was always met at the top of Glendochart, where one first comes in sight of the loch, by the whole male population of Ken-lochewe, every man with his flat blue bonnet under his arm, and they followed the laird's cavalcade bareheaded till it crossed the river to the inn. The old inn in those days was on what we should now call the wrong side of the river, and the crossing was often a great difficulty. Sometimes the children were carried over by men on stilts, which was thought great fun by them. The welcome at the inn my uncle described as "grand." The poor landlady was twice widowed, both her husbands having been drowned in try-ing to get people across this wild river on horseback when it was in flood. My uncle fancied that what made the widow suffer most was perhaps the fact that neither husband was ever found, both being at the bottom of Loch Maree, and that she had not had the great relief and even "pleasure" of burying each of them with un-limited whisky, according to custom. I can well remember one of her sons. He was by far the most skilful carpenter in our part of the country, and was always known as Eachainn na Banosdair (Hector of the Hostess). My uncle says that if ever the Gairloch family had a devotee it was Banosdair Ceann-Loch-Iubh (the hostess of Ken-lochewe), and he believed she would cheerfully have gone to the gallows if she were quite sure that would please the laird.

The following morning the party had only two miles to go to Rudha n'Fhamhair, where the family and all the precious goods and chattels were stowed away in a small fleet of boats and rowed or sailed some ten or twelve miles down the loch to Slatadale, where the then comparatively new narrow bit of road, more or less adapted to wheels, ran from this bay of Loch Maree to the old mansion of Tigh Dige nam gorm Leac, which, as my uncle says,

23

"was looked upon by us Gairlochs as the most perfect spot on God's earth." For the sake of the boys a halt was always made at one of the twenty-five islands in the loch for a good hunt for gulls' eggs, but in truth it did not require much hunting, for my uncle says he and his brothers could hardly keep from treading on the eggs, the nests were so plentiful among the heather and juniper. I can remember them equally numerous till I was about fifty years old, when the lesser black-backed gulls very gradually began to go back and back in numbers, until, alas! they are now all but extinct.

In my uncle's description of the arrival of the cavalcade on the Saturday evening at the old home, the most perfect wild Highland glen any lover of country scenery could wish to see, he says that no sheep had ever set hoof in it; only cattle were allowed to bite a blade of grass there. The consequence was that the braes and wooded hillocks were a perfect jungle of primroses and bluebells and honeysuckle and all sorts of orchids, including *Habenarias* and the now quite extinct *Epipactis*, which then whitened the ground, and which my uncle says he used to send as rare specimens to southern museums. May I remark here that in the course of my long life in the parish of Gairloch I have only twice had the pleasure of seeing the *Epipactis ensifolia*—once near the Bank of Scotland at Gairloch about thirty years ago, and one other specimen on the edge of the stream of the Ewe fifty yards above the boathouse at Inveran. I found plenty of them in the woods of the Pyrenees.

My uncle continues: "Having arrived at long last at the end of our three days' journey, we boys wanted but little rocking ere we were asleep in our hammocks. Next morning (Sunday) before six, all who were new to the place called out 'Goodness gracious, what's the matter, and what's all this awful noise about?' for sixty cows and sixty calves were all bellowing their hardest after having been separated for the twelve hours of the night. They were within eighty yards of the château, and, assisted by some twenty herds and milkers screaming and howling, they made uproar enough to alarm any stranger just waking from sleep, who expected a quiet, solemn west-coast Sabbath morning. This was a twice a day arrangement. Eventually the grass in the Baile Mor Glen was eaten pretty bare, and then the whole lot of them went off to the shieling of Airidh na Cloiche (Shieling of the Stone) for the summer.

"There was a dyke about one hundred yards long between the entrance-gates at the bottom of the lawn and the Allt Glas burn which kept the cows and calves separate, to the great indignation of both parties, who bellowed out their minds pretty plainly. Domhnall Donn (Brown Donald), the head cowman, brought his wailing friends the cows to the west side of the wall, and his subordinates brought the calves from their woody bedrooms where they had passed the night on the east side. And then began an uproar of 'Are you there, my darling?' 'Oh yes, mother dear, wild for my breakfast.' Then the troupe of milkmaids entered among the mob of bawling cows by one of the small calf-gates in the wall. They carried their pails and three-legged little stools and *buarachs* (hobbles) of strong hair rope, with a loop at one end and a large button on the other. The button was always made of rowan-tree wood, so that milk-loving fairies might never dare to keep from the pail the milk of a cow whose hind-legs were *buarach* bound.

"All was soon ready to begin. A young helper stood at each gate with a rowan switch to flick back the over-anxious calves till old Domhnall sang out, looking at a cow a dairymaid was ready to milk, named, perhaps, Busdubh (Black Muzzle), 'Let in Busdubh's calf,' who was quite ready at the wicket. Though to our eyes the sixty black calves were all alike, the helpers switched away all but young Busdubh, who sprang through the wicket; after a moment's dashing at the wrong cow by mistake, and being quickly horned away, there was Busdubh Junior opposite to its mother's milker sucking away like mad for its supply, while the milkmaid milked like mad also, to get her share of it. The calf, I suspect, often got the lesser half, for the dairy people liked to boast of their heaps of butter and cheese, leaving the credit or discredit of the yearly drove of young market cattle to Domhnall and his subordinates. I have seen young Busdubh getting slaps in the face from its enemy the milker, who thought she was getting less than her share of the spoil; and then calfy was dragged to the wicket and thrust out, and perhaps Smeorach's (Thrush's) calf halloaed for next. This uproar lasted from six till nine, when, justice having been dispensed to all concerned, Donald and company drove the cows away to their pastures, and the junior helpers removed the very discontented calves to their quarters till near 6 p.m., when the same operation was repeated.

"And then the procession of milkmaids stepped away to the dairy, which was a projecting wing of the Tigh Dige and is now part of the garden, carrying the milk in small casks open at the top with a pole through the rope-handle of the cask, the two milkers having the pole ends on their shoulders. And now as to the dairy. No finery of china or glass or even coarse earthenware was ever seen in those days; instead of these, there were very many flat, shallow, wooden dishes and a multitude of churns and casks and kegs, needing great cleansing, otherwise the milk would have gone bad. And, big boilers being also unknown, how was the disinfecting done, and how was hot water produced? Few modern folk would ever guess. Well, the empty wooden dishes of every shape and size were placed on the stone floor, and, after being first rinsed out with cold water and scrubbed with little heather brushes, they were filled up again, and red-hot *dornagan* (stones as large as a man's fist), chosen from the seashore and thoroughly polished by the waves of centuries, which had been placed by the hundred in a huge glowing furnace of peat, were gripped by long and strong pairs of tongs and dropped into the vessels. Three or four red-hot stones would make the cold water boil instantly right over, and the work was then accomplished. But oh, the time it took, and the amount of good Gaelic that had to be expended, and more or less wasted, before the great dairy could be finally locked till evening came round again."

In my grandfather's day no colour was considered right for Highland cattle but black. The great thing then was to have a fold of black cows. No one would look at the reds and yellows and cream and duns, which are all the rage nowadays. Though the blacks have since become unpopular, I have been told by the very best old judges of Highland cattle that there is nothing to beat the blacks for hardiness, and that the new strains of fancy-coloured cattle are much softer, and have not the same constitutions.

The Tigh Dige (pronounced *Ty digué*), or Moat House, was so called because the original house belonging to us, which was down in the hollow below the present mansion, was surrounded by a moat and a drawbridge. The first Sir Alexander, my grandfather's grandfather, the Tighearna Crubach (the Lame Laird), finding it inconvenient, started building the present house about 1738, and as it was the very first instance in all the country round of a slated house, the old name Tigh Dige was continued, with the addition given to it of nam gorm Leac (of the Blue Slabs). I believe iron nails were used. But I remember the late Dowager Lady Middleton telling me that when they bought Applecross and had to take off a part of the old roof of the house they found that the original slates had been fixed to the sarking with pegs of heather root. She had been told that a man had been employed a whole summer making heather pegs with his knife, right up in Corry Attadale, in the heart of the Applecross deer forest. This shows the difficulty of getting nails in those days.

It was long after this that some English tourists, finding the lovely Baile Mor Glen peculiarly rich in wild-flowers, proposed to my ancestor that it should be named Flowerdale. I am thankful to say I have never once in the course of my whole long life heard the house called otherwise in Gaelic than the Tigh Dige and the place am Baile Mor (the Great Town or Home). The cause of the flowers being so plentiful in the good old times was that neither my grandfather nor his forbears would ever hear of a sheep coming near the place, except on a rope to the slaughter-house. The stock consisted of sixty Highland milk cows and their sixty calves, besides all their followers of different ages. These were continually shifted from place to place, and this gave the plants and bulbs a chance of growing. I never saw the black cattle on the Baile Mor home farm, but my mother, who was married some years before I was born, saw the whole system in operation, and often told me all about it.

CHAPTER II

FAMILY HISTORY

SOME of my readers interested in genealogy may be glad to know something of our Gairloch ancestor, Eachainn Ruadh (Red Hector). It is since his day we have been known as Clan Eachainn Ghearloch. Hector was the second son of Alexander the sixth of Kintail; so that we were not by any means what would be called "upstarts" even in A.D. 1400. Hector Roy's mother was a daughter of the famous Ruairidh MacAlain of Moidart and Clanranald, whose wife was a granddaughter of the first Lord of the Isles by his wife Lady Margaret Stewart, daughter of King Robert II. Hector Roy also had royal blood in him on his father's side as well as on that of his mother; for his grandfather, Murdo the fifth of Kintail, married Finguala, daughter of Malcolm Macleod, third of Harris and Dunvegan, whose wife was Martha, daughter of Donald Stewart, Earl of Mar, nephew of King Robert the Bruce. The Gairlochs also have Norwegian blood in their veins, as Tormod Macleod, second of Harris and Dunvegan, and father of Malcolm, was a grandson of Olave the Black, the last of the Norwegian Kings who owned the Isle of Man, and who died about 1237.

Gairloch belonged to the Macleods in the earlier part of 1400. When Hector Roy was a young man it was owned by his brother-in-law, who had married Alexander the sixth of Kintail's daughter. Allan Macleod of Gairloch married as his second wife a daughter of Macleod of the Lews. The Lews Macleods were also otherwise nearly connected with Allan of Gairloch. Well, it seems that two brothers of Macleod of the Lews had sworn an oath that no one with a drop of Mackenzie blood in him should ever succeed to Gairloch, and crossing from the Lews they landed at Gairloch. Allan Macleod, perhaps from having heard some whispers of the ideas of his relatives, had placed his family for safety on a small crannog or artificial island stronghold in Loch Tollie, along which the road from Gairloch to Poolewe now runs, which must have been an uncomfortable residence for a wife with her own young daughter and her three stepsons.

It seems that these Macleods, the day after their landing, got word of the fact that Allan had left the island that morning, and had gone to fish on the Ewe. They found him asleep on the river-bank at Cnoc na michomhairle (the Mound or Knoll of Bad Advice), and at once made him "short by the head," which was the term then in use for beheading. Retracing their steps to the island, they managed to get ferried across to it, and, informing the unfortunate widow of what they had done to her husband, they tore the two boys from her knees—the third boy was for-tunately absent—carried them along to a small glen through which the Poolewe road now passes, and at a spot called Meall bhadaidh na Thaisg (the Rock of the Place of Burial) stabbed them both to the heart with their dirks. Their stepmother man-aged, through the strategy of one of her husband's retainers, to secure the blood-stained shirts of the boys, and sent them to their grandfather, Alexander the sixth, either at Brahan Castle or Eileandonan, and Alexander at once despatched his son (our ancestor Hector Roy) with the shirts along with him, as evidence of the atrocious deed, to report the matter in Edinburgh. His Majesty, on hearing of the crime, granted Hector a commission of fire and sword against the Macleods, and gave him a Crown Charter of the lands of Gairloch in his own favour, dated 1494. The two murderers were soon afterwards slain near South Eara-dale. But it took Eachainn Ruadh some years with his small army of Kintail men before he could drive the Macleods out of their stronghold of the Dun, or fort, on the rocky peninsula not far from the present Gairloch Parish Church, and he had many a tussle with them. For instance, one morning he had reason to believe that some of the head-men of the Macleods in the Dun were to try to find their way to the south round the head of the small bay of Ceann t-Sail, so, hiding himself behind a rock which jutted out on the shore just below the present Gairloch Bank, he waylaid them. The Macleods, not having any suspicion that the enemy was anywhere in the vicinity, came along singly, and as each one passed he rushed at him, stabbed him with his dirk, and dragged his body behind the rock, and was quite ready for the next. So his "bag" was three Macleods before breakfast, and thus he avenged the deaths of his two little nephews.

But peace by no means came at once, for the Macleods made various attempts to regain Gairloch, as will be seen from the following story taken from the *History of the Mackenzies*: "A considerable number of the younger Macleods who were banished from Gairloch were invited by their chief to pass Hogmanay night in the castle of Dunvegan. In the kitchen there was an old woman known as Mor Bhan (Fair Sarah), who was usually occupied in carding wool, and generally supposed to be a witch. After dinner the men began to drink, and when they had passed some time in this occupation they sent to the kitchen for Mor Bhan. She at once joined them in the great hall, and, having drunk one or two glasses along with them, she remarked that it was a very poor thing for the Macleods to be deprived of their own lands of Gairloch and to have to live in comparative poverty in Raasay and the Isle of Skye. 'But,' she said to them, 'prepare yourselves and start tomorrow for Gairloch, sailing in the black *birlinn* (war-boat), and you shall regain it, and I shall be a witness of your success when you return.' The men trusted her, believing she had the power of divination. In the morning they set sail for Gairloch. The black galley was full of the Macleods. It was evening when they entered the loch. They were afraid to land on the mainland, for they remembered the descendants of Domhnall Greannach (Rough Donald, a celebrated Macrae) were still there, and they knew the prowess of these Kintail men only too well. The Macleods, therefore, turned to the south side of the loch and fastened their *birlinn* to the Fraoch Eilean (Heather Island) in the sheltered bay beside Leac nan Saighead (Slab of the Arrows), between Shieldaig and Badachro. Here they decided to wait till morning, and then disembark and walk round the head of the loch. But all their movements had been well and carefully watched. Domhnall Odhar MacIain Leith and his brother Iain, the celebrated Macrae archers, recognised the *birlinn* of the Macleods and determined to oppose their landing. They walked round the head of the loch by Shieldaig, and posted themselves before daylight behind the Leac, a projecting rock overlooking the Fraoch Eilean. The steps on which they stood at the back of the rock are still pointed out. Domhnall Odhar, being of small stature, took the higher of the two ledges and Iain took the lower. Standing on these, they crouched down behind the rock, completely sheltered from the enemy, but commanding a full view of the island, while they were quite invisible to the Macleods on the island.

"As soon as the day dawned the two Macraes directed their arrows on the strangers, of whom a number were killed before their comrades were even aware of the direction from which the messenger of death came. The Macleods endeavoured to answer their arrows, but, not being able to see the foe, their efforts were of no effect. In the heat of the fight one of the Macleods climbed up the mast of the *birlinn* to discover the position of the enemy. Iain Odhar, perceiving this, took deadly aim at him when near the top of the mast. 'Oh,' says Donald, addressing John, 'you have sent a pin through his broth.' The slaughter continued, and the remainder of the Macleods hurried aboard their *birlinn*. Cutting the rope, they turned their heads seawards. By this time only two of their number were left alive. In their hurry to escape they left all the bodies of their slain companions unburied on the island. A rumour of the arrival of the Macleods had during the night spread through the district, and other warriors, such as Fionnlaidh Dubh na Saigheada and Fear Shieldaig, were soon at the scene of action, but all they had to do on their arrival was to assist in the burial of the dead Macleods. Pits were dug, into each of which a number of bodies were thrown, and mounds were raised over them which remain to this day, as anyone landing on the island may observe."

Almost the last fight with the Macleods was when Murdoch Mackenzie, second surviving son of John Roy Mackenzie, fourth of Gairloch, accompanied by Alexander Bayne, heir-apparent of Tulloch, and several brave men from Gairloch, sailed to the Isle of Skye in a vessel loaded with wine and provisions. It is said by some that Murdoch's intention was to secure in marriage the daughter and heir of line of Domhnall Dubh MacRuairidh (Donald Macleod). It is the unbroken tradition in Gairloch that John Macleod was a prisoner there, and was unmarried, and easily secured where he was. In the event of this marriage taking place—failing issue by John, then in the power of John Roy—the ancient rights of the Macleods would revert to the Gairloch family and a troublesome dispute would be finally settled. Whatever the real object of the trip to Skye, it proved disastrous. The ship found its way, whether intentionally on the part of the crew or forced by a great storm, to the sheltered bay of Kirkton of Raasay, opposite the present mansion-house, where young MacGillechallum of Raasay at the time resided. Anchor was cast, and young Raasay, hearing that Murdoch Mackenzie of Gairloch was on board, discussed the situation with his friend MacGillechallum Mor MacDhomhnaill Mhic Neill, who persuaded him to visit the ship as a friend and secure Mackenzie's person by stratagem, with a view to getting him afterwards exchanged for his own relative, John MacAilain Mhic Ruairidh, then prisoner in Gairloch. Acting on this advice, young Raasay, with MacGillechallum Mor and twelve of their men, started for the ship, leaving word with his bastard brother, Murdoch, to get ready all the men he could to go to their assistance in small boats as soon as the alarm was given.

Mackenzie received his visitors in the most hospitable and unsuspecting manner, and supplied them with as much wine and other viands as they could consume. Four of his men, however, feeling somewhat suspicious and fearing the worst, abstained from drinking. Alexander Bayne of Tulloch and the remainder of Murdoch's men partook of the good cheer to excess, and ultimately became so drunk that they had to retire below deck. Mackenzie, who sat between Raasay and MacGillechallum Mor, had not the slightest suspicion, when Macleod, seeing Murdoch alone, jumped up, turned suddenly round, and told him that he must become his prisoner. Mackenzie of Gairloch instantly started to his feet in a violent passion, laid hold of Raasay by the waist, and threw him down, exclaiming, "I would scorn to be your prisoner!" One of Raasay's followers, seeing his young chief treated thus, stabbed Murdoch through the body with his dirk. Mackenzie, finding himself wounded, stepped back to draw his sword, and his foot coming against some obstruction he stumbled over it and fell into the sea. Those on shore, observing the row, came out in their small boats, and seeing Mackenzie, who was a dexterous swimmer, manfully making for Sconsar on the opposite shore in Skye, they pelted him with stones, smashed in his head, and drowned him. The few of his men who kept sober, seeing their leader thus perish, resolved to sell their lives dearly, and, fighting like heroes, they killed the young laird of Raasay, along with MacGillechallum Mor, author of all the mischief, and his two sons. Young Bayne of Tulloch and his six inebriated attendants, who had followed him down below, hearing the uproar overhead, attempted to come on deck, but they were killed by the Macleods as they presented themselves through the hole. But not a soul of the Raasay men escaped alive from the swords of the sober four, who were ably assisted by the ship's crew.

Eventually matters became a little more peaceful, and we Mackenzies got Gairloch, which has never yet been bought or sold. I have occasion very frequently to pass the little island in Loch Tollie and the spot where Hector Roy slew the Macleods. And though I have been passing there now for over seventy years, I never do so without realising that but for the tragedy of the island in Loch Tollie, we should never have been Mackenzies of Gairloch, my nephew would not be Sir Kenneth Mackenzie, seventh baronet of Gairloch and thirteenth in direct succession to Hector Roy, and I should not be at Inverewe.

I may mention that for many generations the few Macleods left in the district were naturally very unpopular in the parish, even as late as my grandfather Sir Hector's time. If he asked a question as to the name of a man, and the man happened unluckily to be a Macleod, the answer to my grandfather was certain to be apologetic, and as follows: "*Le bhur cead Shir Eachainn se Leodach a th-ann*" ("By your leave, Sir Hector, it is a Macleod that is in him"). There is one thing, however, I must add in favour of the Macleods. My dear mother and I often remarked about the few scattered remnants of that clan among our crofter population, that they were distinguished by a very superior personal beauty. Often on our making enquiries regarding a specially handsome family of Mackenzies or some other clan, it would turn out that the mother or grandmother had been a Macleod. Another thing we noticed was the similarity of the type of face of our crofter Macleods to our friends the Dunvegan and other Skye Macleods. They are usually tall, with pale, oval faces, blue eyes, and specially fine aquiline noses, never with flat and broad faces, with sandy hair, snub noses, and red cheeks, such as are to be found in other clans.

And now I ought perhaps to say something about what Gairloch did in the '45. Well, I fear I can tell very little except that my grandfather's grandfather, Sir Alexander, the second baronet, called the Tighearna Crubach on account of his being lame, did not turn out as did many of his clan, and although a good many Gairloch, Poolewe, and Kenlochewe men were at the battle of Culloden, they were followers of the laird of Torridon and other smaller lairds, and were not led there by my ancestor, who succeeded to Gairloch on his coming of age in 1721, and therefore must have been about forty-six and in his prime at the time of Culloden. He had hardly finished the building of his mansion, the new Tigh Dige, and was doubtless proud of having accomplished the great feat of covering it with *leacan gorma* (blue slabs), and could not be bothered with such dangerous politics at the time. Sir Alexander was a great improver of his property, and was in all respects a careful and good man of business, and, after Culloden, when John Mackenzie of Meddat applied to him in favour of Lord Macleod, son of the Earl of Cromartie who took so prominent a part in the rising of 1745 and was in very tightened circumstances, Sir Alexander replied in a letter dated May, 1749, in the following somewhat unsympathetic terms: "Sir,—I am favoured with your letter, and am extremely sorry Lord Cromartie's circumstances should obliege him to solicit the aide of small gentlemen. I much raither he hade dyed sword in hand even where he was ingag'd then be necessitate to act such a pairt. I have the honour to be nearly related to him, and to have been his companion, but will not supply him at this time, for which I believe I can give you the best reason in the world, and the only one possible for me to give, and that is that I cannot."

My uncle, however, refers in his Notes to the '45 period in Gairloch, and tells a story of his great-grandfather as related by the family bard, Alasdair Buidhe Maciamhair (Yellow Sandy McIver). I shall quote from my uncle's Notes about the bard:

"This reminds me that one of our summer evening's amusements was getting the bard to the dining-room after dinner, where, well dined below stairs and primed by a bumper of port wine, he would stand up, and with really grand action and eloquence, give us poem after poem of Ossian in Gaelic, word for word, exactly as translated by Macpherson not long before then, and stupidly believed by many to be Macpherson's own composition, though had Alasdair heard anyone hinting such nonsense, his stick would soon have made the heretic sensible. Alasdair could not read or write and only understood Gaelic, and these poems came down to him through generations numberless as repeated by his ancestors round their winter evening fires; and I have known persons as uneducated, who could not only repeat from memory interesting poems like Ossian, but could work out uninteresting complicated sums in arithmetic. Alasdair related as follows: 'Behind the western Tigh Dige rose a mass of rock covered with wood, with a charming grassy level top about one thousand feet above the sea, which in the sheltered woody bay flowed within a thousand yards of the old château.' Alasdair told us that in 1745, when men-of-war were searching everywhere for Prince Charlie, one of them came into the bay, and the Captain sent word to our ancestor to come on board. The latter, who really had not been at Culloden, although some of his people had, thought he was quite as well ashore among his friends, so sent his compliments to his inviter, regretting he could not accept his invitation, as he had friends to dine with him on the top of Creag a Chait (the Cat's Rock), where he hoped the Captain would join them. The reply was a broadside against the Tigh Dige as the ship sailed off, and I can remember seeing one of the cannon-balls sticking half out of the house gable next to the sea, apparently an 18-pound shot. Had it hit a few feet lower it might have broken into a recess in the thickness of the gable, the admittance to which was by raising the floor of a wall-press in the room above, although

35

this had been forgotten till masons cutting an opening for a gable door to the kitchen broke into the recess, where many swords and guns were found. Then it was recollected that Fraser of Foyers was long concealed by our ancestor, and of course in this black hole."

CHAPTER III

CHILDHOOD

I CANNOT say I can remember my first coming to Gairloch, as I was then only about two years old, but there were soon to be very trying times there, during the great famine caused by the potato blight. I have quite clear recollections of my own small grievance at being made to eat rice, which I detested, instead of potatoes, with my mutton or chicken in the years 1846–1848, for even *Uaislean an tigh mhor* (the gentry of the big house) could not get enough potatoes to eat in those hard times. Certainly things looked very black in 1846–1848 in Ireland and the West of Scotland, though, but for the potato blight, when should we have got roads made through the country? My mother never left Gairloch, not even for a day, for three long years when the famine was at its height.

In Ireland a very stupid system was started—namely, the making of roads beginning nowhere in particular, and ending, perhaps, at a rock or in the middle of a bog. It was thought that working at an object which could never be of any use to anyone would be so repugnant to the feelings of the greater portion of the population that only the dire stress of actual starvation would induce them to turn out for the sake of the trifle of money, or one or two pounds of maize meal, which constituted then the daily wage. My mother was totally opposed to this ridiculous plan in our district, and also against merely giving miserable doles of meal, which were barely sufficient to keep the population alive. Her plan was to pay all the able-bodied men a sufficient wage in money or food to enable them to do good work themselves and to support their dependents. So with the help of Government and begging and borrowing (I think) £10,000, she and my uncle undertook the great responsibility of guaranteeing that no one would be allowed to starve on the property. Thus the Loch Maree road was started, and this was about the only thing which could possibly open up the country.

Both my half-brothers were absent from the country at the time, so I, as a small boy, had the great honour conferred on me of cutting the first turf of the new road. How well I remember it, surrounded by a huge crowd, many of them starving Skye men, for the famine was more sore in Skye and the islands than it was on our part of the mainland. I remember the tiny toy spade and the desperate exertions I had to make to cut my small bit of turf; then came the ringing cheers of the assembled multitude, and I felt myself a great hero. I must have driven or motored past that place thousands of times since that day, but I never do so, even if it be pitch dark, without thinking of the cutting of the first turf, and the feeling of great gratitude to the Almighty for His having put into the hearts of my mother and uncle the strong determination to carry through the great work. Nor did they cease with the finishing of the Loch Maree road, but went on with local roads, such as from Kerrysdale to Red Point, Strath to Melvaig, and Poolewe to Cove; and instead of the little narrow switchback road from Slatadale to the Tigh Dige, an almost entirely new road was made from Loch Maree to Gairloch through the Kerry Glen. After the good example of the Gairloch trustees, other neighbouring proprietors followed suit, and the lairds of Gruinord and Dundonnell in course of time made a road the whole way from Poolewe, via Aultbea, Gruinord, and Dundonnell, to join the Garve and Ullapool road at Braemore. This gave the whole of the coast-line from the mouth of Loch Torridon to Loch Broom the benefit of more or less good highways, which are all now county roads. How well do I remember the first wheeled vehicle, a carrier's cart, that ever came to Gairloch, and the excitement it caused.

My uncle says: "There being no need of wheels in a roadless country in my young days, we had only sledges in place of wheeled carts, all made by our grieve. He took two birch-trees of the most suitable bends and of them made the two shafts, with iron-work to suit the harness for collar straps. The ends of the shafts were sliced away with an adze at the proper angle to slide easily and smoothly on the ground. Two planks, one behind the horse and the other about half-way up the shaft ends, were securely nailed

38

to the shafts, and were bored with holes to receive four-foot-long hazel rungs to form the front and back of the cart and to keep in the goods, a similar plank on the top of the rungs making the front and rear of the cart surprisingly stable and upright. The floor was made of planks, and these sledge carts did all that was needed for moving peats, and nearly every kind of crop. Movable boxes planted on the sledge floor between the front and back served to carry up fish from the shore and lime and manure, and it was long ere my father Sir Hector paid a penny a year to a cartwright. The sledges could slide where wheeled carts could not venture, and carried corn and hay, etc., famously."

My readers will perhaps wonder how we got our letters before the Loch Maree road was made. Well, there was a mail packet, a small sloop which ran between Stornoway and Poolewe and carried all the Lews and Harris letters for the south, and which was supposed to run twice a week, though, as a matter of fact, she seldom did it even once. There was a sort of post office at Poolewe, to which the Gairloch and Aultbea letters (if there were any) found their way, and the whole lot was put into a small home-made leather bag which Iain Mor am Posda (Big John the Post) threw on his shoulder. With this he trudged, I might say climbed, through the awful precipices of Creag Thairbh (the Bull's Rock) on the north side of Loch Maree, passing through Ardlair and Letterewe, and so on at one time to Dingwall, but latterly only to Achnasheen. Imagine the letters and newspapers for the parish of Gairloch and Torridon (part of Applecross), with about 6,000 souls, and the Lews, with a population of nearly 30,000 inhabitants, all being carried on one man's back in my day.

The only possible way of getting baker's bread in those days was by the packet from Stornoway, and a big boy, John Grant, came over to us at Gairloch with the bread and the letters once or twice a week. How well I can remember him standing, usually dripping wet, shivering in the Tigh Dige kitchen, while the cook expressed lively indignation because the bread-bag was soaking wet. That lad served me as a man very faithfully for many years as grieve after I bought Inverewe in 1862.

Only a few years ago a party of us went from Inverewe and

back in order to visit the Bull's Rock. In more than one part of it we could let ourselves down and pull ourselves up only with the help of our stalwart stalker! On one occasion a Post Office overseer from London, who was being sent to Stornoway, and was following Big John on foot, fainted *en route*, and Big John managed to carry the fat official on the top of the mail-bag for several miles till he reached Ardlair.

When the first Sir Alexander built the Tigh Dige the timber was all cut in the natural Scotch fir forest of Glas Leitir (the Grey Slope) on the shores of the upper end of Loch Maree, and boated down the loch to Slatadale, and from there dragged by innumerable men and ponies for seven miles over that wild hill that separates Loch Maree from the sea at Gairloch. There was not a single mark of a saw to be found on the timbers of the roof of the Tigh Dige, and they are squared only by the axe.

I spent the nine years of my childhood, from 1844 to 1853, in the Tigh Dige, and did ever boy spend a happier nine years anywhere? When I was between three and four, my dear mother, who was enthusiastic about Gaelic, started me with a little nurse-maid who did not know a word of English, Seonaid nic Mhaoilan (Janet MacMillan). Well do I remember her first lesson. She took me to a looking-glass, and, turning the glass up opposite me, she said, "*Thainig e*" ("He is come"), and then, reversing it, "*Dh'fhalbh e*" ("He is gone"). I learnt Gaelic in a very short time. My good old English nurse, Emma Mills, I fear, felt very much snubbed, as she was told when out with us to sit on a stone and merely watch us two playing together, but not to interfere. Nurse Emma's favourite walk was to what she was pleased to call the "Heagle 'Ouse" (where a tame eagle was kept), and she did not at all approve of my calling it Tigh na h-Iolaire (the Eagle House), which was much prettier and more appropriate.

My mother was one of the very few instances of a grown-up person learning to speak Gaelic quite fluently, but in this she succeeded thoroughly, though she always retained a little of *blas na beurla* (taste of the English). She started going regularly to church when she understood only the one word *agus* (and), and she ended by understanding every word of the longest and most eloquent sermons preached by ministers like Dr. Kennedy of Dingwall and others of that calibre. How I always bless my mother for her determination that she herself and her two stepsons and I should know Gaelic. Life for me, living in the west as I have done, would not have been worth living without Gaelic. No servant on the place, inside or outside, was allowed ever to speak English to the young gentlemen under pain of being dismissed. Dinner was ordered in the kitchen in Gaelic, and all meals were announced by the butler Sim Eachainn in Gaelic—"*Tha am biadh airleadh le bhur cead a bhaintighearna*" ("The food is on the table, by your leave, my lady"), so the whole atmosphere was thoroughly Gaelic. My younger brother Francis, who was very fluent in the language, did not lose it whilst for some years in the Navy. When he took a big farm in Orkney, where no Gaelic is spoken by the natives, he had so many Gairloch workmen there with him that Gaelic was the order of the day; and how proud he was when John Mackenzie, the *clachair mor* (the big mason), and his three stalwart sons were able to beat seven of the best-picked Orkney men at dry-stone dyking. It was a race between Gaelic and English, and Gaelic always won in a canter. At the death of my elder brother, Sir Kenneth, one of the doctors in attendance, Dr. Adam of Dingwall, told me that he went out of this world and entered his eternal rest repeating verse after verse of the Gaelic Psalms, which had been taught him by my mother in his childhood.

I ought to mention here that when my mother took charge of the property there was only the one parish school, but she started nine or ten, and her rule was that no child should be taught English until he or she could read simple Gaelic first. What a success her schools all were, and what intelligent scholars they produced. Not long ago I was in a school where the teacher was an Aberdeenshire woman and the infant class all Gaelic-speaking. They were being taught a little story about a dog running after a lamb. How could the poor teacher instruct intelligently when the little pupils did not understand what dog and lamb meant? I had to come to the rescue and tell them that dog meant *cu*, and lamb meant *uan*. Now, this sort of thing would never have happened in my good mother's day, when all teachers were bilingual.

And now for some more about those delightful nine years of my life spent in the old Tigh Dige. The house used to be full up every summer and autumn. My uncle, John Mackenzie, who was factor for the estate, with his wife, two sons, and five daughters, were often there, and lots of Hanbury relations from the south also came. We were such a merry party. On one or two occasions when Gairloch was let my mother and I resided at Poolewe, either at Pool House or in Inveran Lodge, and that gave me the opportunity of acquiring a wider knowledge of the enormous Gairloch property and its population. I saw comparatively little of my mother for some years at Gairloch, owing to her being away on horseback from Monday morning to Saturday night superintending the making of those miles of road I have spoken of. She was also engaged in abolishing the old runrig system, under which the wretched hovels of some five hundred crofters had been built in clusters or end on to each other like a kind of street, so that when typhus or smallpox broke out there was no escape. All the new houses had to be built each one in the centre of the four-acre croft.

There had never been a doctor in Gairloch, and my mother doctored the whole parish for over three years—a population of about 5,400. She was most successful, and so famous did she become that on one occasion they brought a good-sized idiot, carried on a man's back in a creel from Little Loch Broom, to be healed, such was their faith in her. But after the doctor arrived her work became a little easier, and she began to take me constantly with her on her riding expeditions, my little Shetland pony carrying me everywhere. I then started fishing, both on sea and loch, and took up ornithology and egg-collecting, in which she encouraged me in every possible way. When I was about seven and knew Gaelic perfectly, she sent for a French boy of twelve from a Protestant orphanage at Arras to come as a sort of page, and to go out with me, and I never had any trouble in learning French, which seemed to come to me quite naturally. Édouard, the French boy, learnt Gaelic as quickly as I learnt French, and could be sent all over the country with Gaelic messages.

How different from nowadays many things were when I first remember Gairloch. Such a thing as a lamp I never saw in the Tigh Dige. Only candles were used; paraffin was quite unknown and had not even been heard of; and the black houses depended for light chiefly on the roaring fires in the centre of the room, with, perhaps, an old creel or barrel stuck in the roof to let out the smoke. For use in very exceptional cases the people had tiny tin lamps made by the tinkers and fed with oil made out of the livers of fish which were allowed to get rotten before they were boiled down. But the main lighting at night was done by having a big heap of carefully prepared bog-fir splinters full of resin all ready in a corner, and a small boy or girl did nothing else but keep these burning during the evening, so that the women could see to card and spin and the men to make their herring-nets by hand. I do not remember hemp being grown, as it was, I believe, at one time in special sorts of enclosures or gardens, and prepared and spun for the making of the herring-nets. But it was commonly done in the west. I do not think they grew flax to any great extent, but on the east coast they grew it quite extensively, and all the Tigh Dige sheets and damask napkins and tablecloths in lovely patterns were spun in Conon House, our east-coast home, and woven in Conon village.

I shall now quote from my uncle to show what a good house-keeper my grandmother was. He says: "I doubt if there ever was a much better housekeeper than my dear mother, or more busy and better servants than in those times. They cheerfully put hand to work, the very suggesting of which would startle the modern ladies and gentlemen who serve us. A common sight in the Conon kitchen after dinner was four or five women all the evening busy spinning and carding flax for napery, or putting wicks into metal candle moulds in frames holding, say, a dozen, and pouring the fearful-smelling tallow into the moulds. In those days I seldom saw any candles but of tallow anywhere, unless in chandeliers or against walls where they could not easily be snuffed; so my wise

43

mother made heaps of as good candles as she could buy from the spare suet in the house. Then, where could a storeroom be seen like my mother's at Conon? The room was shelved all round with movable frames for holding planks, on which unimaginable quantities of dried preserved edibles reposed till called for. There were jam-pots by the hundred of every sort, shelves of preserved candied apricots and *Magnum Bonum* plums, that could not be surpassed in the world; other shelves with any amount of biscuits of all sorts of materials, once liquid enough to drop on sheets of paper, but in time dried to about two inches across and half an inch thick for dessert. Smoked sheep and deer tongues were also there, and from the roof hung strings of threaded artichoke bottoms, dried, I suppose, for putting into soups. In addition, there were endless curiosities of confectionery brought north by Kitty's talents from her Edinburgh cookery school, while quantities of dried fruit, ginger, orange-peel, citron, etc., from North Simpson and Graham of London must have made my dear mother safe-cased in armour against any unexpected and hungry invader. Then every year she made gooseberry and currant wines, balm ditto, raspberry vinegar, spruce and ginger beer. I remember they were celebrated, and liqueurs numberless included magnums of camomile flowers and orange-peel and gentian root bitters for old women with indigestion pains."

My dear old foreman of works, Seoras Ruairidh Cheannaiche (George of Rory Merchant), who was at the head of everything, and who did everything for me at Inverewe when I began there in 1862, used to tell me the difficulty there was in his grandfather's and even in his father's day in getting any kind of planking and nails for coffins. It was a common thing, he said, for a man going to Inverness on some great occasion to bring back a few nails for his own coffin, so that they might be in readiness whenever the last call came. In Loch Broom wooden pegs were often used for coffins.

The ordinary way of interment in the time of George's grandfather was to have the dead body swathed in blue homespun, carried on an open bier to the graveyard, and slid down into the grave. His grandfather could remember when, if one lost a hook

44

when trout-fishing, the only way of replacing it was to go to Ceard an Oirthire, the old tinker at Coast (a little hamlet on the bay of Gruinord) and to get him to make one, and to tell him to be sure to put a barb on it. And in the days of old Jane Charles, who was a sort of connection of the Gairloch family, there was only one looking-glass in the district other than in the Tigh Dige, and the girls had to arrange their hair for church or for a wedding by looking at their faces in a pail of water. I can quite well remember when not a sack made from jute was to be seen, and one saw the big sixteen or eighteen feet rowing-boats on fine winter days arriving from the outlying townships at the mills at Strath or Boor piled up with bags of oats and barley (or rather bere), all in sheep-skin bags, with a certain amount of wool still on their outsides to remind one of their origin. It was rare then to see such a thing as a hempen rope. Ropes for retaining the thatch on the cottages were called *seamanan fraoich* (heather ropes) and made of heather. Ropes to hold small boats were generally made of twisted birch twigs, while the very best ropes for all other purposes were made of the pounded fibre of bog-fir roots, and a really well-made *ball maith guithais* (a good fir rope) could hardly be beaten by the best modern ropes.

I never saw a wire riddle for riddling corn or meal in the old days; they were all made of stretched sheep-skins with holes perforated in them by a big red-hot needle. Trout lines were made of white or other horsehair, and when one stabled a pony at an inn, it always ran the risk of having its tail stolen. Also, the only spoons in the country were those the tinkers made from sheep and cow horns melted down. How one used to smell the burning horn at the tinker encampments after dark.

Knives and forks were hardly known in the crofter houses, and everything was eaten with fingers and thumbs. Even now I hear them say herrings and potatoes never taste right if eaten with a knife and fork. My mother was one day visiting some poor squatter families who in those days resided on Longa Island, and one woman was very anxious she should partake of something. My mother was hungry, for she never carried luncheon with her on her long daily expeditions from early morning to night, trusting to her chance of getting a bowl of milk and a bit of oatcake or barley scone from those she visited. Well, the poor woman confessed to having no meal in the house and consequently no bread; all she had was a pail of flounders just off the hooks, and she asked if the *bantighearna* (lady) would condescend to partake of one of them. My mother said she would, and a flounder was instantly put in a pot. When it was boiled the woman took it out, neatly broke it in two or three pieces, and placed them on a little table without plate or cloth, knife or fork. My mother set to it with her fingers, and afterwards declared it was the sweetest fish she ever tasted. When she finished the woman brought her a pail of water to wash her hands in.

When people chanced to have a bit of meat they could not make what we should call broth, because they had no pot barley and no turnips or carrots, onions or cabbage, to put in it; so they thickened the water in which the meat had been boiled with oatmeal, and this was called in Gaelic *eanaraich* (broth). It was placed in the middle of the table, and everyone helped themselves with their horn spoons.

Perhaps a few of my readers are aware that almost within my own recollection the blacksmiths on our west coast did all their own smithy work with peat charcoal. Coal was rarely imported before 1840, and all the oak had been cut down, turned into charcoal, and used by Sir George Hay in his small furnaces or bloomeries towards the end of the sixteenth and the early years of the seventeenth centuries, so there was nothing to fall back on but peat charcoal, which I have always been told was quite a good substitute. I can just recollect the Gobha Mor (the Big Blacksmith) at Poolewe. He was the last smith who used it, and with whom died the knowledge and skill required to make it.

I wonder also if it is known that on our west coast, before tar was imported from Archangel, the inhabitants produced their own tar. When the late Lord Elphinstone bought Coulin in Glen Torridon he used a great deal of the old native Scots fir in the building of the lodge. One day, after a large number of the trees had been cut down, he and I started counting the natural rings on the stems of the trees, and found that they averaged about two hundred and fifty years old. My attention was drawn by Lord Elphinstone to the fact that nearly every one of the trees had had a big auger-hole bored into it just above the ground-level. He was told by the old folk in the neighbourhood that these holes had been bored by the Loch Carron people to produce tar for their boats. We could see the marks of the auger-holes in numbers of the trees that were still standing, as well as in those that had been cut down.

What far happier times those good old days were than these we are living in now. Even the seasons seemed more "seasonable" and the summers far hotter. What an abundance of cherries there was at Gairloch even in my days in the 'forties and 'fifties, and these crops were supposed to be degenerate in comparison with the grand fruity years of the 'twenties. There were about four or five big trees of red early cherries and one of black late Guines, and never did they seem to fail. No amount of blackbirds, ring-ouzels, nor any number of boys and girls, seemed to have the slightest effect on them, and they never, in my recollection, failed to be laden. At long last, however, they had to give in to old age and were blown down one by one; but though my elder brother took great trouble to plant new ones of specially good varieties, there has never, I believe, been another cherry in the Baile Mor garden, the new kinds evidently failing to suit the soil or climate.

I now quote from my uncle as to the seasons in his day: "What long, hot days we used to have then compared with the present short, lukewarm ones, that no sooner begin than they end disgracefully. Astronomers tell us their registers show that the present seasons are just the same as in, say, 1812—seventy years ago. What stuff and nonsense! In those happier times everybody had summer as well as winter clothing. Who dreams of such extravagance now in the north? Not a soul at least of the male animals, who for months in summer wore nankeen jackets and trousers; I was grown up ere I could give up my large stock of Russian duck summer clothes. How a clothier nowadays would stare if I asked for a suit of nankeen or duck for summer clothing! Well do I remember days before we migrated to the west in May, going down to the Conon River to bathe with my brothers and dawdling away our time naked, making mill dams or dirt-pies on the sandy shore, and on putting on my shirt feeling as if there were pins inside. On examination there were several big water blisters on my back, needing a needle to empty them, and many days elapsed before they were healed up. Whoever nowadays hears of such blistering sun? Then in our Conon garden, the extensive walls of which were covered with apricot, peach, and nectarine trees, every year there were loads of fine and well-ripened fruit for five most healthy urchins who had a free run of the garden to eat up as fast as it ripened. And where, in that garden, or now in my own still warmer garden, is a living, growing peach or nectarine to be found? Every one dead for want of sun to ripen the wood ere winter killed it. In our Conon garden a splendid filbert-tree, perhaps twenty-four feet high, with a stem as thick as my body, every year bore bushels of as fine full filberts as were ever exhibited, till old John Fraser, ruined by having a vinery put up for him about sixty feet north of the filbert, actually cut it down on the sly when we were in Gairloch, from an idea that it might possibly shade the vinery. I never saw my father in a hurry or passion or heard him swear, but sure I am that when he came to the vacant site of the filbert, friends would have avoided listening to his *sotto voce* comments on that day. But old John, perhaps, was only looking forward to the shocking seasons to come, when money could not discover a ripe common hazel-nut. There have been no nuts of late years in our woods, which used regularly to produce splendid crops. Hundreds of sacks of nuts, every one full to the neck, were sent in cartloads to the Beauly markets and to every town and village; the nut-crackers became a regular nuisance, paving every street and road and room with shells for months; the whole people in the country seemed to live with their pockets full of nuts, and the price was fabulously low. What utter nonsense to talk of the temperature now being what it was seventy years ago.

"We used, I believe, as a matter of duty always to be settled in the west for the summer before the 4th of June, which was the King's birthday, and on that day we never failed to have a big

48

china bowl after dinner with a pail of cream that "wad mak a cawnle of my fingers" to wash down the first strawberries of the season. Don't I remember their delicious smell in the house, and their taste too! *North Carolinas* the gardener called them. And now in the same garden, but certainly not the same climate, no strawberry thinks itself called upon to ripen until a month later. The same temperature as seventy years ago. What fools we must be supposed to be by those rascals of astronomers!

"And we always had a few cherries to serve up on the 4th of June also. Was there ever such a mass of cherries either before or since as in the Tigh Dige garden, sheltered from every cold wind and held up to the sun by all that could be desired in woods and mountains? And were there ever five boys and a tutor better able to make an impression on the cherry-trees? Our beloved tutor told me years afterwards of one thing that was a weight on his mind—namely, that having dropped one forenoon 999 cherry-stones from his mouth into his fishing-bag, he was suddenly called away and prevented finishing his thousand at one go. Our old Nathaniel, John Fraser, our eastern gardener, having two sons at Conon with the same turn for fruit as we had, schemed to save the peaches and nectarines he wanted for his employer. Every night before stopping work he raked nicely all the soil borders ere he made himself cosy at the fireside with his slippers on instead of heavy wet shoes. Yet he was much surprised to miss many a lovely peach he was sure he left on the tree the previous evening. And lo and behold, there were the thief's footmarks all over the raked border. So he out with the foot-rule and thought he would soon discover the criminal. But the mystery deepened when he found that the shoes which fitted the footmarks on the border were his own. It never occurred to the old innocent to imagine that his son had put on his shoes while he was at tea, and thus safely supped on apricots and peaches, without any risk of the footmarks betraying the thief."

Before bringing to an end this talk about our changed climate I shall give one more proof of it—*viz.*, the almost entire disappearance of the wild bee.

I often heard, when I was young, that in the Lews (whose poetical name in Gaelic is Eilean an Fhraoich (the Heather Island) bees were so plentiful in the olden times that the boys were able to collect large quantities of wild honey, which, by applying heat to it, was run into glass bottles and sold at the Stornoway markets. Hunting for wild-bees' nests was one of the great ploys for the boys in the autumns, but nowadays this amusement is never thought of. Even in the 'sixties my good and faithful grieve John Grant, when at the head of his squad (long before mowing machines were ever thought of), used to be quite annoyed at the continual hindrance to the scythe work through men stopping to raid bees' nests in the grass, and losing time in eating the honey and the *ceir* (bee-bread), and pretending they could not go back to their work owing to the attacks of the infuriated bees. Now-adays, even if one by any chance comes upon a wild-bees' nest, it contains little or nothing in the way of honey. My old sheep manager, Alexander Cameron, better known to his many friends as the Tournaig Bard on account of his being such a good Gaelic poet and improvisatore, owned a collie dog in the 'sixties which learned to point at bees' nests. On one occasion when he was taking quite a short turn on one of his beats on my property his dog found thirty bees' nests for him, some of which contained quite a saucerful of honey and bee-bread. Nowadays an egg-cup would hold all the honey one could find in a long summer's day.

Cameron tells me that, as a young boy, before he left his home, there was an island in Loch bhad a chreamha (Lake of the Clump of Garlic) where there was no necessity for hunting for bees' nests, as the whole island seemed under bees, the nests almost touching each other in the moss at the roots of tall heather. As may be imagined, that island was a very popular resort of the Naast boys. My stalker, too, informs me that his home at Kernsary used to be quite famous for its wild bees, but they finally disappeared just nineteen years ago.

So much for our degenerate climate!

CHAPTER IV

BOYHOOD

My dear mother was indefatigable in finding amusements for me and for all the rest of the young people. Collecting gulls' eggs on the islands of Loch Maree was a favourite pastime. We went on many an expedition in May and June, and, under the best of guides, Seumas Buidhe (Yellow James), the weaver at Slatadale, and his big apprentice, we used to get from 150 to 200 eggs in an afternoon. With the exception of perhaps three or four pairs of herring gulls and about the same number of the greater black backs (which always bred singly on isolated rocks), the whole gull population consisted of thousands of lesser black backs, which are, I believe, our only migratory gulls. Before my time the great breeding-place of the gulls was the big island of Eilean Ruaridh Mor (Rory's Big Island). Then the gulls suddenly left, the popular belief of the cause of their desertion being that some party had gone birds'-nesting on a Sunday. But I believe my father cleared up the mystery; he found out that a shepherd with his dog had landed on the island in the winter following the desertion of the gulls, and that the dog had caught and killed a big pine marten. The animal was so thin as to be little more than a skeleton; it had evidently driven the gulls to such a pitch of exasperation by eating their eggs and young ones that at last they had suddenly deserted Eilean Ruaridh Mor and made for Garbh Eilean, Eilean Suthaninn, and other smaller islands where we used to go. It is interesting to speculate how the marten got to the island, seeing that Loch Maree never freezes.

How certain memories stick to one through life. Never shall I forget one birds'-nesting expedition when I was a very small boy, perhaps about six. I was wandering alone through the tangle of dwarf trees and tall heather intent on trying to get more eggs than anyone else of the party, and had managed to fill every pocket I had, besides having two or three eggs in each little hand.

Suddenly I slipped among the rocks, and my reader can imagine the state my clothes and I were in when I rose to my legs!

In June and July our expeditions consisted in going to one of the best trout lochs in Scotland, Loch na h-Oidhche (the Night Loch), so called because the trout in it were supposed to take all night long. Fly was never thought of. We had three or four stiff larch rods with rowan tops, string for lines, and a hook at the end baited with earth-worms. Two men rowed the boat, we trolled the lines behind, and we used to get perhaps from 80 to 100 lovely golden-yellow trout, from half a pound to a pound in weight. They ran rather heavier on the Gorm Lochanan (Blue Lakelets) a little beyond Loch na h-Oidhche. Sometimes we put up at the Poca buidhe (Yellow Bag) bothy, but its roof in those days was very leaky, and there was little to be gained by being under its protection.

I used sometimes to long to pass the night instead in Uaimh Bhraodaig, a spot where my father and uncles had spent many nights when deer-stalking, and where there was room for two or three fellows to lie down close together. *Uaimh* is Gaelic for "cave," but it was hardly a cave: it was only a sort of hole under a gigantic fragment of rock in the wildest cairn I ever saw, with, perhaps, the exception of Carn nan Uaimhag, at the back of Beinn Airidh Charr. I shall give my uncle's description of it:

"When we went to the hill for deer, expecting to be home at night, after an early breakfast, we never dreamt of taking anything but a heel of cheese from the dairy with some thick barley scone, a favourite bread downstairs, and handy as never crumbling in one's pocket. But it happened to me when I came on deer late at night, as I have often done, I could not get home till next day. Once night fell on me when alone ten miles from home with a stag and hind that I had not finished gralloching ere it was so dark that I could hardly see my way to a large stone called Uaimh Bhraodaig, which gave tolerable protection to two or three people in need from the rain and wind in those hills. I managed, however, and on my way startled a foolish old grouse, who, not caring a straw for me, perched on a great stone so nicely between me and the evening star that he got a little round hole from my rifle that qualified him for supping with me, when skinned hot and made into a spatch-cock that needed no sauce to be enjoyed extremely, the cheese and scone having disappeared by midday. My friend and I just reached Uaimh Bhraodaig in time to gather some of the large heather sticks found near such rough ground, and with my flint and tinder box (for lucifers were a pleasure yet to come) I got up a little fire for cooking and warming my wet feet before I rolled my plaid about me as bed and bedding. That reminds me that, often as I have slept on the hill sound enough till cockcrow, I never saw anyone who could sleep through the early morning chill, even though dry and stuffed into a heap of dry heather. Uaimh Bhraodaig was half-way up the eastern shoulder of Beinn an Eoin (the Bird Mountain), and for, say 500 yards all round it was a heap of great stones left there by Noah, bad enough to clamber over in daylight, but detestable in the dark, and only to be endured in preference to a long, cold, wet night on the open hill. I had roasted and finished my much-admired grouse, and had, of course, taken off my wet shoes— wet leather ensuring cold feet all night, whereas even with wet stockings, if I stuffed my feet into a bundle of dry heather they generally got warm enough not to prevent sleep. I was just dozing lulled by the croaking of some ptarmigan (their song sounds so different from that of the red grouse or black game) as they flew from the hill-tops in the evening to sup on the heather they can only get lower down. A Yorkshire farmer who had been sent to our parts used to insist that gravel must be their food, as nothing else was within their reach on the hill-tops! Suddenly I heard a very different music from that of the ptarmigan, evidently the voices of people, some of whom were so out of temper that it was anything but psalmody which in the dead calm night floated up some hundred yards to my annoyed ears quite clearly. The sweet songsters of the hill were benighted poachers making for Uaimh Bhraodaig, and as we were alone and preferred having no bed-fellows, I handled my rifle and went outside. I distinctly heard very ugly language regarding the quality of the road over which they were scrambling and stumbling much more than they liked in their iron-shod shoes; so, making my voice sound as unearthly as possible, I groaned out loudly in Gaelic, 'Who is there? Wait till I get you.' There was instant silence, and then such a scrimmage and capering about on the big stones as sent me back to my bundle of heather delighted to be left with no comrades but the ptarmigan till daylight. Years after I learnt that two lovers of venison more than of law had been out on a private stalk, and had a miraculous escape from Satan, who nearly got them on the hill at night!"

I myself was told as a boy a terrible story connected with Uaimh Bhraodaig, and I give it here as told to me. A *brocair* (fox-hunter), being benighted on the hill somewhere near the upper end of Beinn an Eoin, thought the only thing to do was to pass the night in Uaimh Bhraodaig. Some time during the night a terrible apparition appeared to him, and he fled before it, accompanied by his two *lethchoin* (lurchers), and ran as never man ran before. Across his path was the Gharbhaig River, which flows into Loch Maree. He took a flying leap across one of its chasms, which was quite beyond the powers of any ordinary human being, and landed on the other side, but both his dogs, which attempted to follow him, fell into the river and were drowned. The *brocair* was quite a young man, and had not a grey hair in his head when he entered Uaimh Bhraodaig, but by the time he reached the first house in Talladale his head was as white as driven snow. This story was believed to be quite true by everyone when I was a boy.

Birds'-nesting expeditions were also made to the islands of Loch Maree after ospreys' eggs. There were two eyries there, one of them in a real curiosity of a place—namely, in Eilean Suthainn, one of the biggest of the islands in Loch Maree. There is a small loch, and in this loch (the depth of which is about double that of the neighbouring Loch Maree), there is an island on which stood one big Scots fir. In it was the ospreys' nest, as large as a waggon-wheel, with three eggs. It was lined with lumps of wool and bits of cow-dung, and lying at the foot of the tree I found a dead mallard, which appeared to have been freshly killed by the ospreys. There was another fir-tree where they bred on a promontory nearly opposite Isle Maree, from which I got two eggs But, alas! the birds have been extinct in that region for at least sixty-five years.

There were expeditions to eagles' nests on the Creag Cheann Dubh (the Black-headed Rock) in Beinn a Bhric and on a rock opposite the Garbh choire of Bathais Bheinn. There, wonderful to say, we were able to walk into the nest. We were too late for the eggs, but we found two good-sized eaglets, and there were five whole grouse, quite freshly killed, lying near them, as beautifully plucked by the parent eagles as any well-trained kitchen-maid could have done.

I had often heard that shepherds made great use of eagles' nests to fill their larders, and my uncle corroborates as follows: "Eagles sometimes built where not even a rope-dancer could get at them —a sad case for shepherds, who were accused of concealing the whereabouts of their nests when in accessible places. It was said that they tethered the eaglets to the nest long after they could fly, because until the young birds left the nest the parents never ceased to bring quantities of all sorts of game to feed them, quite half of which was said to go to the shepherds' larder. A shepherd admitted to me that he once took a salmon quite fresh out of a white-tailed eagle's nest. Fawns, hares, lambs, and grouse were brought in heaps to the nest for months—an agreeable variety at the shepherd's daily dinner of porridge and potatoes and milk."

We also made expeditions seawards to Eilean Fuara and the Staca Buidh (Yellow Stack). My pet terrier Deantag (Nettle) was the first in my time to discover the stormy petrels nesting in large numbers in the cracks of the dry, peaty soil. None of the natives had been aware of this fact, because the petrels when breeding never show themselves in the daytime. Fuara thus became quite famous among ornithologists, but of later years steam drifters have been in the habit of leaving their herring-nets stretched out on the island for days to dry, and that finished the poor little "stormies," which, like so many other birds, have disappeared.

This is what my uncle says about stormy petrels in Longa: "On Sundays when there was no service in Gairloch Church my father often booked us boys for a sail in his charming thirty-foot-keel barge to visit some of the townships round the coast and have a kindly word with the people, or even a scold, though that was rarely needed. Sometimes we landed for a walk on Longa Island. It was about half a mile in diameter, all glens and moor, with good grass, which was kept for wintering for the young of the sixty Tigh Dige cows, so that they might be in the best of condition when ready for market the following year, dressed in their beautiful long, shining coats, the pride of Highland cattle. We often came home with faces nicely painted with blaeberry juice and also crowberries, for that most coveted wild fruit grew in Longa. When it was found out that Longa was our destination, a little dog was often put into the barge to help us to discover if one of the stormy petrels ('Mother Carey's Chicken'), who loved wild Longa as a breeding-place, was at home in the peat-holes or under flat stones, which were generally chosen by 'Mrs. Carey' as a waterproof covering for her wee white egg or little black, tiny pet. Doggie always knew by the wild, fishy smell whether 'Mrs. Carey' was at home or not, and thus saved us much Sunday digging in our endeavours to bring her to Tigh Dige to be shown to the dear mother."

In winter and early spring, when there were no birds' eggs to be got, my mother and I used to fish vigorously. We had a good crew always ready, and setting cod-lines was great sport. I remember that on a certain fine sunny February morning the long lines had been set as usual overnight close off Longa Island, and we thought it a good opportunity to try for otters. There was a spring tide, and big George Ross, the keeper, with his gun and terrier formed part of the crew. We lifted our lines, and our small fourteen-foot row-boat could hardly contain the fish—sixty full-sized cod and two giant haddocks. Then we landed and tried the cairns along the shore without success, so we began cutting off the cods' heads and getting rid of their insides to lighten the boat. While engaged in this we missed the terrier, Bodach (Old Man), and soon we heard a faint yelping high up in the interior of the island, where he had discovered otters. We followed him, and the keeper, leaning down and peering in, thought he could see the eyes of an otter a good way inside the cairn, so he let off the gun into the hole and killed it. Immediately another otter bolted and made across the heather for the sea. Everyone tore downhill after it, and someone giving it a lucky blow with a stick, it was secured before reaching the water. We came back with a nice mixed cargo.

My uncle was not so lucky. He says: "We boys had offers out for young otters which we meant to train to fish for us at command, and one day, to our great delight, a lad brought to Tigh Dige a creel with four young otters. They were the size of kittens a month old, such dear little pets, and we instantly procured a tub of their native element, into which we emptied the little darlings. To our amazement, they yelled and strove like mad to get out of the tub. Then came old Watson the keeper and took a look at them, and he ruined all our hopes by quietly telling us they were young polecats!"

In this manner the days and the years passed by very happily. Nor was my education being neglected. I was always being taught a little, first by my old nurse, and afterwards by my mother's lady companion, who taught me English and Gaelic. I also went to a Gaelic Sunday-school class and thoroughly learnt my Gaelic Shorter Catechism; and the French boy read French with me under the direction of my mother. It was not the fashion in our family for the boys to be sent to school. My grandfather's plan was to have tutors, who spent the summers and autumns with the boys at Gairloch, and who went with them during the winter to Edinburgh, where they attended classes. None of my four uncles nor my father was ever at school, and it was my father's special wish that his sons should be brought up in the same manner.

I do not think it could be possible for any two young men to turn out greater successes than my two half-brothers, the late Sir Kenneth S. Mackenzie and his brother. Sir Kenneth was far and away the most esteemed man in the county of Ross. He was appointed Chairman of the Commissioners of Supply and Convener of the County Council, was at the head of everything that was good, and, like his grandfather, was Lord Lieutenant of the County. My second brother, Francis, was quite as great a man, and equally beloved and respected. I quite agree with my grandfather and father that Eton and Harrow, Oxford and Cambridge, do not by any means produce the best men as Highland proprietors; such training only turns them into regular Sassenachs. It is surely better that a Highlander should be something a little different from an Englishman. When they are sent to English schools as small boys of eight or nine years old, and their education is continued in the south, they lose all their individuality. They may be very good, but they have nothing Highland about them except the bits of tartan they sport, which were probably manufactured in the south and their kilts tailored in London. My uncle writes that his father, Sir Hector, and his wife, the *bhanti-ghearna ruadh* (the auburn lady) as she was always called, spoke Gaelic to each other as often as they did English. To-day my daughter and I do the same. Why should the present chiefs and lairds call themselves Highland if they can't speak a word of the language of their people and country? One would not call a man a Boer in South Africa if he could not speak a word of Dutch, nor call a man a French-Canadian if he could not converse in the French of his country, even though it be something of a patois. Then, again, many of the lairds are so unpatriotic as to have forsaken the Church of their forefathers. Instead of worshipping with their tenantry and their servants in the Presbyterian Church in their neighbourhood, they motor great distances to some chapel where they can find ritualistic services and probably hear only a very poor sermon.

A distinguished lady remarked to me quite lately that the three best educated and most intelligent and most charming men she had ever come across in the course of her life had never been to a public school; and if I were asked who was all round the most intelligent and best educated man I ever came across, I should say it was my uncle John Mackenzie. He also was never at a public school.

One of the charms of the good old times in the Highlands was the strong family affection shown to relatives, even if not very

58

near kin. My grandfather, Sir Hector, had two younger half-brothers, General John Mackenzie and Captain Kenneth Mackenzie. The General was known as "Fighting Jack," and had distinguished himself in the Peninsular War and fought also at the Cape, India, Sicily and Malta, while the Captain was in all the great battles of his time in India. When they were disbanded after the great war they were naturally drawn to the homes of their youth, and my grandfather gave the younger one, Captain Kenneth, the farm of Kerrysdale, A Chathair bheag (the Little Throne or Seat), which then included part of what is now the Gairloch deer-forest. There he built a house and reared a large family of children and grandchildren, and thus he resided within about a mile of the Tigh Dige for, I think, about seventy years. General John passed a good part of his life at Riverford, and at Balavil Farm, close to the east-coast family mansion of Conon. In these modern times I often hear the horrid and unnatural assertion that it is disagreeable having one's relatives all round one. So much for the culture of the twentieth century!

How I loved my two old grand-uncles. They were such pattern gentlemen of the old school. The General always accosted me in Gaelic when I was taken to see him in Inverness, where he latterly lived, and would ask me which parts of Loch Gairloch were fishing best. He said his heart was in Gairloch, and a common saying of his was that he would rather meet a dog from Gairloch than the grandest gentleman from any other place. I always felt it a feather in my cap having known so well my grand-uncle, who had served under the Earl of Cromartie, who had fought at Culloden on Prince Charlie's side. General John raised a whole company of a hundred men for the 78th Regiment of Ross-shire Highlanders, every man of them from the Gairloch property, and he died in 1860, aged ninety-seven, honoured and beloved by everyone. He had been sent to France as a boy and spoke French like a Frenchman, and his good Gaelic was a great help to him among his devoted men when fighting the French in the Peninsula. Speaking of his manners, my mother often told me that when living at Riverford, near Conon, he used to look in constantly in the afternoons, and, after a chat, when he left the room he always found his way out without turning his back on his hostess.

It was such a joy to me as a child walking over to Kerrysdale and being spoilt there with the kindness and hospitality of old Uncle Kenneth and Aunty Flora and their charming daughters and grandchildren. I remember so well in 1861 or 1862, when I was about nineteen, going to call on my old grand-uncle Kenneth at Kerrysdale, he being then past ninety. On my telling him that I was thinking of buying Inverewe, he brightened up, and told me that, when he was an ensign of only fifteen, one of the first jobs he had to do after getting his commission was to go with a party of non-commissioned officers and men to get recruits from Aird House, the home of the laird of Gruinord. The lady of Gruinord, the *Bantighearna bhuidh* (the Yellow Lady), was at the time very keen to get a commission for her son. This could be managed if she provided a certain number of so-called recruits, so she turned her ground officers into a press-gang; they kidnapped a number of lads, sons of her numerous small tenants, and these she had safely confined in a black hole under the Aird House staircase. It has always been said that she greased the soles of the feet of these lads and semi-roasted them opposite the fire until they were so tender that even if they escaped from the black hole, they could not go far. And it was to fetch these unfortunates that my grand-uncle was sent as a boy with his armed force. They made a very early start from Aird House, and he breakfasted with our relatives, the Lochend Mackenzies, at Inverewe, where they then lived in a long, low house thatched with heather. I give the menu of his breakfast, which he distinctly remembered. It consisted of a roast leg of mutton and a big wooden bowl of raspberries and cream. And he finished up his story by saying: "And if you, Osgood, make a garden there, I guarantee you will grow good raspberries in it."

We were not very expert at flowers in those days in the Baile Mor garden, but *Lios na cathracha bige* (the Kerrysdale garden) was more up to date, my grand-uncle being, like most of the Gairlochs, keen on flowers and trees. I shall always remember the smell of *Daphne* and *Ribes* there, and the big clumps of *Gladiolus cardinalis*, which was not common in those days, and the lines of Christmas roses, which flourished and bloomed in winter and early spring and formed edgings to the garden walks.

CHAPTER V

W<small>HEN</small> I was about eight years of age a tutor was got for me, and I had one with me from then till I was eleven, when I left Gairloch for Germany. I was very keen about sport of every kind, and one day, when I was about nine, my mother told me that as soon as I could swim twenty yards she would order a little gun for me. I quickly learned to swim at the lovely big sands at Gairloch, being taught by two or three girl cousins who were expert swimmers; so one day a twenty yards length of rope was bought, each end was held by a very pretty lassie, and after a fearful struggle I accomplished my task. That night a little single-barrelled muzzle-loader weighing only three pounds was ordered from a gun-maker in London. Some wise folk thought my mother was making a great mistake by letting me start shooting so early, one of the chief reasons brought forward being that I should soon become quite blasé and should not enjoy sport when I grew up to manhood. But all these prophecies were completely falsified, as I was the keenest of sportsmen all my life, until I gave up the gun when I was over seventy.

Few men have done more shooting in the course of their lives than I have. Before I began to shoot I used to love to go out with our old butler, Sim Eachainn, with a six-barrelled flint gun. I fancy there are few now living who can remember the use of flint guns, but I am one of those who can, and this special gun invariably misfired when some rare or interesting bird was shot at. But this was not so much the case, I fancy, when my grandfather and his sons all shot with flint "Joe Mantons," because their flints worked better.

It is interesting to note what there was to shoot in those far-back days of my grandfather. Well, there were grouse, but not too many, my father and his brothers always going to Leacaidh, in the heights of Kenlochewe, which was the best grouse ground then. There was nothing like the number of grouse killed in the parish of Gairloch in those days as in the 'seventies and 'eighties; and there were not so many deer either. But there were lots of black game in the woods, and ptarmigan on the high tops, and a good many partridges; and though there were plenty of fine, fat brown hares all round the crofter townships and wherever there was cultivation, there were few blue hares to be found except as great rarities on the summits of the highest hills. As for rabbits, they were unknown in the county, until my grandfather introduced them to Conon from England. I give my uncle's account of this introduction of the bunny:

"My father, alas! sent for rabbits to England. In due time they arrived, having finished every turnip with which they had started and seemingly none the worse of their travels—the darling lovely little pets! Our minds were distracted wondering how best we could protect them from the nasty, greedy foxes. We carried the hamper to some sandy banks in Dugarry, and, as the rabbits might weary if left to dig holes for themselves, busy hands and spades soon built up twenty or thirty foot refuges of turf, like six-inch square drains, at the end of which, if they pleased, they might in due time dig holes for themselves. To our great joy, the dear little innocents every morning showed plenty of new holes dug, so that they soon were safe from their enemies. In a very short time we found troops of little bunnies trotting about, so that one or two were shot as samples of such a wise investment in game. This took place over seventy years ago, and from this colony the whole north is now swarming with the pests. And yet I have never heard of anyone, planter, farmer, or gardener, who has suggested a monument to my father for conferring such a benefit on the Highlands!"

There was so much vermin in those days that the so-called gamekeepers were in reality only game-killers, and vermin trappers were only just then being started. In the old times all the lairds had in that line was a *sealgair* (hunter) who provided their big houses with venison and other game; for, until my father and uncles started stalking, not a Gairloch laird had ever troubled himself to kill deer either for sport or for the larder. The vermin consisted of all kinds of beasts and birds, a good many of which are now extinct. The fork-tailed kites swarmed, and I have heard that the first massacre of them that took place was when my father poisoned with strychnine the dead body of a young horse which had been killed by falling over a rock on Creag a Chait (the Cat's Rock), behind the Tigh Dige. The last kite had disappeared before my time. There were plenty of pine martens and polecats and some badgers even in my young days. My mother used to have an average of forty or fifty skins of martens brought to her by the keepers every year, of which she made the most lovely sable capes and coats for her sisters and lady friends. The pine martens, the polecats and the badgers are all quite extinct with us now, but they were all still in existence when I bought Inverewe.

My uncle in his Notes says that when he was a lad the Magnum Bonum plums were being raided from off the south wall of the Tigh Dige garden, and to try and guard them the gardener covered the tree with several folds of herring-net. On the following morning what did my uncle see struggling in the net but a big marten, which he shot. Its inside was found packed full of the yellow plums, but it was clever enough to avoid swallowing the stones, which were found in heaps on the top of the wall.

I was stalking when a boy of sixteen on the steep braes above Loch Langabhat in the deer forest of Morsgail, in the Lews, and as I was crawling along on my hands and knees I saw in front of me, jammed up against a low gravel bank, a dead sheep. It happened that owing to the formation of the ground my keeper and I and the Morsgail stalker were able to raise ourselves to standing position without spoiling the stalk, and on turning over the sheep what should we find under it but a large marten squashed pretty flat. We understood at once what had happened. The marten had pinned the sheep by the throat, the sheep had torn downhill, and just as it was on the point of giving in from loss of blood had jammed itself with all its might against the gravel bank. Unfortunately for the marten, there was a sharp stone sticking out of the bank, and the sheep, with more luck, I fancy, than good management, had rammed the marten, about the region of the heart, against this stone and so had its revenge. I doubt whether anyone else has ever had such an experience.

Before finishing my marten stories I shall tell what happened at Inverewe about the 'forties. Lambs and sheep were being killed, and the fox-hunter was sent for. Right up on a very wild part of the property in Carn na craoibhe caorainn (the Cairn of the Rowan-tree), near the Fionn Loch, the hounds had several times lost the scent of what was supposed to be a fox at the foot of an enormous perched boulder which we now call Clach mhor nan Taghan (the Great Stone of the Martens). To look at the boulder one would imagine it was impossible for anything but a bird to alight on its top, but a pair of martens had managed to do so by making tremendous springs from the ground on to a slight ledge half-way up the stone. There was a huge mass of peat and heather on the top of the boulder.

Spades having been sent for, the martens were unearthed, and, as they sprang from the diggers, they and their young ones jumped into the mouths of the fox-hounds and lurchers. Thus ended the martens of "Castle Marten," as a friend of mine, the late Dr. Warre, Provost of Eton College, christened the boulder. Readers will wonder that martens would kill sheep. I was once, however, informed by a very intelligent *brocair* (fox-hunter), who had been head fox-hunter for the whole county of Sutherland, that when a marten started killing sheep it was worse than a fox, and would kill even three-year-old wedders.

My uncle tells of a fox-hunter's pack which found the scent of something that was supposed to be a fox on the hillside above the Tigh Dige. The hounds ran the track for three or four miles, the fox-hunter and his gillies following as best they could, until the pack came to a dead stop on the shore of Loch Tollie, just opposite the small island where the awful tragedy connected with our family in the days of the Macleods took place. Thinking it was a fox which had crossed to the island, the fox-hunter swam over, followed by his mongrel pack, and what did they find there but a huge wild-cat, still dripping wet, and its six kittens, the latter hard at work eating a freshly killed grouse which their mother had brought them. They needed no more grouse after that interview! What a deal of thought pussy must have given to the matter before she made up her mind that the only chance of saving her kittens from the detested fox-hunter was to keep on swimming across Loch Tollie, until they were old enough to leave the island.

My uncle used also to mention the case of a gauger searching for a sack of malt.or the copper worm of a still he had heard was hidden in the Castle Leod Raven Rock above Strathpeffer. He poked his stick into a wild-cat's nest among her kittens, and in a second, unable to escape past him, she flew at him, so that he missed his footing, fell to the bottom of the rock, and broke his leg. Had not some tourists visited the rock two days afterwards he would have lain and died where he fell.

A fox was lately found dead and quite fresh on an island in one of the lochs on my own property. There was no doubt that, though foxes are not fond of water, this one had made the island his home during the daytime. On his way back after a night's ramble he had eaten an egg containing strychnine, and had only just managed to swim over to the island when he dropped down dead.

I soon became a good shot with my little gun, though it weighed only three pounds, and, strange to say, I started on snipe. Of course I could not kill them flying, but to help me there came a very severe snowstorm and hard frost, and whilst the grown-ups were shooting woodcocks in the coverts my tutor and I went snipe-shooting at the few streams and springs which were still open. I had very good eyes, but my tutor's eyes were even better, and he could generally see the snipe squatted among the dead grass and bits of ice, and he would call out, "Shoot two inches to the right of that red leaf," or "three inches to the left of that black stone," and as soon as the smoke had disappeared (and there was a lot of smoke in those days of black powder) there would be a dead full-snipe or jack-snipe, and very occasionally a woodcock. In this manner I got fifty or sixty snipe in a week, which I was proud of being able to send to friends in England. Before I grew old enough to use a big double-barrelled "Dickson" I did perfect wonders with my little three-pounder, and was the cause of the

death of two wild swans and several roe, my mother having persuaded Eley to make me little half-charged wire cartridges loaded
with BB shot and slugs. As I grew older and became a better shot
I was given a small rifle, and ornithological expeditions of several
days were made to the Shiant Islands in a smack with a tent, etc.

Never shall I forget the joy of those trips on lovely hot days at
the end of May or beginning of June. The Shiant Islands are in the
Minch about thirty miles from Gairloch, and much nearer the
shores of the Lews and Harris. They were a revelation to us, not
only on account of the myriads of sea-birds of every sort and kind
on them, but because their geological formation was quite different from that of our mainland or that of the Long Island, for
they are composed of trap rock and are basaltic, and show
columns like Staffa and the Giant's Causeway.

On each of these expeditions to the Shiant, before reaching
them we ran into Loch Na Shealg (Loch Shell) in the Lews, and
landed at a big crofter township named Leumrabhaigh (I believe
the Sassenachs now spell it *Lemmerway*). There we got a good
supply of herring, partly for our own consumption, but chiefly for
bait for our long lines, which the crew set and we lifted, in the sort
of horseshoe bay formed by the three islands, though according to
my recollection two of them are joined together at low tide. What
hauls of fish we got! Often there were cod and ling and huge
congers on almost every hook; but the best of all in our eyes were
the *Bradanan leathan* (broad salmon, as the halibut are called in
Gaelic). It is a rule among the fishermen that if one feels something
extra strong on a long line, which might be a halibut, the name
Bradan leathan or halibut must never be uttered until the monster
is safe at the bottom of the boat, otherwise it is certain to escape!

The natives of Leumrabhaigh told us they made expeditions to
the Shiant Islands for puffins, and brought back boatloads of them
because they valued the feathers. They also enjoyed big pots of
boiled puffins for their dinners as a welcome change from the usual
fish diet. They told us how they slaughter the puffins. They choose
a day when there is a strong breeze blowing against the steep braes
where the puffins breed, and the lads then lie on their backs on
these nearly perpendicular slopes holding the butt-ends of their

fishing-rods. These stiff rods would be about nine or ten feet long. Holding them with both hands, they whack at the puffins as they fly past them quite low in their tens of thousands, and whether the puffin is killed outright or only stunned he rolls down the hill and tumbles on the shore or into the sea, where the rest of the crew are kept busily employed gathering them into the boat.

The puffin-killing reminded me of the way I used to get hauls of rock-pigeons in a cave at night on the wild rocky coast beyond the crofter township of Mellon Charles, and actually in sight of the Shiant Islands. There are a number of caves which used to be well stocked with rock pigeons in the 'sixties and 'seventies, and one of them had comparatively smooth sides with a square mouth. Just before dark we used to drive the pigeons from the other caves into this one, which we called the netting cave, and then, when it was pitch dark, a herring-net weighted with stones at the bottom was let down from the top of the rocks over the cave's mouth. By lifting the net our boat glided in. We were armed with two short, stiff fishing-rods, and carried a big pot of burning peats and splinters of resinous bog-fir, which lighted up the cave. To make the pigeons fly out of the innermost recesses, we flung burning peats from time to time in as far as we could, which made a fresh batch of birds fly out against the net. Oh, the excitement of it as we whacked away at them flying round and round the big cave! The pigeons had a good sporting chance of escape, for the net could never be made to fit the inequalities in the edge of the cave, and we were quite contented if we got from twenty to twenty-five birds. To add to the excitement there were generally several shags (cormorants) roosting in the cave besides the pigeons, and we always did our best to get them, though they very soon found out that their safety consisted, not in fluttering up against the net like the pigeons, but in taking a header into the water and escaping to the ocean by diving under the net.

In 1851 my mother, who was always fond of showing me everything, planned a little tour in Normandy, finishing up with Paris, and this was a real joy. It was mostly done in *diligences*; we generally had the *coupé*, while Sim Eachainn (Simon Hector), the butler, swore at the beggars in Gaelic from the *banquette*. What an amount of delicious greengages and pears I consumed on that journey! The only drawback to the trip was the remarks of rude little French boys, who, because I was dressed in the kilt, mistook me for a Chinaman, and called me *le petit Chinois*. What a lot of good that trip did me, and how it opened my eyes! If my dear mother had not had me thoroughly taught French in Gairloch I should not have benefited by it half so much.

That summer also we visited the first great Exhibition in London. How well I remember seeing the Duke of Wellington and other celebrities! I thought more of the Duke than of any of the others, because my dear old uncle, the General (Fighting Jack), had fought and done such great deeds under him in Spain.

CHAPTER VI

VOYAGE TO ST. KILDA

My next experience was what I might almost call "The Voyage to St. Kilda," for so it seemed to me as a boy. The following detailed narrative was written by my dear mother, Mary, Lady Mackenzie of Gairloch, on our return. In that far-off island I found what to me were quite new birds, such as gannets, fulmars, shearwaters, fork-tailed petrels and eider-ducks, specimens of which I was able to shoot with my own little gun.

"On Monday, the 30th of May, 1853 (having had all our provisions and packages prepared on the Saturday), we were called at three o'clock in the morning with the good news that it was a beautiful day for our start to St. Kilda. Dressing was soon accomplished, and off we set on foot for the quay, about half a mile from the Tigh Dige. The weather did not please me so well as it did my housemaid, for I found on looking on the bay that it was a perfect calm with a sea mist over the Isle of Skye; so, instead of getting into the *Jessie*, the vessel we had hired for the occasion, we continued in the smaller rowing-boat, proposing that Osgood should shoot and amuse himself in some way. We, for a wonder, could not see any guillemots or cormorants, and then George Ross, the keeper, said spearing flounders would be grand sport, so to shore we went for a spear, and in about an hour we got seventeen fine flat-fish, besides a large cat-fish or 'father lasher,' and also a sea-devil, both frightful in the extreme. I had never seen a sea-devil before, and when the spear went into it it turned round and bit the spear, leaving the distinct marks of its teeth on the steel prongs. We also found a rock-pigeon's nest with two young ones in it, but left them till they should grow larger and be fitter to leave their nest.

"We stopped at Little Sand, where the fish were cleaned and some of them sent to a cottage to be boiled, whilst we sat on the rock, and along with the excellent fish came fresh oat-cakes from

Iain Buidhe's wife. There we made a good breakfast, and then got again into the small boat to go to Longa Island, at the farthest end of which I had ordered the *Jessie* to call for us. It was nearly midday before we went on board, and by that time a nice breeze had sprung up from the north-east. Our crew consisted of the Skipper Ali Ban, the Gillemor (or Alexander Fraser), and Sandy Longa (a Maclean). Besides these three, I had engaged two extra hands, Alexander Macmillan and William Grant, both capital fellows. The former is considered the best seaman in Gairloch, and neither of them cared what they did nor how much they worked so that they did but please us and add to our comfort.

"Besides the five seamen and myself, Osgood and his tutor, there were four more persons—namely, George Ross, the keeper, Simon Fraser, the butler, and the two hall-boys Ali and Duncan—Just a round dozen of folks leaving home with the determination to be delighted with the voyage of discovery. I am at least sure that eleven of them were joyous: I am not quite so sure about the captain. I think he was too anxious for our safety and satisfaction to be quite happy.

"We went sailing along the Minch nicely for a while, but the breeze lulled at four or five o'clock, and by degrees it became perfectly calm. We were then within about three miles of Eilean Trodda, at the north end of Skye, so we got into our boat and rowed to it, and there Osgood shot away at some puffins and guillemots. The rocks were very picturesque, and I saw several stacks or rocky pillars and some dark, deep chasms. After remaining about an hour, we saw our vessel slowly rounding the island, and, thinking it time to join her, we rowed to meet her. There was a swell, but no wind. We found that the tutor during our absence had not been so good a sailor as he had expected, and Osgood immediately he went on board was ill, so to bed we went. To those who may wish to know what sort of beds ours were I will describe them, and also the arrangement of the vessel.

"As to her make, she was neither yacht nor clipper built, but a good ordinary-sized sailing smack. She had one cabin aft with two small berths. These I gave to the tutor and the keeper, whilst Osgood and I had two grand beds, with mattresses, blankets, and sheets, made in the stern end of the hatchway or cargo-place, and a long curtain placed across to make our bedrooms snug. The middle of the hatchway was open and contained sundry hampers, boxes, etc.—in fact, it was our larder and crockery-place and sort of general receptacle for waterproofs, plaids, guns, ammunition. Beyond this open space was another curtain concealing the sleeping apartment of Simon and the boys, and occasionally William Grant and Macmillan. In the bow was the crew's lodging-place.

"The floor of our bedroom was rather uneven, being merely hay placed on the top of the stone ballast; but once in bed we were well off—at least, whenever the *Jessie* behaved herself, but when she pitched and tossed, as she did on the following Thursday, then Osgood and I neither praised the bed nor anything else.

"On waking on Tuesday morning we found ourselves very near Lochmaddy (the Loch of the Dogs), there being at the entrance of the loch two rocks that bear the name of "The Dogs" (*na madaidh*). We sailed to the head of the loch, and the captain went ashore to try and get a pilot, a Colin Macleod, who was highly recommended. Unfortunately, he had gone seven miles from home, and thus we were detained five hours waiting for him. During those hours we went on shore. The appearance of the place, which is not at all pretty, is rendered strange by the very numerous lochs, many of which are affected by the tide. We went to see a small steamer belonging to Lord Hill, the shooting tenant of Macleod's country in Skye, and also of Lord Macdonald's North Uist shooting. He resides chiefly at Dunvegan Castle, but occasionally goes over to Lochmaddy in his steamer from Monday to Saturday. He killed a great many seals last season. One day he got six. We also visited a small school where the children read English and translated it into Gaelic very well. Osgood saw a strange bird, black with some white. He could not make out whether it were a sort of tern or some dark-coloured gull. He thought it more resembled the former species than the latter.

"Towards three o'clock the pilot arrived. The breeze, that had been very fresh and favourable, was lulling, and fell almost completely soon after we got out of Lochmaddy. As the evening advanced we got tired of the *Jessie*, as she was rather going back-wards, so again we ordered the boat and four rowers and away we went to one of the numerous islands that bounded us on the left. There were scarcely any birds there; it was not sufficiently steep and rocky. Osgood had a bathe, notwithstanding that the shore was very rough and stony, and Deantag, our terrier, discovered the former retreat of some kind of petrel. The nest we got after a great deal of tearing up of clods, but, much to our sorrow, there were no eggs. The nest was fresh and much larger than the nests of the stormy petrels—I should think about twice the size—and it must have been that of a shearwater. Deantag scratched and whined at several other holes, but having no spade and no time to spare (for we saw the vessel retreating from us) we were obliged to leave the hidden treasures untouched. Our men did not spare their arms, and by dint of hard rowing we gained upon and at length reached the *Jessie*, which the current was fast taking back to Lochmaddy, and there, in fact, we were next morning, much to our annoyance. At the turn of the tide the current changed and helped us on our course northwards to the Sound of Harris, and after going at the pace of a snail for hours, and with innumerable tacks, we reached *Bun an t-struidh* (the Stream End) or *Òb* (the Pool), three miles west of Rodal, at one or two o'clock in the afternoon. There we cast anchor, as the wind, north-west, was dead against us and it was beginning to blow very hard. We saw one seal in the water, but not near enough to get at it.

"We landed on Harris, and I like the appearance of the country much better than that of North Uist. The hills are much higher, and I heard that the country was more fertile. The bere gives wonderful returns, they say—sometimes twenty or twenty-five fold. Our sailors got in fresh water for the vessel, for fear we might run short on our passage to the 'back of beyond.' After a lounge about for some time a young girl addressed us in Gaelic, and asked whether we should like to go to the Ladies' Flowering Work School so Osgood and I set off with her, and made enquiries as we went. The school was established by the Countess of Dunmore, whose only son, the proprietor, is a minor about twelve years of age. We reached the school-house, a neat little building, in about twenty minutes. Nothing mental is taught there, only the embroidering of collars and sleeves. The teacher was a young Irishwoman, who mentioned that she was under the guidance of a society of ladies for the promotion of fancy work, and that they had offered her services to Lady Dunmore, but that they were going to remove her next year so that other places might have the advantage of her to instruct them, and whichever girl she recommended to Lady Dunmore as the best worker would be appointed to supply her place. The cleverest hands could earn two or three shillings a week or more did they apply themselves entirely to the occupation. They were working for a shop at Glasgow, and also for the Countess, who had sent them nice patterns from Paris. There were not more than about fifteen girls present when we were there. They are allowed to come any time they like from 6 a.m. to 6 p.m.

"On returning to our people I proposed to go to see Rodal, to which there was a good road. After some trouble I hired a pony for Osgood and myself to ride by turns. It was only a three-year-old, and had never had anything on but a rope round its head, and perhaps creels on its back. It did not look remarkably fresh, yet it managed to throw William Grant over its head when he mounted it to bring it to us. Notwithstanding this freak, we determined to venture, and after borrowing a bridle and a man's saddle from a person who kept a little inn and shop together by the roadside, Osgood mounted with William Grant as his attendant. He is so strong and active and so devoted to Osgood that in his charge I always think my little man in safety.

"As we approached Rodal the scenery became very picturesque. We passed through a gate on the right hand, and on rising ground was a long extent of plantation containing a great variety of trees, apparently about fifteen or twenty years of age. There were larch, birch, beech, oak, elm, alder, and ash. The whole appearance of the grounds was that of the approach to a gentleman's seat, but in reality there is no family mansion anywhere on the property. I had heard there were the ruins of an old cathedral, and I saw it on the left hand, so having got an intelligent-looking man as a guide, we went into the burying-ground which surrounds the ruins. The ground is high, and the view from there extremely pretty. The broken edifice contains a good many monuments. It was the burial-place of some of the Macleod chiefs of Skye and Harris and other noted folk of the days long gone by. There were some very curious figures on the wall. The building had been, unfortunately, nearly destroyed by fire years before.

"At Rodal there is a quay with a small snug harbour which can be entered from two directions, but, I believe, not at low tide. We returned as we came. The evening was fine, but the wind high. Having paid for the use of the pony, that had behaved well, and got some milk we wished to go on board, but on account of the tide being out our boat could not come for us, so we were obliged to have some men at a cottage roused up (it was past 10 p.m.), and they ferried us across a sort of inlet that was in our way, and then after a little walk we came to the shore, where our boat was waiting us. On our talking to the pilot, he said the tide would serve soon after break of day, and he would then endeavour to proceed. Once out of the sound, which was in all eight miles in length, the north wind would not be so much against us, for as soon as we reached the open Atlantic we should go direct west. The Sound of Harris is considered very dangerous for the navigation of vessels. It is full of rocks, numbers of which are sunken at a short distance from the surface of the water, and, again, the current is always so strong during a calm that there is great difficulty in keeping a vessel off these dreaded skerries.

"The noise of the pulling up of the anchor soon wakened me in the morning, and I quickly found out I was at sea. Poor Osgood, too, was not happy. As we neared the ocean our vessel pitched and tossed even more than our pilot liked. He told me afterwards he was really alarmed for our safety; but the *Jessie* was a gallant barque, and she bore us bravely, notwithstanding that the rough weather and the great swell in that place tried her goodness. I kept as quiet as I could in the hopes of Osgood's sleeping between the fits of coughing. Everyone was ill except the sailors, even Simon and Ali and Duncan, who had all scorned the idea of being seasick. We had a wearisome day of it. Occasionally I sent for one of my favourite sailors and asked how matters were going on. One of William Grant's replies, translated into English, was: 'She is

carrying full sails at present, my lady, so there is no fear of her.'
There were as heavy seas where we were as in any part of the
Atlantic between here and America, and the passage was rendered
worse by these strong currents.

"At seven or eight in the evening we began to draw near to the
far-famed St. Kilda. When I heard that we were not above a mile
from shore, I begged to get out in the boat, as the wind had sunk,
but I was told that four men were in her, rowing away with all
their might, trying to keep the vessel from driving on the rocks
by the force of the current. The rest of our crew were toiling at
two enormous sweeps belonging to the *Jessie*. Well, I waited
another hour, and on finding that instead of being nearer we were
fast receding, and that we might now have the boat, as we had
(against our will) gone out of the little bay and exchanged its steep
rugged rocks for the wild ocean, I told Simon to put clothes on
Osgood in some sort of way and ordered the boat to the gangway.
Poor child, he looked most wretched. Putting on his and my own
swimming belts, we somehow or other got into the boat. There
was a heavy swell, but fortunately no broken waves. I was not
much alarmed, and said nothing at any rate; but the tutor and
others who were left on the *Jessie* watched us a little while, and
then we sank so low that they could not see us at all, and were
half afraid we had been swamped. But we had been more merci-
fully dealt with, and landed at length quite safely and comfortably
on the shore of this wonderfully striking, picturesque island.

"I had been told there was but one small flat stone on which one
could land, and that the natives would pull me up from it. That
is not quite the case. There are twenty or thirty yards of shore on
which you might put foot, but there is one spot more convenient
than the rest and yet not altogether good, for the rock is covered
with seaweed of the most slippery sort, and you are almost sure to
tumble on your nose. You can never land when the wind is from
the south-east, for that is the direction of the bay, and a very little
breeze thus raises an awful swell. I was told by the people that the
ast time the factor came to visit them he was three days before he
could land. When at last he did accomplish it, it was by tying a
rope round his body and throwing the other end to the people on

shore, and waiting till one of the enormous waves went back-wards, when he flung himself out and was drawn up on the flat rock, the usual landing-place. Another story was also told me, but after I got home. A man from our parish met William Grant at Poolewe. 'Weel,' said he, 'so I hear you have been to St. Kilda. Could you manage to land?' 'Land,' said William. 'Oh yes, we landed safe enough, and passed three days and three nights there.' 'You were in luck,' replied his friend; 'the last time I sailed there, when in the service of Macdonald of Lochinver, who had the islands, I was twenty days beating about and round St. Kilda in the *Rover's Bride* and never could land after all.'

"The only gentleman I ever conversed with about St. Kilda was the Rev. James Noble, Free Church Minister of Poolewe. He went there with one or two other ministers in Lord Breadalbane's yacht about three or four years ago. They intended to remain three days, but a frightful hurricane arose one night after they had gone to the vessel, and they were in great danger for twenty-four hours. It was impossible to put out a small boat, and they were every instant expecting the anchor would give way. Although the anchorage-ground at the end of the bay is fairly good, it is ex-tremely shelving, the sea becoming deep so suddenly, and thus an anchor is liable to shift. The captain had a great many fathoms of spare chain which he threw out to help to steady the vessel. She could not sail out; the wind was right ahead of her. The next night it changed, and then they started, only daring to put up the jib, and in the midst of a frightful hurricane reached Harris in nine hours, thankfully wondering that their existence was thus pre-served. It was the same storm which on the east coast destroyed so many of the Caithness herring fleet with their crews.

"Besides St. Kilda itself, there are three other islands and the two 'Stacks.' Two of the islands, the Dun and Soa, almost join, but the third, Borrera, is near the Stacks of the solan-geese, which are about five miles off. Nearly all the male inhabitants of the island were assembled to meet us when we landed, and well might they welcome us, for they had not seen a creature but themselves for nine long months, and they were very anxious for news from Australia about their friends who had emigrated the previous autumn. Eight families containing thirty-six souls had then gone. Only fifteen heads of families remained, the population now being but sixty persons. Formerly it was always about one hundred, but it never materially increased, and this was owing to the mortality of the infants, the greater part of whom die at the early age of five or six days, owing, it is supposed by medical men, to the heat and dirt in which the child is kept and the want of proper washing and attending to. The poor parents themselves attribute it to no human cause, and calmly say that it is the will of God. In no family are there more than six children. Generally there are not above one or two. I saw one little boy who was the only child left out of fourteen who were born to his parents. The oldest man in the island was fifty-seven, but there was one old woman nearly eighty.

"Both the men and the women are rather undersized and not at all strong-looking. Their complexions are a sort of dingy yellow. I did not see anyone with red hair, but many with light hair, sandy and brown, and several of the women had black hair and very dark eyes. Their persons and houses and everything belonging to them smell of fulmar petrel oil, which, by the way, is not at all fragrant. They told me they were usually healthy, and they were not subject to any particular disease, but the poor men often meet with accidents among the rocks, and thus their days are short-ened. As to their dress, I remarked that they wore homespun and home-woven woollen shirts sewn together with worsted yarn. Their trousers were of a sort of blue tartan check, probably dyed in the island, the indigo being purchased by them from elsewhere. Nearly all of them were without shoes or stockings. Some of them had a little piece of blue cloth under their heels. The few shoes I did see were very round and ill-shaped. They are all able to do shoemaking and tailoring, and many of them wove, but not all. They have no mill, but grind with the quern. One woman works the quern alone. They did not appear to grind above a quart or two of corn at a time. I observed several men and women with lamb-skin caps. The girls had a great deal of hair, very un-tidily arranged, and the wives had equally untidy caps, and, for what purpose I know not, they had two strings tied round their bodies, one just under their arms and the other a quarter of a yard below, making their second waist very low. Their gowns were some of them of dark cotton and some of homespun. Neither the men nor the women had any politeness in outward manner. I did not notice any of them bow or curtsey at any time, but they are kind and gentle in speech and obliging and friendly in actions. Yet this does not prevent them from being keen for money and still more for tobacco. They would part with any of the commodities of the island for half their value if paid in tobacco.

"Their houses are built rather in a crescent form about one hundred yards above the shore at the head of the bay, and extend for nearly a quarter of a mile. I counted twenty-five dwelling-places besides the little barns or outbuildings. The byre is on the left-hand side as you enter, and above it is the only aperture for letting out smoke, which, in fact, they wish to keep in as much as possible for the sake of the soot, which they use to enrich the land for the barley and the potatoes in the spring. I was told that they never clean out their byres at all till they take away the manure in April, and previous to that time it is almost impossible to get in and out of the door. I visited the island too late in the season to see this bad arrangement, and was surprised at the cleanly appearance of the walls and roofs of the houses, and the nice dry walk which went all along the sides of the houses. The walls of the houses are built just as they are in Harris—that is, double, being very thick and the middle filled with earth. The roof extends only to the inner wall, and you can walk round the top of the wall quite easily. The form of the roof is oval, like a big bee-hive. They are made with wood covered with turf and then thatched with straw above, and on the outside are straw ropes like a network put across to keep the wind from blowing away the thatch. The houses have generally a sort of window with a tiny bit of glass, and they have a plan of their own for locking their doors with a wooden key made by themselves. It appears to keep matters quite secure. Osgood observed that the beaks of the solan-geese were used as pegs to keep down the straw on the buildings. The houses are built on a gentle slope, the highest hill, Conacadh, gradually rising to the west. The land between the shore and the houses and up some way above them is cultivated, and at the back is a capital high, strong dyke to keep the cattle and sheep out. I did not hear how much arable land they have, but by making a rough guess I should say between thirty and forty acres. Each head of a family or crofter pays £1 for the arable land, 7s. a year for his cow's grass, and 10s. for ten sheep at 1s. per head. Besides this £1 17s., he has to pay 7 stones of 24 pounds weight of feathers, which is reckoned to him at 5s. a stone. I heard various accounts as to how many birds would be required to supply sufficient feathers to make up a stone weight. One lad told me about two hundred fulmars and another eight hundred puffins; the latter, of course, are much smaller, and the feathers are not so plentiful nor of such good quality, I should think.

"There are two burns or very small streams running from Conacadh by the houses to the shore. There is a capital natural well or spring in the arable land, and another in the glen two or three miles off. This one is celebrated. On the right side of the village and near the shore is a storehouse where the feathers and cloth and wool, etc., are kept. The factor also keeps a small supply of meal, planks, and coals there, and the elder has the key. Not far from the store are the manse and the church, both of which are built with stone and slated. The former is always kept locked during the factor's absence, and he inhabits it during his visits. The church is a plain building, probably thirty feet by eighteen feet, and in it we slept on hay and ate our meals. The famous Dr. Macdonald of Feristosh, the Apostle of the North, visited St. Kilda four times. His first visit was in 1822, when he remained eighteen days. I believe it was through his instrumentality that the church and manse were built, but being erected before the Disruption, they belonged to the Established Church. The Rev. Neil MacKenzie was minister there for fourteen years, and left, I think, in 1843. Since then there has been no regular pastor, but the Breadalbane yacht with a Free Church minister generally visits them or a few days once every summer. Neither have they any schoolmaster just now, but all can read Gaelic except the younger children, and they have a little library of all the Gaelic books, which are circulated among them. They told me they assembled in the church for worship every evening of the week excepting Saturdays and Mondays, and met on the Sabbath before breakfast and in the evening.

"Though the people are far from large and robust-looking, yet they informed us that they were very healthy, and were not subject to any of the great diseases of the Long Island or the mainland. There did not appear to be any abject poverty or scarcity of food amongst them. They all at that season (the 3rd of June) had still a little corn. Barley grows best with them. I thought the grain looked small, and they told me that the reason was the sea-breeze dries and whitens it too soon before it is properly ripened. There is one small elder-bush near the manse. I did not remark any other kind of bush or tree of any description. The grass on the hills was looking very dry and apparently suffering from drought, but on the Dun amongst the cairns, where the puffins built, the grass and natural clover was most beautiful and luxuriant. The people described the weather as being usually very dry during May and June, but dreadfully stormy in winter, with frequently much snow. I wondered to hear them say so, as, being so exposed to the sea-breezes on all sides, even if the snow fell I could not have imagined it would have lain long. Perhaps they think more of a little snow than a Perthshire man would of three times the amount.

"There are four sorts of sheep—the *lachdann*, which are of a dull yellow or amber colour; the *gorm*, which are of a bluish-grey; the white sheep and the black. In Soa the sheep belong to the proprietor, a Mr. John Macleod, son of a Colonel Macleod and grandson of a minister that was at St. Kilda. I was told that there were in all between two and three thousand sheep on the islands. The ewes belonging to the people are milked every morning, and the lambs shut up every night to keep them from their mothers. The milk is chiefly made into cheese. The cows seem to me of a good size, rather larger than many in Gairloch, and of ordinary Highland colour, not spotted. There are no peats to be got anywhere in the island, and the poor people are obliged to burn the green turf, which they cut and dry and put into little stone buildings with great trouble and care.

"The bird that is most esteemed amongst the natives for its flesh and feathers is the fulmar. It much resembles the herring-gull, but has no black tips to its wings, which, along with the back, are of a French grey, the head, throat, and breast a pure white. They belong to the petrel tribe of birds, and have a bill, curved at the point, which is yellow, and nostrils in a tube which has only one external hole. They have a great many soft and rather long feathers, and skim along the air noiselessly. They are very tame, and when we were rowing they passed close over our heads. None of our party shot at them, for fear of vexing the people. They did not mind the other birds being fired at. The fulmar builds on the grassy ledges of the highest and most precipitous rocks, some twelve hundred feet high. They lay but one egg, which is white and larger than a very large hen's egg and quite oval. The St. Kilda folk catch these birds with a noose made of horse-hair and fastened to a stick like a short fishing-rod. Near the ends it is rendered stiffer by pieces of the shafts of the solan-goose's feathers plaited amongst the horse-hair. The man who is to descend the rock has two ropes, one of which is fastened round his waist and the end held in the hands of his companion, who stands on the top of the rock. The other rope is in under the foot of the man above, who plants his heel firmly on it in a sort of hollow he has made for the purpose, and it is with this rope that the fulmar-hunter descends, letting the rope slip through his hands as a sailor does. They are very expert in killing the birds by breaking their necks in an instant, and as the fulmars are killed they are tucked into the waist rope. When many are taken they are tied together to the end of the loose rope, the bird-catcher meantime standing on a ledge, and they are drawn up to the top. It is said that the fulmar lays but one egg, and if this be taken she does not lay again that year. It was from the face of Conacadh that we saw them descend for the fulmars. One, a little boy apparently not more than twelve years of age, was let down by his father. They all say the same Gaelic words, *Leig leatha* ('Let her go,' meaning 'Let out the rope'), in going down. They use their feet much in descending, and go, as it were, by starts and bounds. They seem to have no fear, though so many have been killed on the rocks.

"The puffins, or sea-parrots, are very numerous, but are chiefly caught by the dogs under the stones or cairns or by snares. They are very plentiful on the Dun, and where they build the grass is beautiful. The dogs appear to be of a small, lean, mongrel kind of collie dog. There seem to be numbers of them, and some I saw at the houses had a rope round their neck and one foreleg passed through it to prevent them running far away.

"The people have no means of killing the eider-ducks, as they have no gun on the island. Osgood and George Ross went after them on Friday and killed between them three drakes. Osgood killed one positively and another doubtfully. Two other drakes were killed afterwards. They are very beautiful large birds with much white in their plumage, the top of the head velvet black, and a pea-green colour at the back of the neck. The duck is of a handsome, dark, mottled brown plumage, something in colour like a grey hen. The eggs are large and of a light opaque-looking green. It was in the East Bay that we saw the eiders, perhaps a dozen or twenty pairs. The people said they were getting much more plentiful on the other side, between Soa and the Dun. Their nests are composed entirely of the softest down, which in Norway is collected in such quantities for pillows and quilts.

"The solan-geese build on the two Stacks, Stac an Armuin and Stac an Ligh. We went to the latter on the Friday in the afternoon, about three o'clock. I ordered the only boat in the island. It is large and heavy, with mast and sail and eight oars. It is used for going to the Stacks and to Borrera and Soa, and also generally once a year, about Whit-Sunday, a party of the natives go over in it to Harris to purchase little things and to hear the news. Osgood and I had gone to the *Jessie* for our luncheon, and when the big boat came alongside there were no fewer than nineteen persons in it. We sent nine of them on shore, taking ten St. Kilda men and six of our own men with us. The Stacks are a good five miles away from the main island, and though the day was fine there was a pretty heavy roll. The whole of the way the ten St. Kilda men kept singing a sort of song at the pitch of their voices, the refrain of which consisted of the following words of encouragement in their rather funny St. Kilda Gaelic:

" 'Iomru illean, iomru illean,
     Robh mhath na gillean, robh mhath na gillean,
     Shid i, shid i, shid i, shid i.'

A rough translation of which is—

" 'Row, lads, row, lads.
     Well done, the lads! well done, the lads!
     There she goes, there she goes.'

As we approached the Stacks the gannets came to meet us in their thousands, and one could hardly see the sky through them. There is no possible landing-place on the Stacks where a boat can be drawn up, as they rise sheer out of the ocean. At one place for which we steered there had been an iron pin three feet long let into the rock perhaps ten feet above high-water mark, and from the boat a rope with a loop at the end of it was thrown over this pin and the boat drawn in near enough for some of the best of the St. Kilda climbers to spring on to a small ledge. Then they ascended very carefully and very slowly with their rods with the nooses at the end, and soon they had caught and killed a large number of the solans who were sitting on their eggs. The Stacks and their feathered inhabitants were a sight never to be forgotten. The gannets are the main food-supply of the St. Kilda people. They told us they caught the old ones when they first arrived in the spring, but made their chief raid on them just before the fat young ones leave the nests. They salt them down by the thousand, and they told us they tasted like salted bull beef. Of course, the natives live very much upon eggs all through May and June, and we asked them whether they were very particular as to the eggs being quite freshly laid. From their answers we inferred they ate a lot of eggs that had been more or less sat upon, for they said: 'Of course, if you don't like the young bird you can throw it away, and just eat the rest.'

"On our return to Uist to land the pilot at Lochmaddy we noticed that he had a large washing-tub on deck full of guillemots' and razor-bills' eggs, most of them evidently quite hard set, and we asked him what he was going to do with them, and he said they were to be given as a present to Lady Hill, who was so fond of blowing eggs!

"The return voyage to Gairloch was uneventful and safely accomplished, and the trip to St. Kilda was most thoroughly enjoyed by every one of us."

Thus ends my mother's story, but just to show the very primitive manner in which not only the St. Kilda islanders, but also more or less the whole population of the Long Island, lived in the early 'fifties, I must tell the story of a visit I paid as a boy to a typical house in South Harris on our way back from St. Kilda.

We reached *Bun an t-struidh* (Stream End) or, as it is now more often called, *Òb* (the Pool), on the Sound of Harris, late on a Saturday night, and having no milk for our Sunday breakfast porridge, I was landed, accompanied by our faithful butler Sim Eachainn (Simon Hector), to try and get some from one of the many crofters' houses which were dotted about among the rocks opposite to where we were anchored. The habitation we selected for our visit was, like most of the native houses, very long, considering its height and its width inside, because these Hebridean houses have to contain not only the family, but also the whole stock of cattle, not to mention sundry pet sheep and innumerable hens, with no division of any kind between the animals and the human beings. I should say the house was a good forty-five feet long, with the usual low, broad walls, six feet thick, built partly of stones, but mostly of turf, and only some five feet in height, on which grass grows and sheep and sometimes even a calf may be seen grazing happily. What surprises a stranger at first sight is that instead of the thatched roof extending, as in all other parts of the world, a little beyond the outside of the walls, so that the drip from the roof may fall clear of the dwelling, the couples which sustain the roof invariably rest on the inside edge of these wide walls. This arises chiefly from the fact that there is no wood on the Long Island, with the exception of the few comparatively young trees in the plantations round the policies of Stornoway Castle and Rodal; so the natives have always had to do their best with very short lengths of timber, such as stray bits from wrecks washed up along the coast or wood brought with great trouble in their fishing-boats from the mainland. That houses built on apparently such a wrong principle as this must be frightfully damp goes without saying, but notwithstanding, they often turn out as fine specimens of men and women as can be found in any part of Britain.

We entered the house, which was very narrow (only about twelve feet wide inside), by a door near one end, and had to make our way along through manure and litter, there being only just room between the tails of the eight or ten cattle beasts and the wall for us to squeeze up to the end where the fire was burning against the gable and where was also the bed. We were most politely and hospitably welcomed. The good wife, like all the Harris people, had most charming manners, but she was busy preparing the family breakfast, and bade us sit down on little low stools at the fire and wait till she could milk the cows for us.

Then occurred a curious scene, such as one could hardly have witnessed elsewhere than in a Kaffir kraal or an Eskimo tent or Red Indian tepe. There was a big pot hanging by a chain over the peat fire, and a creel heaped up with short heather, which the women tear up by the root on the hillsides and with which they bed the cows. The wife took an armful of this heather and deposited it at the feet of the nearest cow, which was tied up within two or three yards of the fire, to form a drainer. Then, lifting the pot off the fire, she emptied it on to the heather; the hot water disappeared and ran away among the cow's legs, but the contents of the pot, consisting of potatoes and fish boiled together, remained on the top of the heather. Then from a very black-looking bed three stark naked boys arose one by one, aged, I should say, from six to ten years, and made for the fish and potatoes, each youngster carrying off as much as both his hands could contain. Back they went to their bed, and started devouring their breakfast with apparently great appetites under the blankets! No wonder the bed did not look tempting! We got our milk in course of time, but I do not think it was altogether relished after the scene we had witnessed, which impressed me so much that I have never forgotten it.

CHAPTER VII

THE LEWS

I SHALL now have a good deal to say about the Lews, and I may mention that the oldest story that I know concerning that interesting island is the following:

About 1780 Lord Seaforth persuaded my grandfather, Sir Hector, to accompany him over to Stornoway. The Seaforth Lodge, which then stood nearly on the site of the present castle, happening not to be in a very good state of repair for the reception of its owner and his guest, they repaired to the Stornoway Inn, and a queer sort of hole it must have been in those days. It was a great day for the landlady, and she did her very best. For dinner she proudly uncovered a big dish of boiled grouse, but nearly fainted at the outcry made by his lordship on seeing that his grouse had been poached in May!

Let me now quote my uncle's experience of a Stornoway whale-hunt:

"One day when I was fishing for salmon in the Ewe a lawyer came to me with a letter from a political coterie saying a county election was imminent, and I found it was decided that I was the proper party to go with this limb of the law to canvass the voters in a distant island, as being well known by name, person, or reputation to them all. A yacht waited to carry me there and back again at my command. That abominable yacht made it impossible for me to say, 'But I'll not go. I'd rather catch salmon than voters.' So with a heavy heart I left my country—for my country's good we shall hope, but, at all events, for an aquatic battle such as I have never seen and never shall see again. As the old ballad did not appeal to me which says—

    " 'Up in the mornin's no for me,
      Up in the mornin' airly;
     I'd rather gae supperless to my bed,
      Than rise in the mornin' airly,'

it was soon after dawn on a calm grey morning that I found my-self parading Stornoway Pier, whence the long harbour was visible down to the open sea about three miles away. I observed people looking seaward with their spy-glasses, and wondered what they were taken up with. In a few minutes all but myself and some of the wise men with glasses were scampering away up the town like mad bulls, roaring their loudest for all hands to get out the boats, and ere one could cry 'Peas' every male in the town seemed gone crazy, shouting out, 'Mucan mara, Mucan mara!' ('Whales, whales!') Many, half-dressed and hatless, were carrying oars and guns, boat-hooks, old broadswords, and other kinds of lethal weapons, one of them even bearing a kitchen spit with its wooden wheel at the end like a gallant lancer's spear. They all tumbled into the many boats at the pier and on the shore, first throwing into them heaps of smallish stones, evidently to be used as round shot for the enemy. I just sucked a finger of astonish-ment, wondering if I was living in an asylum, until a telescope-holder kindly told me the people were expecting a catch of whales.

"Then between tongues and telescope I became aware that a line of six or eight boats were acting in concert with the harbour boats, some of the men rowing and others standing up on the thwarts and waving hats and jackets to indicate something not yet visible to us landlubbers. In a few minutes some thirty boats were steering down the harbour close to the land on our side, rowing as if for dear life or a £1,000 prize. We saw them very soon pass the eight boats at the harbour mouth, which, it seemed, had gone off early to their ordinary long line fishings, when they fell in with a great school of whales that were capering about like lunatics in the sea. The moment the supporting boats passed those which had discovered the whales, we saw them wheel round out-side them from the shore, and soon a regular barrier of boats was formed quite across the bay about one hundred yards beyond the original fishermen, who then left their stations to join the new flotilla. Meanwhile another line of boats, arriving later, formed a second barrier one hundred yards or so nearer the ocean than the first one. All this time our telescopes showed us that the chase was going on vigorously. The crews of the boats were waving coats and throwing stones at the coveted mammals, and the sea was boiling with the capers of the monsters, who were growing alarmed at their danger. Oh dear, dear! they have dived under the first line of boats and are off back to sea! What a loss of booty! But all is not over, for the fugitives have taken fright at the second line of boats, and the first line has divided in the middle, passed farther out in two columns, to reform their line again beyond the second. This game went on for rather longer than the fishers desired, for the demands upon wind and limb were severe, and they had started early, without food or liquor, their only breakfast being deferred hope, which does not take long to digest.

"However, about noon the whales seemed to have had enough of men and boats, and their leader, distinguished by the name of *Delphinus deductor*—or *caaing*, that is, 'driving whale'—steered up the harbour and was soon nearly opposite the town. All was most quiet and silent there, lest any noise on shore might frighten the whales out to sea again. The harbour grows so much narrower near the town that the boats came gradually closer together, and showers of stones were thrown at every whale who showed above water. I fetched my double rifle and its ammunition from the hotel, and became so excited that when the leading whale raised his head high enough to show his eye, I fired without asking anyone's leave, feeling certain I could extinguish it. A universal groan and some unmistakable bad language from land and sea rather shocked me for a moment; but I am certain the shot was a wise one, for the leader, instead of turning away to sea as my groaners were sure he would do, quietly continued his course up the harbour till he grounded. It was high water or nearly so, and ninety-five others of his large followers ran ashore also or hung about him like a swarm of bees round their queen, though there was nothing to prevent all of them going back to sea if they had resolved to do so.

"As soon as the boat people learnt the leader was ashore, the boats dashed in among the shoal, busy with every deadly weapon they could lay hands on, till the sea was mere bloody mud. I saw my spit-bearer poking his spit into shining backs as they emerged from the water alongside his boat, and I saw also a leather-cutter busy with his knife, imagining he was killing whales also, while in reality he was only spoiling their leather, for below the skin, which naturally he cut, was a mass of blubber. I soon expended all my bullets at point-blank distance. The sea seemed pink, nearly scarlet.

"Every now and then a boat was upset by a whale rising to the surface underneath it, and the noise of the killers and the semi-drowning people and the onlookers on the shore was astounding, a whale sometimes getting his head so much above water that he could join in the uproar, which he did with a will. One boat struck near the shore, and a badly wounded whale took to spouting blood in a stream as thick as my arm from his blow-hole. He anchored exactly astern of the stranded boat, and rather astonished its crew by regularly deluging them with a continuous stream of pure blood. The water was too deep for the men to jump ashore, and in a few minutes, in spite of their seeking shelter under the thwarts or at the side of the boat, any one of them might have applied for a place as the Demon clothed in scarlet in *Der Freischutz*; and instead of their receiving pity from the spectators, the shore just rang with yells of laughter.

"When it was low water I went among the ninety-six captives, and forgetting that they were not fish, who died when out of water, got rather a start when one of them, which I poked, opened his mouth and gave an alarming roar, making me feel quite sorry for him and his. They were of all sizes, most of them about twenty to twenty-four feet long, but some were down to four feet, and in several places in the mud I could have taken up bowls of milk that had run out of the mother whales. One of them opened its mouth and spat out an eight or nine pound salmon as fresh as if taken out of a net, and I doubt not it made a dinner for some people that day, after having itself dined with a whale. It was evidently a salmon that intended to go up the River Creed, but had fallen in with the school of whales as they passed along, and had very naturally been gobbled up. The whole of the townsfolk were busy as bees making sure that there was no risk of any of the whales swimming out to sea again at the next high tide, and in due time slices of whale were being boiled for oil in every hole and corner of the town. For many a day everything smelt, if it did not taste, of whale oil! It was a wild mess, ending most child-ishly in each whale being towed out to sea after its blubber was pared off and cast adrift, whereas if made into manure it would have made a great piece of land grateful for years."

When I was ten years old I paid my first visit to Lews Castle with my mother, accompanied by our keeper, and I brought my new little rifle. We were sent to Morsgail, the deer-forest on the west side of the island, about thirty miles away, and were to remain there some time till I got a stag. Although no one believed such a small boy could kill a stag, I got two the very first day, one of them with a funny little head of twelve points which I still possess, and on the third day we returned to the castle in triumph. For years afterwards I went there for long visits, and what bags I used to make of grouse and golden plovers, besides stags! One day I got five stags right away on the Harris march. I remember as a lad of fifteen or sixteen starting on foot from the castle, and on the home beat shooting thirty-six brace of grouse over dogs with my muzzle-loader, and after my return dancing all night at a ball given in the castle to the townspeople.

The Lews was a wonderfully sporting island in those days. A connection of mine, a Captain Frederick Trotter, used to get as many as twelve hundred brace at Soval, besides endless snipe and golden plovers, while hundreds of woodcock used to be shot out on the open moors over dogs in the winter. And now, as on the opposite mainland, game is nearly extinct.

That summer, when I was ten, I made my first attempt at salmon-fishing in the Ewe, and was much more successful than I have ever been since. There had been a great drought, and towards the end of June came a big flood, and I was given a small new salmon-rod and put in the charge of Sandy Urquhart. He and his older brother Hector, whom he succeeded, were the best hands who ever cast a fly on the Ewe. Wonderful to say, I killed twelve fish in the first two days, the heaviest $27\frac{1}{2}$ pounds, and my little arms were so tired each day by about two or three o'clock that I could fish no longer and had to go home. But I got thirty fish in those nine or ten days. If I had been eighteen or twenty years of age and an experienced fisherman, what would I not have caught if I had fished from six in the morning till ten at night! My first salmon-fishing took place in the year 1852, and I do not think my record has ever been beaten, though before my time I have heard of my grandfather doing wonders and getting sometimes as many as thirty fish a day to his own rod.

I have heard a story about my father and Fraser of Culduthel fishing the Ewe. Culduthel was catching fish after fish, and declared they would take any mortal thing. He removed his fly, put on a bare bait-hook, to which he tied a small tuft of moss, and cast with it. No sooner had the hook with the tuft of moss touched the stream than he had a fish on. When the fish was landed he threw down his rod in disgust, saying it was no sport fishing the Ewe, as the salmon would take anything.

Certain families served the lairds in the good old times generation after generation. For example, my teacher in salmon-fishing, Sandy Urquhart, and his brother Hector were grandsons of my grandfather's head herdman, Domhnall Donn, who had charge of Sir Hector's sixty black cows at the Baile Mor of Gairloch. How well I remember their mother! Such a handsome old woman and of such size and strength! I have heard that as a girl, when helping her father with the cattle, she could catch a heifer by the hind-leg and hold her. Many a good lunch I have had from her when fishing the Ewe! Her boiled salmon was better cooked and tasted better than that of anyone else. Her recipe was to boil the salmon overnight and leave it all night in the water it was boiled in. In the morning each slice was encased in its own jelly. There were few flour-scones in those days, only either good hard oat-cakes or softer barley-scones, generally made with a mixture of potato. Nothing nowadays can come up to Bantrach Choinnich Eachainn's (Kenneth Hector's Widow) salmon and barley-scones, with those most delicious of all potatoes the *seanna Bhuntata dearg* (old red potatoes), which, alas! did not resist that awful plague, the potato disease, and very soon entirely disappeared.

Describing salmon-fishing fully one hundred years ago, my

uncle says: "Our father at breakfast would say: 'Boys, salmon are crowding into the bay now and we must help some of them out. See and get your lessons finished and we'll dine at two, and have a haul of the seine-net at Inverkerry.' 'Hurrah, hurrah!' was the ready response, and by three we were off in the long-boat, and soon found the net people with all set ready for a haul, and quite cross at our being so late, for a shoal of salmon had cruised all round inside the bight of the net laughing at them, but they dared not begin till we came. So we sat down on the Scannan rock, and in a few minutes there was a grand fish springing in the air close to the net and a crowd of his admirers hauling on at its shore-ropes like mad. Old Iain Buidh was furious at us urchins for making such a row, as he knew noises often frightened away fish. One end of the net is always close to shore, but the other end of the semicircle may be over one hundred yards out at sea, and it was the rope from it to the shore that we were all hauling at like demons—not nearly such tame ones as old Iain would have liked. The smaller people were set to throw white *dornagan* (fist-sized round stones) along the line of the hauled rope to prevent fish swimming away from the net as it kept closing in. Both ends of the net are now ashore, but much caution is needed yet, lest it be raised above the ground ere all is high and dry; for Mr. Salmon has a good eye, and would instantly dart out to sea through the gap!

"Hurrah! they are all safe. There is the leader springing in the air, just to see what all this contracting of their sea means. Alas! very soon he is capering on the rock with all his friends, while many of his young admirers are busy as bees with their shillelaghs, made for the purpose of administering vigorous head-whacking opiates to ensure the peace. At one such haul I once saw over three hundred salmon, grilse, and trout, from 2 or 3 pounds up to 25 pounds, brought ashore. Usually two or three hauls of the net landed as many as our father cared to take home, for all but the few needed for home use were that evening allocated for tenants or poor people. It takes more planning than folks would imagine, first to settle where each fish is to go, and then who is to take it.

"By the time the net was hung up in the boathouse roof, sledges were up at Tigh Dige with the fish, which were always laid out on the grass in front of the house, that the dear mother might admire the really beautiful sight, and with paper and pencil, supported by her devotee and housekeeper, Kate Archy, plan the fishy distribution. I have sometimes wondered how my father and mother would have looked at anyone who suggested their selling salmon or game! So when Kate had selected her fish for kipper-smoking—and no one ever matched her at that trade, for the Tigh Dige breakfast without hot plates of kipper was not to be tolerated—and when Mrs. Cook had secured her share, every other fish was despatched to the tenants and crofters, and they were legion, within reach. And now, instead of those happy, exciting times, there are horrid bag nets all round the coast, which keep up a melancholy stream of fish, all going to greedy London in exchange for horrid, filthy, useful lucre. My father, luckily for him, died ere the Gairloch salmon came to such degeneration."

Kate Archy was widow of Fraser, our gardener, and mother of a daughter who succeeded her and remained with the family all her life. I see her now in the high white mutch, herself considerably above ordinary height, stalking over the lawns and along the roads with a strong apron fastened round her, containing, perhaps, seven or eight live chickens, and at her right side a huge pocket. With her right hand she hauls a squalling chicken out of the apron. In a second the left hand holds the feet, the knuckle of the right thumb (did she not teach me herself carefully?) dislocates chicky's neck, and a large handful of feathers goes into the pocket, till in an amazingly short time the featherless victim is thrust away among the survivors in the apron. Then another suddenly goes through the same ceremony, till all are served. When Kate's walk round the place ends in the kitchen of the Tigh Dige seven or eight chickens, merely needing "flamming", are lying on the table for the housekeeper's orders. And don't I remember her sometimes allowing me, as a reward for being good, to flam the feather-plucked flesh, passing the bird suddenly through the flames of some paper, which burnt off all the small feathers or down? My uncle writes further:

"I don't believe Kate was ever aware of what she was doing when stalking about with an apron full of chickens. It never for a moment stopped her singing or holloaing any advice or warning to A, B, or C, who crossed her path or eye. Was there ever a more valued, entirely trusted, loving family friend? I doubt it. Christie, her daughter, was hardly behind her. What did Kate and Co. care for their own interest compared with ours? Not a straw! These were the kind of people that cheerfully 'gaed up to be hangit' just to please the laird.

"How ashamed Monsieur Soyer would have been had he competed with Kate in a dish of venison collops for breakfast at Tigh Dige! Such collops were never made before or since. And as for her kippers, who nowadays could settle like her the exact quantities of salt, sugar, and smoke each dried salmon and grilse required, to suit the date of their consumption, whether immediate or deferred, confidentially imparted to her by the dear calculating mother? Until salmon close time ended the family was never disgraced through being out of salmon or wonderful kipper, not to mention venison, and venison hams. Sir Hector would only eat heifer beef; no bullock beef for him.

"Our father took much interest in our fishing and shooting, even planning our expeditions and sometimes taking a drove of us on ponies to fish in the then celebrated Ewe, a seven-mile ride from the Tigh Dige. We were always off by 6 a.m., so as to have fresh salmon cutlets for breakfast in the old inn. He would land six or eight fish before we went to gorge ourselves, keen with hunger, at breakfast with dish after dish of fried slices of salmon. One day I remember he landed, besides many others, two fish each about 40 pounds weight, one of which took him right down into the sea, whence it was landed. Nowadays salmon are all killed (at least, on the Ewe) ere they approach that weight, for there are nets everywhere. In the old times there was a haul of the salmon-net, twice a day or so, at the mouth of the river opposite Pool House, and once in the evening in the pool below the cruives. Heaps of salmon were caught every day but Sunday in the cruive-boxes, and I once helped to draw ashore over three hundred in one sweep of the net from the cruive pool.

"I must admit that I removed the cruives to please the Government Drainage Commissioner, who would not in 1847 sanction drainage in Kenlochewe till the cruives, which he said dammed up Loch Maree, were removed. Since then there has been no trouble taken to make pools in the river. The salmon scoffed at our efforts and rushed up to Loch Maree, very few resting so long in the river as to get hungry, and running fish seldom care for fly or bait. I never would have removed the cruives had I imagined the river, which is not a mile long, was not to be made into a series of pools instead of flowing in rough runs broken up by big stones, behind one of which, when the river was furnished with cruives, a fish was obliged to rest and get a good sight of our flies. There was no bridge on the Ewe until, I think, 1836 or so, and the present much altered Cliff House was then the smoky, whisky-perfumed Poolewe Inn."

Apropos of salmon-fishing, my uncle tells a story of a lawsuit his father had: "My father was his own factor and clerk, as every wise landlord will be till too old for work with mind or body. He just pities landlords who knew not the pleasure of guiding their tenants through all the many difficulties, which no factor can remedy like their landlord, and when the factor was a mere lawyer his pity was greatly increased. He detested law and kept out of court with wonderful success, till all at once a litigious fool of a neighbour drew him into no fewer than seven lawsuits. The River Ewe was the Gairloch march in one direction, and Seaforth had bought Kernsary, which was on the north side of the Ewe. Like many people who are very clever but not wise, he discovered that my father was using rights belonging to Kernsary, etc. He soon found lawyers glad enough to back him in his folly. I need not detail more than one of the complaints to court—namely, that my father drew the seine-net at the mouth of the Ewe on the Kernsary seashore. No use telling him that this had been done without any objection for more than a hundred years. He would soon make people wiser, and into court he went ding-dong. Then he discovered that a ship pier erected on this, the only spot where a net could be drawn at the river mouth, would be a grand thing to upset the netting, so Brahan Quarries were all busy and ships

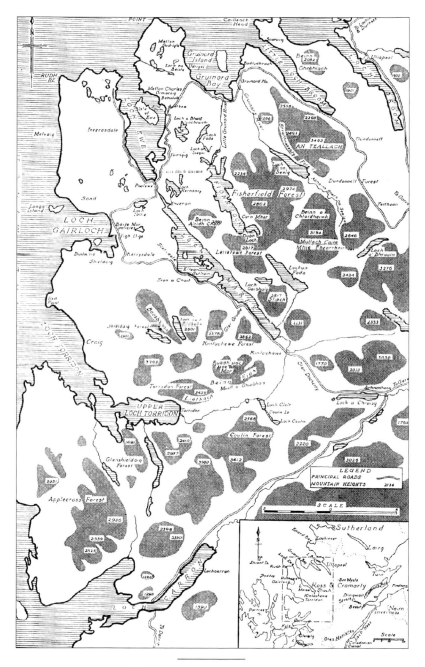

Map of Gairloch and surrounding country.

John MacKenzie of Eileanach

The Old Gairloch Mansion House, *An Tigh Dige*, The Moat House
(from a painting by Finlay MacKinnon)

But these digressions are very anti historical, so I
must hie back to my main thread at present viz
my fathers story.
Wire fences were unborn in his day, & enclosing
by paling, every tree he took a fancy to plant here and
there at Flowerdale too expensive — So he adopted a
most simple & most effectual protection to his young
trees, wherever planted. He had a nursery, whence
hardwood trees were always ready to be transplanted
8 to 10 feet high, to a carefully prepared pit. In Gairloch
myriads of wild roses grew everywhere often 8 to 10 feet
high — For every hardwood tree planted out, a carefully
taken up wild rose with many stems was found and
planted in the same pit, its stems fastened to the
hardwood tree by wire ties. The result being that
the most itchy beast would go a mile for a scratch,
rather than touch a tree so thorn protected. So every
tree thus planted by my wise father was perfectly safe
from injury by cattle by such protection, the briars
living for many years or for ever —
I have observed many cases where a young
man married a much older woman than himself, and
in every instance but one, have seen that they remained

as if to kill a cow or sheep; get their shot, & never forget the
luncheon hour!
When we went to stalk we were always off ere
daylight. (I have walked miles on the moor, to reach
the spying spot, long before day) — We had a bite ere we
started to diminish carriage, but what we needed till we
returned home, was of course (probably barley scons and a
reel of a kebbuck) in our pockets, while we never dreamed
of any "pocket pistol" except the best water we met with.
Then such excitement & enjoyment as we had but
which the sleepy sassenach entirely misses, watching every
step of the deer, feeding hillwards to their look out front
& considering how to get safely before them & have a shot
before 9, at which hour they lie down, with heads towards
every direction, to discuss their nights feed & examine every
thing suspicious like in their horizon. For unless one gets a
stalk & shot ere they lie down, they had better be let alone till
they get up again, at 12 —
Sometimes we went to a distant beat, not coming home
at night, but sleeping in the heather, or if possible below a
rock or stone, tolerably rain proof — Then our stalker had prog
put up for two days, & when that comprised a leg of mutton
as it often did, I never saw the bone bare that the keeper or gillie

---

Facsimile Extracts from Dr John MacKenzie's 'Memories'.

Inverewe House built by Osgood Hanbury MacKenzie in 1862.

Top. Inverewe House on fire, 1914.

Bottom. Inverewe House, the remains after the fire, 1914.

Inverewe Gardens. This magnificent Highland garden, in its impressive West Highland setting, celebrated the centenary of its foundation in 1962. Famed for its profusion of exotic plants. Presented in 1952 to the Nat onal Trust for Scotland.

The splendour of Inverewe Gardens in the 1980's.

loaded with dressed freestone for the pier, and were instantly discharged into the sea on the pier site. When the lawyers had seen him well into the courts they suddenly advised Seaforth to throw up the sponge, and the result was that he offered to withdraw the seven lawsuits and pay all the costs. These, of course, were no trifle, but the fishing up of all those ship-loads of stone out of the deep below at the river mouth (for every one had to be removed) must have been a wild expense. He also had to pay my father damages for the loss of two seasons of fishing there, and the affair became the standing joke of the county wherever the parties were known."

CHAPTER VIII

EARLY SPORTING DAYS

I LEFT my home for Germany in the autumn of 1853, when the Crimean War was in full blast. My mother's intention was to remain abroad for perhaps three years, but the first summer at Heidelberg proved too hot for me (the thermometer going up to 92° in the shade), so we had to go to Switzerland for three months. Ross-shire saw us back again (at least, for a good long holiday) in 1855, because I was beginning to get very homesick, and in consequence was not thriving quite to my mother's satisfaction. ·

Now, as all the shootings on the Gairloch estate were let at this time, I proposed to my mother that we should hire Pool House, which was empty, and which had been our home on one or two previous occasions, and that we should try to get the sporting rights over Inverewe, which was quite near. It was then just a neglected outlying sheep-farm, belonging to the Coul estate, without even a resident farm tenant on it, and in charge only of two shepherds, who looked after its stock of Cheviot ewes. One of these shepherds generally carried a gun instead of the regulation shepherd's crook! There were also one or two other men in Poolewe and in the crofting township of Londubh (Black Bog) who occasionally shot over it; but as grouse were so very scarce, they more or less confined themselves to sporting along its shores, on the off-shance of getting a shot at an otter, a merganser, or, still better, a great northern diver. Well do I remember one of them telling me that a Muir Bhuachaill (sea herdsman, the Gaelic for the northern diver) was far better than any three fat hens. I can certainly vouch for its being bigger and heavier, if not better flavoured, for the first northern diver I ever shot weighed 17 pounds!

Accordingly we approached the then laird of Coul, Sir Alexander Mackenzie, on the question of shooting rent; his ideas were very moderate, for he only asked £10 per annum for something like 7,000 or 8,000 acres, on condition that we put on a good keeper, who would stop poaching and destroy the vermin. And so I started my life as a regular sportsman at the early age of thirteen years. The keeper who was engaged came of real good old stock, who had served the Gairloch family more or less for generations, and had been with us as hall-boy for some years in the Tigh Dige. He rejoiced in the modern anglicised patronymic of Morrison, which would sound so much nicer in its old original Gaelic form of *Mac ille Mhoire* (Son of the Servant of St. Mary).

The next thing was to get a good dog of some kind, and as I was so young someone suggested that a sort of retriever, which would occasionally point at his game, might suit me, instead of having a regular team of pointers or setters. There was nothing in the way of a kennel at Pool House, so my first and only dog, "Shot," a curly retriever, made himself quite at home in front of the kitchen fire or under the kitchen table, along with various terriers, and there my pet otter used to enjoy many a rough-and-tumble game with them!

How distinctly I remember my first day out on the hill in August, 1855! I was armed with my little gun, which weighed only three pounds; but I had a real licence to shoot game, and this made me feel very important and quite a man. Away Uilleam (William) and I started, with great hopes. On our way we met the poaching shepherd, Alasdair Mor nan Geadh (Big Sandy of the Geese), who was known by that name because he had been born at a place called *Achadh nan Geadh* (Field of the Geese), on the shores of one of the Inverewe lochs, where the greylags ate all the little patches of oats. The only news he could give us was that he was sure there were one or two coveys of black game in Coille Aigeasgaig, the only bit of wood on the whole property, which consisted of dwarf, scrubby birch with lots of bracken growing between the trees. I was for making straight for the wood, but Uilleam wisely argued that we should keep it for dessert, and first of all try the open moor by the side of Loch a Bhad luachraich (the Lake of the Tuft of Rushes). I remember everything as well as if it were yesterday. All we and Shot found in the open were two coveys (if they deserved to be called such)—*viz.*, a pair of grouse with one cheeper, which Shot promptly caught in his big ugly mouth, and another pair with two young birds, out of which small lot I contrived to shoot the old cock as he ran in front of me. Then off we went to the haunt of the black grouse. What a big pile it would make if all the black game I shot there between 1855 and 1900 were gathered into one heap. Now, alas! there are none, and why, who can tell? Shot was not long in finding one of the coveys Big Sandy of the Geese had told us of. Up they got in ones and twos, fat young cocks, with their plumage half black and half brown. I blazed at them more than once, but was so excited that I felt sure I could not have hit anything. However, Shot, who was, as a matter of fact, quite unbroken, tore off after them, and soon returned with a fine young black-cock in his mouth; of course, it was supposed I must have wounded him, though there were no signs of any pellets. The next covey Shot put up out of range of my poor little scatter gun, but notwithstanding, he brought back another young beauty and laid it at our feet. It seemed as if my firing or not was quite a matter of indifference to Shot. As for blue hares, even a well-grown leveret had not a chance if Shot got a sight of it, unless it went to ground, and then he would come and ask us to help him to dig it out. If ever there was a real poacher, it was Shot, so he was voted a very useful dog in helping to make up a bag. We came home quite pleased with ourselves, though we should not have thought much of the day's work in the 'sixties and 'seventies, after the wildcats and foxes and the falcons and hoodies had been mostly destroyed.

The following year we returned again from Germany, and I began rather to look down on Shot, and aspired to getting a brace of properly broken pointers or setters. Hearing of two for sale in Loch Broom—*viz.*, at Foich Lodge, which was then tenanted by a friend of ours, a Mr. Gilbert Mitchell Innes— Uilleam and I crossed the hills by way of Carnmor, Strath na Sealg, and Dundonnell—a very long wild walk it was—and I spent the night with my friends, leaving again in the morning, accompanied by the Foich keeper and two pointers, which he was to show off to us.

They were of an unusual colour for pointers—*viz.*, black and tan—and we found any amount of grouse as we went along, though I believe they are all but extinct there now. We made a bee-line for home, crossing the dreary high-road to Dundonnell, where there used to be a tiny wayside pub, well known by its Gaelic name of Tigh Osda na feithean mora (the Inn of the Great Swamps). The dogs behaved well, and I decided to buy them, but we already perceived that they would be very determined about returning to their homes with the keeper, and would refuse even to be dragged in the contrary direction by us. Ross, the keeper, however, was a match for them; he asked us to hold them and stay where we were, giving him a quarter of an hour's start; then he walked straight ahead as if making for Poolewe, and as soon as he got well out of sight over a top, he slipped round, and returned to the big strath of Loch Broom. Then we started, the dogs always thinking Ross was in front of them, and, straining on their couples, they dragged Uilleam, who held them, all the way back to Pool House. They proved useful dogs, were as hard as nails, and never got tired or gave in, but they required constant flogging, as nothing could ever cure them of running hares or of quarrelling and fighting; and though they were brothers, of the same litter, before very long the one killed the other. We always thought they must have had a dash of foxhound or some other blood in them, as they took such a fearfully vicious grip of anything they got hold of. I remember one day, when shooting grouse along a hillside on Inverewe, we heard a most awful row going on ahead of us, and there were the black and tan brothers, quite in their glory. They had come on a badger which had got its foot in a small steel trap, set for a weasel or crow, and had gone off with it. One would have thought they had bulldog blood in them by the way they tackled the badger and killed it straight off.

We still have in use a big rug of badgers' skins in front of our smoking-room fire, all caught on this place, though, as in the case of the eagles, we had no wish to exterminate them like wildcats and foxes; in fact, we should have liked to preserve them, but they would not keep out of the vermin's traps, and so they soon became extinct.

At last I determined to start breeding setters of my own, as the grouse and all other game had increased greatly, and I secured a pedigree bitch from Sir Alexander Cumming of Altyre. She was "Gordon Castle" on the one side and "Beaufort" on the other, and proved a really good investment. Indeed, I was never, perhaps, quite as successful with anything else as I was with my setters from 1858 to 1914. For many a long year they had such a good name that I used to sell from £80 to £140 worth every season, and I always had more orders than I could possibly supply. In 1914 we were compelled to give up the setters. My gamekeeper and faithful friend and companion, John Matheson, who was such a wonderful dog-breaker, had, alas! died, and it was impossible to get food for a kennel of dogs during the war, while the grouse had decreased greatly in number.

Among the first litter I had from the Altyre bitch was one jet black pup, "Fan." She and I were inseparable friends during the fifteen best years of my life, and it would fill a book if I attempted to describe what she did for me, and what marvellous powers of reasoning she had in that dear old head of hers. There really seemed to be nothing in the way of sport that Fan was not up to. Although she was not a "show" dog, not being quite correct, it was much more interesting to be out with her than with any other dog I have ever seen or possessed.

About the time Fan made her début, Lord St. John of Bletsoe (who was my brother's shooting tenant at Gairloch) very kindly gave me the winter shooting of those twenty-five lovely islands in Loch Maree, the very place for Fan to show off—in fact, it was the islands that taught her so many of her clever tricks. With the exception of parts of Eilean Suthainn, the islands were more or less covered with trees, but they also had some open spaces with heather where grouse came in for shelter from the neighbouring deer-forests in wild weather in November and December. There were a good many black game and woodcock, and just enough roe and wild ducks and geese, and even wild swans, to raise one's expectations and make it exciting; indeed, I did get one wild swan on a long shallow loch on Eilean Suthainn after a tremendously exciting stalk with my little three-pound gun and with the help of an Eley cartridge duly charged with slugs!

No ordinary dog was of any use in the islands, as one could not keep it in view for a moment among the Scots firs and birches; but with Fan all that had to be done on landing was to start her and sit comfortably on a stone or stump and wait developments. She would not be long before she came back to tell the story of her discoveries. We used to fancy we could guess by her face what kind of game she had found, and that she put on a sort of apologetic expression when it was a woodcock and not a grouse. She never wasted a moment at her point, unless we were actually in sight or she felt sure we were following at her heels. She evidently argued that the only thing to be done was to find us as quickly as possible, put on a solemn face, and lead us carefully up to the game. Even black game feeding on the birch seed in the tops of the trees did not escape her, and back she would come to give us notice. She seemed to know perfectly well if birds were wild or not, and, if they were wild, she would sneak along, keeping herself as low as possible, and thus giving us the tip to do likewise; but, if she felt they would lie close, she would go boldly up to them. If we had Fan with us we never had to take a retriever.

There are numerous lochs in this Gairloch district. The grouse seem always to prefer the loch sides, and when shot often fall into them, and not unfrequently into the sea; but whether it was a duck or a snipe or a grouse, distance was nothing to Fan if she saw it fall on the water, and you were as sure of your bird as if you had a boat and crew with which to fetch it. With the experience of the many years she had worked the ground, she would find about twice as much game as most other dogs. She knew the sedgy pool where a jack snipe was to be found, and the smooth greenish slopes where the great flocks of golden plover spent their days sunning themselves and waiting for the dusk, when they could get on to the crofters' potato patches; and also where the brown hares and partridges were likely to be, and the cairns which held blue hares. She always did her best to get us hares, though she never chased them, and what a dab hand she was at a woodcock!

One of her wonderful talents was always appearing to know in a moment if a bird were hit or not. She would stand up on her hind-legs so as to try to mark it down as far as she could. She had another marvellous quality, which was that she could gauge whether a bird was mortally wounded or not, and she knew if she could make sure of grabbing it, or whether it would rise again and require another shot. So if we saw Fan pointing a wounded bird and waiting for a gun to come up, then we knew it was only slightly hit; otherwise Fan managed the business herself and spared us all trouble by stalking up to it like a cat, and then, with a sudden rush, seizing it and bringing it back to us in her mouth without the mark of a tooth on it.

After a year or two of the sporting rights on Inverewe only, I added three outlying portions of the Gairloch property to my shooting, by hiring from my brother the Isle of Ewe, the extensive hill grazings of the Mellan, Ormscaig and Bualnaluib crofter townships, and the small farm of Inveran. That gave me a good deal more room, and my annual bags became much heavier and more varied. Especially was this the case after the year 1862, when I became the actual owner of Inverewe, and added some five thousand more acres to it by the purchase of Kernsary. Mellan was some distance away, and motors had not even been dreamed of then; but my younger brother, Francis, had built and endowed a beautiful Girls' School at Bualnaluib for the benefit of the daughters of the numerous surrounding crofters, and had placed in it as teacher a daughter of John Fraser, my grandfather's old gardener at Conon, who looked upon herself as one of the family retainers. I used, therefore, to put up at the Bualnaluib school-house for two or three nights at a time and shoot over the crofter hill grounds, which made three good beats. This I did chiefly in November and December, and delightful shooting it was.

I did not, perhaps, make what farther south would have been called big bags, but I used to get from twelve to fifteen brace and sometimes over twenty brace of grouse a day to my own muzzle-loader, and always a few woodcock or teal, snipe or ducks. As for golden plover and rock-pigeons, there was no place like it for them; and there were besides a good many coveys of partridges and many brown and blue hares. In short, on Mellan and the Isle of Ewe there was everything a boy sportsman could possibly desire. How constantly do I still dream of those happy days even now in my old age.

I see by my game-book that one year—in 1868—I got 99½ brace of grouse off the crofters' hill ground, 60 brace off Isle Ewe, and 30 brace off the small Inveran farm; and my total in that year was 1,314 grouse, 33 black game, 49 partridges, 110 golden plover, 35 wild ducks, 53 snipe, 91 blue rock-pigeons, 184 hares, without mentioning geese, teal, ptarmigan and roe, etc , a total of 1,900 head. In other seasons I got sometimes as many as 96 partridges, 106 snipe, and 95 woodcock. Now so many of these good beasts and birds are either quite extinct or on the very verge of becoming so. I wish I had kept a regular diary in addition to a game-book, because I saw and did many things connected with sport and natural history which would have been well worth recording.

One day on the Isle of Ewe, in a wet turnip field which was full of snipe, I started a thrush which had a broad white ring round its throat, just like that of a ring ouzel. I promptly shot it. Immediately afterwards old Fan pointed at something, evidently close to her nose, which I thought might perhaps be a wounded snipe, though if she could have spoken she would have whispered to me that it smelled like something she had never smelled before; and what should it be but a quail, which I also shot. Afterwards I had both thrush and quail stuffed in the one case. I have heard that one hundred and fifty or two hundred years ago the lairds in Easter Ross used to get quails there, and also that they used to be found in the South of Ireland; but, with the exception of this one on Isle Ewe, I had never, until that year, heard of a quail having been killed in Ross-shire in my time.

Another day on the same island we kept putting up nearly as many short-eared owls as grouse and snipe. Luckily, they rose singly, otherwise Fan would have had fits, for, as it was, she was evidently horrified with this new uncanny kind of game which had taken possession of the heather on her pet preserve! I shot five. That very same day a ptarmigan rose in front of me, which I also shot. It has always puzzled me why it had descended to the very sea-level, seeing that the big hills, where its home must have been, were some ten miles away. I surmise that it must have been driven down by an eagle or a falcon.

Apropos of Isle Ewe, I remember taking the late Dr. Warre, of Eton College, there one afternoon. I did not have my gun, and he did all the shooting himself. His bag was twenty grouse and twenty snipe. When it was getting on towards evening, and we thought the blue rock-pigeons would be back in their caves at the outer end of the island, we rowed there in our boat, and Dr. Warre added a good many pigeons to his bag. As a finish up, and to vary the sport, we lifted a long line, which we had set on our way to the island, and got a fine haul of haddock and other fish. The doctor was good enough to say it was the best afternoon's sport he had ever enjoyed.

Another day on the island we saw a flock of twenty grouse. We soon perceived they were not natives, for instead of being in the heather they sat in a row on the tops of the stone dykes and crowed incessantly. They all appeared to be cocks. So I went at them, and did not stop until I had got nineteen of them, only one escaping. Extra old cocks they were, as most of them had white feathers about their heads and white whiskers! We often wondered where they had come from.

I occasionally had pretty good days at woodcock. Perhaps my best day away from home was once when I was staying at Invermoriston Hotel with my brother, Sir Kenneth Mackenzie, our host being the late Lord Lovat, who had with him his two brothers, Colonel Henry and Colonel Alastair Fraser. We shot part of three short December days, and got, if I remember rightly, 146 woodcock, besides hinds and roedeer, etc., which was supposed to be a record bag in those days. Once at Inverewe a friend and I got fifty-two cock in two consecutive days, and at Shieldaig, on the south side of the parish, the late John Bateson and I had a good day. He got eleven and I nine before luncheon, and after lunch I got eleven and he got nine—forty in all. The keepers sometimes did well right out on the open moors, when after their traps. I remember my keeper getting eighteen woodcock one day with only a retriever along with him, and another day twenty-two in snow by walking along the old whin hedges in Isle Ewe.

I have made many a curious shot in the course of my life. I have twice killed two black-cocks on the wing with one shot, and one day, at the side of the public road, Fan pointed at a clump of bracken, hidden in which was the best covey of black game I ever came across. They began to get up in ones and twos, and I shot five young cocks, leaving the old grey-hen and her four daughters for stock. Another day an old friend of mine, Anthony Hamond of Westacre, and I were shooting, and close to what was then the Inverewe kennel in some heather, now replaced by tall timber, a mixed lot of partridges and grouse got up. We each killed a part-ridge and a grouse, and it was a very rare occurrence, that would not be likely to happen more than once in a century.

On two different occasions I have killed a hare and a grouse with the same shot, and another time I shot a woodcock and a stoat with the one barrel! On one occasion I made quite a name for myself. It was when a small covey of grouse rose in front of me at the Ardlair march; the tenant of the farm, a Mr. Reid, was standing on the opposite side of the boundary at the time, and I happened, by a fluke, to kill three of the birds with the right barrel as they rose and the remaining two with the left barrel as they crossed! Reid afterwards improved on the story by declaring that the covey was a big one of at least a dozen, and that I killed every one of them with the two shots! This yarn he spread over the whole parish—I might even say county—much to my con-fusion.

But really the greatest fluke I ever made was when I let off a rifle, just to see how far away the bullet would hit the water, at three wild swans as they rose on the wing from the sea at the mouth of the River Ewe, I being about one thousand yards away. My bullet actually grazed the tip of one of the swans' pinions, and down he came. We were so long in getting a boat launched—it was full of ice and snow—that by the time we got started the swan was far out to sea. Fortunately, however, for us—and, as it turned out, for the poor wounded swan—another boat was return-ing in the dusk from setting their long lines. The crew turned the swan, and we captured it, I had it put in a room, with a tub full of water into which I threw a lot of barley. For five or six days the barley was never touched, but at last one morning we found the grain all gone, so I took courage, and a fortnight later I sent the swan in a crate to the London Zoo, where the whooper lived eighteen years, and had an easy, if not quite a happy time.

The only good shot I ever had at swans was on Loch Kernsary. There were three whoopers out in the middle of the loch, when a very violent squall came on, with sleet and hail. We noticed the swans come in for shelter under a promontory that jutted out into the loch, so we ran off to circumvent them, and I killed one on the water and wounded another as it rose. The latter we had to chase in a boat, and whilst we were doing so the third one passed high over the boat, and I brought it down. With this swan story I now end the tale of my early sporting days.

My cousin, Col. H. Mackenzie, when quite a young lad made himself a great name in this locality. When out deer-stalking he saw two swans out in the middle of Loch an h'oiche. He had only an old, double-barrelled German rifle with him, but killed both swans right and left, one on the water and the other as it rose.

CHAPTER IX

DEER-STALKING

DEER-STALKING about a hundred years ago is thus described by
my uncle:

"My father never was young enough in my days to become a
deer-stalker, although he was very heavy on Kate Archy's venison
collops and loved a fat haunch, so one day, when I was about
fourteen, says he: 'John, can't you and Suter go to Bathais Bheinn
to-morrow and try and get a deer?' Strange to say, Suter was not
a native, but from the Findhorn country in Morayshire, and never
saw a deer before. Neither had I much experience in stalking—
Hector Cameron, predecessor to Suter, who had been promoted
to Loch Luichart estate, always killing what venison we required.
Suter's father (a poacher, I fear) was actually drowned by a salmon
in the Findhorn River. There is a fall there where salmon are seen
constantly leaping to get up, and some did and many did not.
There was a narrow ledge or shelf of rock where, if one could
reach it and the river was in proper trim, one could stand so near
to the fish when they leaped that a look-alive fisher could whip
them out of the spray with a gaff or clip-hook. Old Suter had got
on the ledge when, unfortunately, an extra heavy salmon sprang
in the spray and was instantly gaffed, but so heavy was it that Suter
could not haul him aside, was overbalanced, and away went both
the salmon and the gaffer down into the pool. The salmon was
found dead from his wound, and thus it was learned how the man
was drowned, although no one was present.

"Rifles in 1817 were not actually unknown, but the only one in
Tigh Dige was an enormous one, say twelve pounds weight,
carrying a two-ounce ball, called the *Claiseach*, meaning in Gaelic
'the grooved one,' and a still heavier one we called the *Spainneach*
(the Spaniard), with the sides of the bore half an inch thick, and,
as Paddy would say, 'Its ball was a plug of lead two to three inches
long, warranted seldom to hit any mark aimed at.' So Suter was

armed with the *Claiseach* and the *Spainneach*, and I had my father's double Joe Manton, with a whittled-down bullet made to fit the bore in one barrel and a lot of slugs in the other. It was past nine ere we climbed the Cosag above Loch Bhad na Sgalaig (Loch of the Ploughman's Grove), walking and talking and exposing ourselves, as we were not expecting deer for miles. On the top, as visible to us as this pen is to me, and about one hundred yards away, was a brown thing like a broken bank of reddish earth with some curious sticks upon it. A minute's look told us the sticks were a deer's horns and he himself was the brown bank, evidently asleep, or otherwise he would have soon said good-bye to us.

"In a minute we two 'innocents abroad' scrambled out of sight, and, sweeping round the brae on which the deer was sleeping, walked, like lunatics, within twenty yards of him ere he awoke. A proper stalker would have got a favourable berth, say fifty yards from him, and would have waited till he woke and stood up. We despised such manœuvres on this our first stalk, and the consequence was that he did not rise up, but flew into the air and away over a flat piece of ground faster than any deerhound. I could shoot decently, and so banged off my slug barrel, while Suter fired the *Claiseach*, but neither of us touched him. This seemed to paralyse me till Suter cried out: 'The other barrel.' I had quite forgotten my bullet till the monster was nearly one hundred yards off. Then I fired, and he rolled over and over like a rabbit, the bullet having broken his neck. We were soon beside him, and while I was reloading, Suter, who was over six feet high and broad in proportion, rushed at the stag and seized him by the horns. He merely bowed his head, threw it up again, and sent Suter yards away like a pair of old boots. It ended with my having to kill the deer outright by a bullet in the heart, and then we two danced *Gillecallum* and hurrahed like two madmen, for though I had seen many deer killed by Hector Cameron, they were all like calves in comparison to our monster.

"Nothing would serve me but cutting off his head and walking home direct with it about four miles, and sending a horse for the body. So, soon after twelve, there was I marching up the avenue to Tigh Dige under the royal stag's head, and Suter with the pieces of ordnance behind me. The story having got about, there were father and mother on the stone stair head outside in little less glee than I was, though a wee thing less tired. The head was handed over to the Jack-of-all-trades, William Fraser, Kate Archy's son, with orders to go with all speed and bring home the corpse. I have killed and seen many a good stag since then, but never was a stag like my number one, passing twenty-five stone, clean and white inside as a prize bullock. Hurrah! my stag had twelve points (he was royal), and is now hanging up on my staircase. My last stag, shot in Glencannich, had thirteen points, all clean, but was under twenty stone.

"I had a hard day once with a fine stag in Coire Ruadh Stac of Beinn Eighe of Kenlochewe. I started with a lad and *prog* (food) for two days, and we roosted at Uaimh Bhraotaig under the big stone there, having seen nothing the first day. We were young, rash stalkers, and next morning started a fine stag, which galloped off towards Coire Ruadh Stac, about two miles off. Now, that corrie is a cul-de-sac, its upper end being one sheet of white quartz gravel, about one thousand feet to the top of the hill, in which man or beast would sink deep every step. I had never before seen a deer in that grand corrie. Probably they knew that if pursued there they must come out past their enemy, although the corrie is about half a mile wide at its mouth and is very rough hillocky ground. Could our friend the stag really have gone into the corrie? Peeping into it carefully, we spied the brown back of a beast near its mouth, and after we had scraped our knees and tummies badly in getting within shot, our deer turned out to be a pony strayed there from Lochcarron or Torridon! Further enquiry, however exhibited our coveted friend lying on a heather *mulcan* (hillock) near the mouth of the corrie, placed so that nothing alive could come near him unseen.

"That was severe on us but I knew that deer often let people come wonderfully near them if they seemed bent on other business, walking smartly past and not stopping and peeping about, and with no gun visible. That was my only chance, so, leaving the lad in hiding, 'Joe Manton' and I sauntered into and up the corrie as far as possible from my friend, 'whistling as I went for lack of thought,' and never even looking at him, though I saw he kept an eye on me. The hillock faced west, and I saw that, if I could get far enough east, a shoulder of it would come between me and him, so on I swung till the shoulder concealed me. Then I took off my shoes in a second, and in a few minutes I was panting at the back of the hillock, hoping for breath to take aim. I was on my knees and seeing if my flint and powder were all right when Mr. Stag thought he had better see where I was going up the corrie. He soon saw I was within fifty yards of him, and, turning like lightning, he just flew away; but my bullet flew also, and by good luck hit his flank, breaking all the ribs on one side and his left shoulder, so on my getting over the hillock there he was, poor fellow, sitting on his end like a dog, thinking how he could pay me off. I was rather below him, but quite near, so he rushed on three legs at me and made me clear out. Then I loaded with small shot, which, applied to his neck, ended matters, and, the lad coming up, we had a light fantastic hop, for he was a trump stag, though only of ten points.

"But we had soon to drop the fantastic and to consider how to get him home. I never went stalking with more than one helper, so I had always to stay to assist him with the deer, and that was often a great bother. After gralloching the beast, I was taught to tear up heathery turf and hide my prize from birds and beasts, of which in those times there were more than enough, and all willing to dine on venison. Then I squibbed gunpowder among the clods all round, and no fox would touch a beast so perfumed. If we only had our friend down at Grudie Bridge, three miles off and twelve miles from Tigh Dige, we could direct a carrier to the deer while we were more agreeably employed.

"But first, where on earth were my shoes? After about an hour's hunt we found them. Then, the brown pony coming in sight, we resolved to try and catch him and saddle him with the stag, but probably he smelt blood on us and would never let us handle him. We went close to a scree of the Beinn Eighe quartz shingle. If we could only rush him into it we had him, but then where were our bridle and ropes to tie the deer on him? Luckily we were both good string-collectors, and had two big handkerchiefs, so when at last we grabbed the stray horse, we brought him below a steep, broken bank, to which we slid the deer, and after about an hour's calming of our terrified charger the deer was on his back with its legs tied below him. Gentle reader, if you have an enemy whom you would like to make miserable and mad, you will give him exactly such a job as fell to our lot for several hours while we were covering the three miles on that dreadful hillside. But ere dark we had our stag near the track and bridge, and the place was marked so that the men with the deer-saddled horse whom we sent off next morning needed not us to direct or help them. That was the worst day's job for fatigue that either of us ever met with. I suppose we had to hoist up the stag on to the pony about fifty times on the way. Had we known what was before us, we would never have handled him, but once we started pride carried us through, and our praise when he was in the larder was great.

"In all my stalking it surprises me that I only once came across a wounded deer. Being abstainers, I believe they soon recover from wounds. I have often found shed horns, but have seldom seen the bones of a dead deer in the forest. Yet they must often die unknown at the time of being shot. Once, trotting along the top of the Glas Leitir wood, I started a hind in the brae about a hundred yards above me. I took a flying shot at her, but felt it was a miss. I loaded and went forward, never troubling to look where she had gone, till, about a quarter of a mile on, I saw a little burn red, evidently, with blood. Walking up it a few hundred yards, I found the hind stone dead, the heart actually cut in two by my bullet. The one wounded deer that I ever got was a fine old stag who for years had been devoted to the Taagan corn at the head of Loch Maree.

"When Hector Mackenzie, at that time I was his factor and farming on his property at Kindlan, complained to me of his loss of crop through deer I said to him, what Sir George Mackenzie used to say to me, 'Shoot them, shoot them.' Hector was no great gunner, but he took a shot at his enemy and made him clear out, at all events for the season. Next year, however, he was back again, though his footmarks only were seen. Having Colonel Inge's keen-nosed lurcher Gill with me for some such lethal purpose, I got some beaters to drive the east end of Glas Leitir wood, where Hector said the stag was seen almost every day, though he hid himself in a jungle whenever disturbed, but whereabouts exactly no one ever could tell. I gave Gill on a leash to the forester, old Duncan—whoever could see or walk or stalk better than he, though then past seventy?—and went out on Loch Maree in a boat, sure that on such a lovely, clear, calm day a hare could not move in front of the beaters without our marking it. But the beaters went carefully through the wood without seeing the stag, though they found his bed in a jungle-hole. It was beaten as smooth as if done with hammers and coated with his cast hair, so he had been there since spring.

"That was disappointing, but Duncan waved for us to come on shore and come up to him, and there was he, nearly pulled in pieces by Gill raving to follow some scent. Gill never gave tongue in any circumstances. Of course we followed Gill, wondering why on earth he was leading us to an almost perpendicular wall of rock down the centre of which ran a small ravine, its bed covered with red gravel that had been washed from the top to the bottom by heavy floods. Up this ravine Gill dragged Duncan, and we followed on our hands and feet till, after about a hundred yards, we emerged on to a flat peat moss, where Gill made us ashamed of having doubted his nose, for there were the quite fresh marks of a big three-footed stag, so we drew breath and opened eyes all around.

"Nothing visible, but from the lie of the tracks we knew our friend must have made for the deep burn half a mile in front of the Allt Giuthais. So we minuetted along slowly till old Duncan dropped down in front of us as if shot, turning round with his tongue out and holding up his spread fingers above his bonnet to signal 'deer's horns seen.' Then we peeped and saw them too, and we had almost to choke Gill, who was mad to get on. A short council of war sent me away to the left to strike the burn half a mile down, and I was soon there waiting till wanted. The two others and Gill took to the right, and soon halloaed to me to look out. The stag as soon as he saw them flew to the burn and crossed it into the fir-wood, which grew out of six-foot-long heather and ferns, and but for Gill we should have seen no more of him. Gill, however, was at his heels in a few minutes and compelled him to fly back to the burn, where the men with stones prevented his keeping the dog at bay, and speedily drove him through the rough ravine and burn past me, where my rifle ended the sad story. And then we found that Hector's bullet the previous year had broken his fore fetlock. The wound had healed, but it was only a flail foot, and a mere nuisance to the poor, beautiful fellow. I think he had nine points, but was well and fat. 'Yes,' said Hector, 'on my corn and potatoes, digging the potatoes out of the pits with his horns, the rascal!' Even with three feet he was a grand beast.

"I was reminded that when Hector Cameron kept the Tigh Dige in birds and beasts he was one day on top of this same wood (Glas Leitir), watching a roebuck feeding some hundreds of yards down in the flat below. He stopped. What is that other red beast evidently stalking the roe? His spy-glass soon told that it was Mr. Fox, so he took a lesson in stalking from him without a fee! In a few minutes the roe was kicking helplessly below the fox, who, holding on by the throat, soon killed him. Hector thought it was then time for *his* stalk, and ere the fox had drained all the roebuck's blood, Hector had potted him, and brought his skin and the roe home.

"Years after this, Frank (Sir Francis Mackenzie) hired the Wyvis shooting, and at much expense in keepers, etc., brought it up to be so good a moor that in the last year of his tenancy, on the twelfth of August, he shot over eighty brace of grouse to his own gun. Having heard of the slaughter, the laird of Foulis, a recluse living in London who had never himself put a keeper on the ground, which, till my brother hired it, was only shot over by poachers, resolved to allow it to recover. I was then nominal tenant of the sheep-farm of Wyvis, my brother being the real tenant, and in my lease I was bound to protect the game from persons trespassing. My shepherds gladly ordered off all who were disturbing the sheep, till one day my shepherd, George Hope, who came from the Borders, on a twelfth of August saw three men with pointers and a pony and creels on his beat, and had to tell them his orders were to allow no one there. The reply was,

'Unless you want your collie shot you had better be off.' Nothing makes a shepherd get 'oot o' that' so quickly as such a threat, so he left the poachers alone, merely watching their movements, suspecting, as there were blankets and pots, etc., in the creels, that they were making for the Smugglers' Cave at Coire Bhacidh behind Wyvis. And so it turned out. His spy-glass showed them making for the cave, into which they carefully emptied the creels, and off they went with pony and creels up a long glen and began business. As soon as they were out of sight Hope made for the cave, and was at least as busy as they were. Every pot and blanket, every bag of meal, all the cold provisions, ammunition, etc., he took to a deep peat-hole he knew of, where the articles are safe and sound to this day, for he kept his secret to himself, for fear of the poachers' revenge, till just when he was leaving my service for the south years afterwards. Then, retiring to a hillock far off, but in sight of the cave, he lay there till the sportsmen's return to the cave in the evening. His glass revealed one of the men entering the cave and rushing out as if chased by wasps. He seemed to be explaining affairs to his comrades, who also ran to the cave and ran out again, all three proceeding to search the hill in the hope of finding the cave robbers. Then Hope retired home; I am sure he was very sorry that he dared not tell his comrades of the fun he had in his burglary.

"Wyvis has been sold since then, and has long been clear of sheep and under deer. It makes a real deer-stalker sick to observe how stalking is generally managed now in the Highlands. I used always to be on the look-out ground if possible before 6 a.m. to observe any deer which had been down feeding on the low grounds, and were stepping away in the morning to their spying posts up above for the day. Now the sleepy, soft-potato fellows must have a grand breakfast ere they can stand the fatigue of the hill. The keepers are sent out very early to find the deer and mark them down for the guns, and when the soft gunners reach the ground, on horseback if possible, they are led up to the shooting spot as if to kill a cow or a sheep, getting their shot, but never forgetting the luncheon hour.

"When we went to stalk we were always off ere daylight. I have walked miles on the moor to reach the spying spot long before dawn. We had a bite ere we started to diminish carriage, but all we needed till we returned home was coarse barley scones and the heel of a home-made cheese in our pockets, while we never dreamt of any pocket 'pistol' except the best water we met with. Then great were the excitement and enjoyment we had, which the sleepy Sassenach entirely misses, in watching every step of the deer feeding hillwards to their look-out post. We had to consider how to get into a good position and have a shot before nine o'clock, at which hour they sometimes lie down with heads towards every direction, to discuss their news and examine anything suspicious on their horizon. Unless one gets a stalk and shot ere they lie down they had better be let alone till they get up again in the afternoon. Sometimes we went to a distant beat and did not come home at night, but slept in the heather—if possible, below a rock or stone tolerably rain-proof. Then our stalker had provisions put up for two days, and when, as often happened, they included a leg of mutton, I never saw the bare bone that the keeper or gillie did not crack for the sake of the marrow, precisely as every bone in caves with prehistoric remains is found carefully cracked by the ancestors of our stalkers and gillies.

"For some years we employed as our gillie Donald Munro of Clare (on Wyvis), the most thorough poacher I ever met with. We could never reconcile him to letting a bird rise before we fired. It would be a clever grouse whose head Donald did not see the moment the dogs pointed; then with a dig at my elbow and a shrug sideways, he would show me two heads in a line, and when I made them get up before firing he was perfectly sick at my folly in wasting two shots when one would have killed both birds had I fired when they were on the ground and in line. He always carried a gauger's iron-pointed stick, and if close when the birds rose he would fling his stick at them with all his might, hoping to knock one down without such lamentable waste of powder and shot. Indeed, one day his iron point flew in among a covey with such force that it pierced a grouse right through, and so it had to stop, while four barrels stopped another four birds. 'Weel done, thon's behter; we'll be coming on by-and-by!' he exclaimed.

"A blue leveret getting up once before us would have come to bag had not Donald, who detested hares as 'no canny brutes,' seized my gun, saying, 'The stirk wasna worth a shot.' He told us he only once had a real proper 'go' at grouse. In a snow-storm he stalked an immense pack of them on Wyvis, a white shirt over him and a white neckerchief covering his face. He had his big musket and a great handful of No. 3 as the gun charge, and on that day he bagged thirty grouse at the cost of only three or four charges. He grinned with horrid glee when telling the tale, like a *Monadh Liath* poacher in whose bothy I was once benighted, and from whom I heard many a shooting story.

"Once in a heavy snow-storm not far from Killin in Perthshire he found about fifty deer packed together like sheep in a *fank* [1] below a rock for some shelter. He crept close above them and let fly a handful of slugs among them. Five stopped where they were, and two more went only about one hundred yards, when they also stopped. His brother was a Killin shepherd living on the west side of the loch, the east side of which was under birch, where deer were frequently seen among the trees from his door. If his salting barrel was getting empty he never needed a gun to refill it, but went round the loch, guided by his daughter's signs, till just above the deer. Then he stalked down close to them, and by hounding on his two very good collies he seldom failed to make one of the deer take to the loch and swim across. Just before it landed his daughter would rise up in front of it, working an old umbrella for all she was worth and advising the deer to recross the loch. This it did, not noticing the shepherd or his dogs till again about to land, when the sight of them made it start for another swim. Thus the shepherd and his daughter so wore it out that a drowned deer was found in the loch—and of course there could be no harm in using it for food!"

[1] Enclosure

CHAPTER X

DEER-STALKING—*continued*

I SHALL now follow up my uncle's account of deer-stalking by some of my own doings in that line in the 'fifties. I was about sixteen and residing with my mother at Pool House, and had Inverewe hired as my shooting, when one day our great friend, the gentleman farmer, Hector Mackenzie of Taagan, Kenlochewe, called. Knowing me to be very keen on deer-stalking, and being aware also that I seldom had a chance of a deer in those days, he remarked that he wondered I did not try to ingratiate myself with my eccentric old English neighbour, who owned some seventy thousand acres, forty-five or fifty thousand of which were the most famous stag ground in the country. It was then still all under sheep, but notwithstanding this, it had a good stock of its original breed of deer on it. Was it not famous even in the Fingalian days, when they killed the monster boar in Gleann na Muic? The very name of Srath na Sealg (the Valley of Hunting) suffices to show its special merits.

The owner, who had then been thirty years in the county, had never even attempted to stalk. My friend of Taagan thought that if I went and made myself agreeable to the young ladies of the house, and could manage to offer something, even a small sum, in the way of rent, there was no saying but that I might get permission to stalk on the famous Srath na Sealg ground, which had never been regularly stalked, and where the deer had only occasionally been killed by poaching shepherds. Wonderful to say, my trip succeeded. I told the old gentleman that I had no money of my own except a little pocket-money. He asked what I could give him, and I told him I could afford only five pounds. Marvellous to say, though almost a millionaire himself, he agreed to take that; so I wrote him out a cheque for the amount and came back in triumph; for had I not got carte blanche to stalk over a huge bit of country of some fifty thousand acres for a whole season? Perhaps that was among the happiest days, if not the very happiest day, of my long life.

But how was the stalking to be managed? There was a broken-down, thatched shepherd's bothy at Carn Mor, some eight or nine miles away from Poolewe, with no road to it; this bothy had not been lived in for many years, but it seemed to be the only chance for me in the way of shelter at night, so I was determined to try it.

We had a favourite sailor and fisherman in our employ at that time and for many years after, William Grant, who was one of those who went with us to St. Kilda. Three or four of these Grants have served me faithfully and devotedly all through my long life, and one of them (Donald) is still serving me, aged seventy-nine.

In 1640 one of my ancestors, Kenneth the sixth of Gairloch, married as his second wife Ann, daughter of Sir John Grant of Grant by Ann Ogilvie, daughter of the Earl of Findlater, and when Ann Grant started on horseback from the door of Castle Grant, her *gille cas fhluich* (wet-footed lad), who led his young mistress on her palfrey, wading through all the fords between Strathspey and Gairloch (and they were many), was a young Grant. From him all the Grants in the parish of Gairloch are descended. Some of the Grants were very powerful men, and when my grandfather, Sir Hector, was young, there were said to be only two men in the whole parish who could take up a handful of periwinkles and crush them; they were my grandfather and Grant, the big bard of Slaggan.

To come back to my deer-stalking. William Grant and our house-boy started away on a Monday morning with a little red Uist pony called "Billy." To a big saddle on his back were attached two large peat creels, into which my dear mother put a week's supply of provisions with her own hands. Away they went to Carn Mor, whereas my trusted keeper and stalker, William Morrison, and I made a bee-line across the Inverewe and Kernsary moors to a tiny sandy bay on the Fionn Loch (White Lake), where we kept a boat. Rowing across the loch, we soon landed on the Srath na Sealg ground, which was in the parish of Loch Broom, landing either at the foot of Little or Big Beinn a Chais-gan, two hills on the opposite side of the loch. I forget if we got anything the first day, though I know as a fact that we were never out on that ground without seeing lots of deer, in spite of its stock of eight or nine thousand sheep.

We arrived in the gloaming at Carn Mor, to find things in a terrible mess in the bothy. It seemed that a few days before Grant and the boy got there, a passing herd of cattle belonging to the laird, being bothered with the heat and the flies, had pushed open the door of the bothy and taken refuge in it, which was not difficult, as the door was barely hanging by one hinge. This was all very well until the beasts began to get hungry and tried to get out, but the door which they pushed inwards so easily, refused to be pushed outwards, and if by the greatest luck a shepherd had not passed that way and looked in, the whole lot of cattle would have been starved to death. The smell made the house almost unbearable, and had it not been a wet night we should rather have laid ourselves down à la belle étoile. Time, however, cures many things, and it at last cured Carn Mor of being "cowy."

The fire, which consisted of heather sticks and bog-fir, was at one end of the bothy against the gable, and I lay on the earthen floor on a bed of heather, with a blanket or two on me, the man and the boy having to do likewise on the opposite side. I was what would be called at the present day very badly armed. All I had were my little rifle, given me by my mother when I was about eleven years old, which required at least two sights to be raised if the animal was one hundred and fifty yards away, and an old, heavy, German, double-barrelled, muzzle-loading rifle lent me by my brother, and a very small, inferior telescope. The second day I was in luck, and got two stags with a right and left. I was very pleased with myself, and, not forgetting that I had got the shooting at a fairly low rent, I thought it my duty to make the eccentric old gentleman a present of the whole lot. So the boy was sent very early next morning to the mansion of the laird with a polite note, and he himself started with a lot of retainers and several ponies to fetch the stags. They carried them home in triumph and with great pomp.

Just to show how eccentric this old gentleman was, his game-keeper told me afterwards that on the arrival of the cavalcade at the door of the big house, they were ordered to stand at attention with the stags still on the unfortunate ponies' backs! Had it been in these modern times the men might have thought the group was to be photographed, but photography was not known then, and so they fondly hoped it might mean a dram all round on the great occasion of the laird's bringing back his first stags (though they happened to have been shot by someone else). From former bitter experience, however, they well knew that treating was not at all in his line; so there they were kept standing for well over an hour, until they nearly dropped; but at long last "himself" appeared, dressed as if for an Inverness Northern Meeting ball, with all the paraphernalia of powder horn and pistols, dirks and daggers. Thus embellished, he walked three times round the stags, ordered the men to give three ringing cheers for "himself," and then dismissed them without either a dram or anything else, and retired indoors to undress himself.

How often have I since regretted not having at the time asked the keeper (who was so well known by his nickname of "Glineachan") whether on that great occasion the laird wore his long or his short kilt. He possessed two, and at the first Inverness gathering which he attended in the 'thirties, soon after his arrival from England, he wore one so long that it reached nearly down to his ankles! Some good friends having ventured to hint that the kilt would have been more becoming to his figure had it been made shorter, he had another one made for a Stornoway ball which reached down a very short distance, to the great consternation and scandal of the assembled company.

I think I got twelve stags in all that season. I might have killed a lot more, but I did not like to overdo it when I thought of the rent! I got one very big stag, the biggest, I fancy, I ever killed, though we had no possible means of weighing him at Carn Mor, as he had to be cut up in bits and packed in the creels on each side of Billy's back; but he had a grand wide head of eight points. He was evidently the master stag on Beinn a Chaisgan Mhor, and we were after him a good many days before I downed him on the flat, smooth top 2,800 feet up, where a coach and four might have driven for a long distance. I think I was in front when I saw the ears of a lot of hinds coming along down wind, probably moved by one of the shepherds, and we had just time to throw our two selves down behind a small boulder which happened, fortunately, to push its head through the otherwise smooth, mossy turf. We both at once guessed that the big stag would be bringing up the rear, and luckily managed to let the long line of hinds file past without their seeing us. When the stag came in sight I got him.

One day in October my stalker and I had crossed the Fionn Loch, so famous for its big trout, and landed at a shepherd's house on the opposite shore at Feith a Chaisgan. The shepherd came down to meet us, and he told us he had the previous day come across the very finest stag he had ever seen—namely, a grand big royal. We had heard for two or three years of an extra good stag being in Slioch, the beautiful hill which overhangs Loch Maree, and we had heard also that the Cornish shooting tenant of Kenlochewe would not allow anyone to stalk on Slioch, not even his own brothers, for fear they might shoot it. Well, we explored our ground most carefully the whole day, and though we saw deer, we saw nothing that resembled the shepherd's description of the royal stag.

It was getting late and the light of day was rapidly departing, so we thought we would venture to descend to Carn Mor, by an awful pass between the twin peaks of Sgur an Laoicionn and Sgur na Feart. All at once, in a tiny green corrie, just above the pass, what should we come upon suddenly but three hinds and the big royal! They were just about within range, so I fired my little rifle at him and hit him, but he was quite able to take himself off after the hinds, and we saw no more of him that night; indeed, we did not expect ever to see him again, as he did not appear to be very hard hit. However, before midday on the morrow, Morrison spotted him about two miles away lying down on the slope of the Ruadh Stac bheag; in fact, it was the size and length of his beautiful antlers, with the three long white-tipped tines on each of his tops, that betrayed him. After a long, difficult stalk, I gave him the *coup de grâce* lying down. There was a big pool of blood under him which he had lost during the night. So precious in my eyes was his grand head that we cut it off at once, for fear of anyone stealing it if left till the morrow.

I cannot quite finish my story without referring to the Cornish shooting tenant of Kenlochewe. He had a habit always of walking down in the forenoon to the hotel to see the arrival of the mail-car on its way to Dingwall, accompanied by his stalkers and gillies, and one day what should they see perched on the top of the car but the head of the big Slioch stag on its way to a taxidermist in Inverness!

I saw just one other very big stag during those most happy days I spent at Carn Mor, but, alas! I failed to get a shot at him. I must say I like the old way of going off alone with one's stalker in the morning much better than the present system of being followed by a retinue of gillies and ponies, in order to get the stags home in the shortest possible time, though I admit this is best for the venison. To me, however, a cavalcade of that sort takes a lot away from the romance of stalking.

While I am dealing with sport I may here quote my uncle's story of Watson and the eagles. Even I can remember Watson when he was a very old man. Though he bore a south-country name, he was, as we say in the north, "as Highland as a peat"; in fact, he had very little English, and he was the first gamekeeper and vermin-killer the Gairloch estate ever had. I think it was he who, when my mother was inveighing against the use and abuse of whisky, replied, "'Deed, yes, my leddy, too much of anything is baad—too much gruel is baad." I wonder who ever exceeded in the way of gruel!

My uncle says: "Watson by daybreak was on the top of Bathais Bheinn with swan shot in one barrel and a bullet in the other, peering over the rock. Away sailed one of the eagles, but the swan shot dropped him on the heather below the rock. Another eagle from the nest on the other side of the hill came to the same end. Then Watson hid himself among the rocks near where a wounded eagle was flapping his wing, and a third eagle, coming to see what this meant, was invited by a cartridge to remain, making one and a half brace of old eagles before breakfast. Then, to shorten matters with the two big chicken eagles, he climbed the

124

hill again, and ere his bullets were all used up both of the young eagles were dead, having got more lead for breakfast than they could digest, and their remains were visible on the shelf of the rock for many a year after. I wait to hear of the gunner in Britain who could show his two and a half brace of eagles bagged in one day before breakfast."

Watson was undoubtedly a first-rate killer of foxes and eagles, but I think we have as good vermin-killers in the twentieth century as were to be found at the beginning of the nineteenth. My stalker, Donald Urquhart, at Kernsary in the winter of 1918–1919, killed twenty-five foxes. He once got two eagles and two foxes in one day. Two seasons running he got ten eagles, and two seasons running he got seven eagles. One day he went out to shoot hinds and visit traps. First he got a wild-cat in a trap. Shortly afterwards he got a hind; he visited three other traps, getting an otter in one trap and a fox in another, and then he shot a hind on the way home—a useful day's work for a stalker.

I often wonder why some County Councils take the trouble to forbid eagles being destroyed. How can the killing of eagles be prevented? Do the County Councils wish no traps to be set for foxes, wild-cats, ravens, or hoodie crows? And if the traps are to be set for these very destructive beasts and birds, how are the eagles to be kept out of the traps? Is it the wish of the wiseacres of the County Councils that an eagle with both or even one of its feet smashed should be let go to die a lingering death of starvation?

The best place for a trap to be set for foxes or hoodies is a tiny island in a pool of water, the bait to be half in and half out of the water, and the big trap set on the top of the hummock of sphagnum moss just immediately above the bait. I dare say very few County Councillors are aware that an eagle depends entirely on his talons for attack or defence, so that if one of them is fixed in a trap you may put your hand or even your face close to his head and he will not touch you. Eagles are terribly destructive. They tear the live rabbits out of the rabbit-trappers' traps, kill lambs wholesale, and the very sight of one scares every grouse off the ground. Only last summer an eagle was seen attacking a hogg (year-old sheep) on our ground and had to be driven away. The

Ross-shire County Council very wisely does not forbid the killing of eagles.

Apropos of eagles, I shall describe what happened to our heronry, which we greatly valued. It was on an island in the Fionn Loch, which was overgrown with a jungle of stunted birches, rowans, and hollies, the twenty or more herons' nests being in some cases so near the ground that I once saw a terrier manage to scramble up into a nest full of young ones. It did not relish the unusual experience, as, unlike the eagle's, the heron's means of defence is his powerful bill, with which even a young one is very handy. One day we thought we would visit our heronry, and as we approached the island we were much surprised at seeing no herons flying about as usual. On our landing there was nothing to be seen but upset nests and quantities of feathers everywhere, and in one holly-bush we found a full-grown dead young heron, covered with blood, but still intact.

We could not imagine what had happened, and thought some evil four-footed beast like a fox must have swum to the island, or perhaps a wild-cat or marten, which are better at climbing trees than a fox. We had some strychnine with us to give poisoned eggs to a pair of hoodies in another island, and we decided to poison the young heron whose body had escaped being eaten, in the hope that we might thus discover the cause of the terrible destruction; so we laid its poisoned carcase on a flat rock on the island. A few days afterwards a dead eagle was washed up on the shore of the loch opposite the island, thus making it quite clear to us that an eagle, or more probably a pair of eagles, had done all this mischief.

We have had far too many eagles in our country of late, and when one can see seven in the air at once it is about time to thin them out. I have only once in my life taken an eagle's nest, and that was sixty-eight years ago. We never set traps for eagles, but when one is caught I must confess we do not mourn very much.

Strychnine is a wonderfully handy drug. I remember once laying a poisoned egg in the hope of killing a pair of hoodies which were doing an immense amount of damage stealing grouse eggs, and returning in a very short time to find both the hoodies lying on their backs dead, though still warm, one on each side of the

126

egg. On another occasion when stalking hinds in January I was crawling along at the foot of a rock when I noticed an egg which I knew to be a poisoned one. Just a little beyond it I saw two small white spots which looked like little lumps of snow, and when I got to them I saw that they were two dead pure white ermines. They must only just have put the tips of their tongues into the small hole at the top of the egg, for it was still quite intact.

CHAPTER XI

THE FIONN LOCH

I HOPE I may be excused if I am often guilty of asserting that Fionn Loch (the White Loch) is the best trout loch in Scotland. In one respect it is certainly superior to Loch na h'oiche, which I have extolled in a former chapter, because the Fionn Loch fish are of a much greater size. It is a magnificent loch, whether regarded from a natural history standpoint or from that of sport and scenery; indeed, the upper end has often been compared to Loch Coruisge in Skye. It was not part of the original Gairloch estate. Some time in the early 'forties, when my brother, the heir to Gairloch, was still a minor, my mother and my uncle (the trustees) bought the Kernsary property for him from the Seaforths, so as to give Gairloch the north as well as the south bank of the River Ewe; for, though Gairloch had a Crown charter of all the salmon rights in that famous river, it was more difficult to look after it and keep down poaching, etc., when the land on one side belonged to someone else. So in 1862, after I bought Inverewe, my brother sold me back the larger part of Kernsary, which adjoined and lay right into Inverewe, retaining for himself only that portion of it which ran alongside the river, and thus I acquired several miles of the shores of the famous Fionn Loch, sharing with the Earl of Ronaldshay the joint right of fishing in all its waters.

The Fionn Loch is some six miles in length and runs nearly parallel with Loch Maree, only that it is very much higher—*viz.*, 538 feet above sea-level, whereas Loch Maree is only 32 feet. I believe there was hardly ever a boat on it until it came into our possession about 1845 or 1846. I think there must have been a boat of some description on its waters on one occasion, for I have often heard the story told that long ago the only scrap of cultivable ground on its shores—*viz.*, the tiny green patch at Feith a

128

Chaisgan—was dug and sown, and that when the harvest-time came the crop was made into a stack on one of the islands (the Eilean Fraoich) to protect it from the deer in winter. So there must have been some kind of a boat to ferry the sheaves across. I was told that once when the owners went to remove the stack in the spring, it was found so full of live snakes that they fled in terror, leaving the stack where it was.

I asked the old yeoman farmer, who was one of many who recounted the story to me, and happened to be telling it in English, if there were many snakes in the stack. His reply was rather quaint: "'Deed, yes, there waas severals of them." This snake story is a strange one, for though adders are so plentiful in many other parts of the Highlands, there happens to be none in the Gairloch district, and slow-worms (which are notoriously very slow) would not have been in a hurry to swim across those cold waters in any numbers!

At any rate, I know there was no boat on the loch when Gairloch got possession, and what a job it was thought to be, when a clumsy sea-boat had to be dragged over nearly five miles of bogs and rocks, and across a ridge of something approaching eight hundred feet high. Many a boat did we drag up to it in succeeding years, until at last I made a private road for carts and motors, with two good iron bridges over rivers, and built a pier and a boat-house up at the loch-side.

When the loch first became ours, a pair of white-tailed eagles had their eyrie on the island, still called Eilean na h'Iolaire (the Island of the Eagle). It was quite small and low, and covered with little trees, but at one end a steep, bare mass of rock rose up suddenly out of the water, and on the top of this rock was the large nest. It was, however, quite accessible, and well do I remember, as a very small boy, clambering up to it, or rather to the mass of sticks of which it had been composed, and collecting no end of skulls and bones of beasts and birds, which lay scattered all around in great profusion.

The white-tailed eagles had evidently trusted entirely for their security to the fact of there having been no boat on the loch for many years, but after being robbed several times they flitted to a shelf in that stupendous precipice at the back of Beinn Airidh Charr just above Carn nan Uamhag (the Cairn of the Small Caves)—that wonderful cairn and stronghold of foxes and wild-cats, where the last of our martens was killed. When I was not more than seven or eight years old, I was already quite a keen collector of eggs, and greatly coveted a clutch of those of the sea-eagle, which were always rare in this district, whereas the golden eagles were comparatively plentiful. I have known only one other nesting-place of the sea-eagles on this coast, where in a sea-cliff they continued to breed till within comparatively modern times. I gave my dear mother no peace until she had arranged an expedition to the nest; it was just beyond our march, but per-mission having been got from our neighbour, away we went on pony-back, with an expert rock-climber and ropes, etc. Though the precipice from the pinnacle of Spidean Moirich down to Loch an Doire Chrionaich (Lake of the Withered Grove) at its base cannot be much under two thousand feet of nearly plumb rock, the eagles had fortunately chosen for their eyrie a fairly accessible shelf near the bottom. But, on our arrival we found we were just a day too late, for a south-country shepherd from the other property, having lately got wind that eagles' eggs had a certain market value, had taken them the previous day. How-ever, a good Caledonian bank-note, if it had *Tir nam beann, nan gleann s'nan gaisgach* (the land of the mountains, the glens, and the heroes), printed on it, was fairly powerful in those days; and for a pound-note of that description my enemy, Jock Beatie (for I fear I hated him in my little heart), handed over the two big, pure white eggs, and I returned home in a kind of semi-triumph on my Shetland pony's back. Just below the north end of the Fionn Loch, which is but one of the many lochs in that wild stretch of moorland, is Loch an Iasgair (the Osprey's Loch). In Gaelic the osprey is called Ailein Iasgair (Allan the Fisherman). How well I remember the excitement over the arrival at Poolewe Inn of Lord Huntingfield and a Mr. Corrance—both, I think, from Suffolk—the first egg-collectors who ever came to this country. Hearing of the ospreys, they made at once for the loch, where the nest was built on the top of a high stack of rock rising sheer out of the water. Their valet swam out, and returned with the two eggs safely in his cap, which he held between his teeth.

I flattered myself for some time that I was the first to find in Britain, or at any rate in Scotland, a goosander's nest with eggs, and that was in an island in the Fionn Loch, but afterwards I heard that a Cambridge professor maintained he had found one in Perthshire prior to my discovery.

A few pairs of black-throated divers still float about on our lochs, and sometimes rear their young, but sad to say they are diminishing in numbers, and many lochs where they used never to fail to breed are now without these beautiful and most interesting summer tenants. The red-throated divers, which I can quite well remember nesting on a small loch near the Fionn Loch, and also on lochs in the Rudhe 'Re point, have been quite extinct for close on seventy years.

The islands in the Fionn Loch, with its heronry and the lands surrounding it, both the high hills and the flat moors, were once upon a time good sporting grounds. The late Viscount Powerscourt hired the stalking of the great Fisherfield sheep-farm, just the year before the sheep stock was taken off it, and had a grand time among the stags. Having noticed, when stalking one day, the number of blue hares on little Beinn a Chaisgean, on the north side of the Fionn Loch, he planned a small hare drive.

There were only four or five guns, and I was one of them. We crossed the loch in a boat, strode up the steep hill, and were posted along the ridge on the very top, while a limited number of beaters walked in line along the sides of the hill. When the first beater came in sight, and called out to me in Gaelic, "How many hares have you got?" I replied that I thought I must have at least fifty, as my gun had got so hot that I could hardly hold it. Well, he gathered forty-seven. Twice I killed a brace of hares with one shot, as two of them happened to cross each other. We got quite a big bag that day.

This hill-top was also famous for ptarmigan in days gone by, and William Grant, who accompanied us to St. Kilda and was my right hand during the season I stalked at Carn Mor, told me that when he was in the service of a sporting innkeeper at Aultbea as a boy, they often used to make expeditions to the Beinn a Chaisgean, the worthy host armed with an old flint blunderbuss. It was, he said, never a question as to whether or not they would get any ptarmigan, but rather how it would be possible for him to carry home what his master shot; for the latter soon made a big bag, not by firing at them on the wing, but by taking pot shots at them on the ground, thus often getting several with one discharge. I am told that now there is not a hare and hardly a ptarmigan to be seen on those forty or fifty thousand acres.

A few years later, when the ground had been cleared of sheep, and the deer had had time to breed and accumulate, one could sometimes almost make oneself believe that the smoother and greener patches on the hill looked red when the sun shone on them, so thickly were they covered with deer. On our side of the loch, though the ground consisted of only bog, rocks, and heather, it was just about the best for grouse in our big parish. Shooting over it with dogs pretty late in the season, a cousin and I got 53 brace one day, and 50½ brace another day. In the year when Lord Medway had our shooting, his total bag was 412 brace, and his lordship got 100 brace in two days on the shores of the Fionn Loch, on the two beats right and left of what was then the new road. These flat moors used also to have, besides grouse, a lot of golden plovers breeding on them, with their charming little satellites, the dunlins, who stupid people often mistook for young plovers, because they also had little black patches on their breasts. Nowadays not a plover or a dunlin is to be seen, and the grouse are very few and far between.

The biggest wildcat we ever caught—and we caught many a big one—was a monster we got close to the Fionn Loch. It measured forty-three inches in length. How I lamented he could not have been tamed, as he would have looked so handsome on a rug, lying warming himself before a drawing-room fire.

I was nearly forgetting the otters. The Fionn Loch is a particularly favourite resort for them, and the Little Gruinord River is their highway from the Fionn Loch, and the twenty or more smaller lochs that empty themselves into it, to the ocean, which the otters much prefer in winter to the fresh water. One could not possibly imagine a more perfect home for otters than the islands of the Fionn Loch. I remember one day when fishing on it, and when right out in the middle, we saw a very young otter swimming along, which must have somehow got separated from its mother. During the chase it happened to come up near enough to the boat to be captured with the landing-net, and after keeping it for some weeks, we sent it to the London Zoo, where it lived and throve for many a long year in the otter pond.

About the year 1860 I had a delightful tame otter, which had been captured when quite tiny, and was brought up on milk. What a fascinating pet it was. It was never so happy as when playing like a kitten with a bit of stick, or tumbling about among dogs and puppies under the kitchen table, and it loved a good hot fire. I got it in April, and in the following winter I used to let it out with a very long cord in the big sea-pool of the Ewe below the bridge. One day the cord came off, the otter disappeared, and after swimming along the coast for two or three miles, came upon some boys fishing for cuddies off the rocks. Not being in the least afraid of human beings, it clambered up the rock, and began eating the fish, but the boys, who did not know it was tame and belonged to me, began belabouring it with the butt-ends of their rods and killed it. They added insult to injury by bringing the skin to me for sale a few days afterwards. How I did bemoan the loss of my otter!

My readers will agree that the records which I propose to give of the various fishermen are truly amazing. From time immemorial the Fionn Loch has been always famous for its enormous trout. As there were no boats on the loch, the old crofter population, who lived around its shores in their shieling bothies, used to catch fish by tying a cod-hook to the end of a long string, baiting it with a good-sized trout, and throwing it as far as possible out into the loch from certain points and promontories best known to themselves. They also used to spear the trout by bog-fir torchlight in the burns and the rivers in October and November.

Soon after the purchase of Kernsary by Gairloch, my uncle

happened to come across the late Sir Alexander Gordon Cumming of Altyre, who was then a very keen young sportsman, both with gun and rod, and on hearing of the reported size of the trout, Sir Alexander determined to try the loch himself. Of all unlikely times of the year for trout-fishing, he chose the middle of March, when no one but himself would have had hopes of catching anything; but in spite of the odds against him he caught plenty of fish, many of which were real giants.

The old people declared there were three different species (or at least varieties) of these big trout, and gave them three different Gaelic names—*viz.*, *Claigionnaich* (skully, big-headed), *Carraigeanaich* (stumpy, short and thick), and *Cnaimhaich* (bony, big-boned). Certainly the trout do vary a lot in shape and colouring.

How perfectly do I remember one evening in April, 1851 (when I was just nine years old), Sir Alexander sending down a message to us at Pool House, asking my mother and me to come up to the inn and to witness the weighing of the fish he had brought back that day, in case his own statements might be doubted in future years. There were four beauties lying side by side on the table of the small drinking-room, and they turned the scales at 51 pounds. The total weight of the twelve fish caught that 12th day of April by trolling was 87 pounds 12 ounces, made up thus: 14 pounds 8 ounces, 12 pounds 8 ounces, 12 pounds 4 ounces, 12 pounds, 10 pounds, 6 pounds 12 ounces, 6 pounds 8 ounces, 3 pounds, 3 pounds, 2 pounds 12 ounces, 2 pounds 8 ounces, 2 pounds.

Sir Alexander did very well on many of the other days, even in March. He was so energetic that, in order to lose as little time as possible in going to and from the loch, he sometimes put up at the Srathan Mor shepherd's house with my enemy, Jock Beatie of the sea-eagle's eggs. Before leaving he gave my mother an exact list of every trout he caught during his stay, with all the dates and weights. This list we always retained in our possession. As Sir Alexander had also a great name as a crack shot, we were keen to see him perform with the gun, so the day before he left Poolewe my mother and my uncle, who was then residing on his model Isle of Ewe farm, planned an expedition with him to the pigeon caves at the point of Cove to test his reputation. The sea proved too rough for him to shoot the pigeons from the boat as they came out of the cave, so he had to do the best he could from the tops of the caves, and the pigeons very nearly beat him, though he did knock over a few. But he did one thing which I never happened to have seen done before, nor have I seen it done since. A great black-backed gull, one of those cruel marine vultures, measuring sometimes nearly six feet from tip to tip of their wings, rose off a rock on the approach of the boat and soared high up over us. Sir Alexander's gun was loaded with one of Eley's wire cartridges, which were then the fashion, and he fired. There was a strong breeze blowing, and the gull fell straight down on to the water, though it was quite alive, and the wing was blown away in quite another direction by the wind; it had been cut clean off by the cartridge, which had failed to burst.

The luncheon was not the worst part of the outing. It was provided by my uncle, and was composed of the produce of his island. The previous day there had been an extra low spring tide, a flat, calm, clear sky, and a bright sun; and he had been out with his landing-net at the end of a very long pole, and had scooped up quantities of the most lovely oysters and big clams. So what with the wonderful butter and cheese from his model dairy and the delicious scones and oat-cakes, oysters and clams, our hero was made very happy in spite of having missed a few pigeons, and declared it was the best alfresco luncheon he had ever sat down to.

In my young days I was taken up rather more with shooting than with fishing. Owing to my living generally at Gairloch, I was far away from the Fionn Loch, and only occasionally able to make expeditions to it. Sometimes when we wanted to make sure of showing some friend a sample of the big Fionn Loch trout we would send a couple of men up the previous evening with two or three lines, each having six hooks on it and baited with small parr caught in the Ewe. These lines were set by tying them generally to a boulder, of which there are plenty in the loch standing up out of the water. One day I remember, as we were approaching the little sandy bay, where we kept the boat in the pre-road days, we noticed a great commotion on the surface of the water. One of the men said, "Oh, that is where we set one of our lines last night." When we reached it there were two twelve-pounders on it. How they dashed about and jumped out of the water before we could get the clip into them! I could point out the very boulder even now, though I am seventy-eight, for one does not forget an event like that in a hurry.

Another day I was fishing with a friend of mine, and trolling along past the Eagle Island, when he caught three fish in quick succession, of 9 pounds, $7\frac{1}{2}$ pounds and 7 pounds. But the most exciting thing that happened to me on the Fionn Loch was the hooking of the biggest fish I ever saw on that loch. It was only a few years ago. I was casting with a light rod, and had on an ordinary cast with three small flies, just where the small burn flows into the loch at the Feith a Chaisgan sandy bay, when I hooked an enormous fish. Some readers might say it was just a big salmon, for both salmon and sea-trout come up into the Fionn Loch by the Little Gruinord River, though they are very seldom taken; but I am a pretty good judge of fish, and my two rowers—my late faithful friend and gamekeeper, John Matheson, who came to me when he was sixteen and I was nineteen, and lived all his life with me, and our present stalker, Donald Urquhart, who has also been all his days with us—were as positive as I was that this monster was a typical Fionn Loch trout, only quite double the size of any we had ever seen before. It jumped three times clean out of the water close to the boat, and we saw it as well as if we had handled it; but in spite of us all doing our very best to ease the tension on the line, it soon carried off everything. Without in the least wishing to exaggerate, I honestly declare that fish to have been a twenty-five pounder!

Just once (perhaps about the year 1863) I set a net in the Fionn Loch which we used in the sea to catch lythe, and got such a haul of fish that the two men who went to lift it could hardly carry them home across the moor. The biggest of the lot scaled eighteen pounds, and I sent it over to my friend Lord St. John of Bletsoe, the grandfather of the present peer, who was then and for many years after my brother's shooting tenant of Gairloch, just to show him a sample of the trout we could catch in our lochs! I have heard of one other having been caught of a similar weight.

The last big fish I handled was one caught a couple of years ago by my son-in-law, Mr. Robert J. Hanbury. He had said that the first twelve-pounder he got on his own rod should be preserved. He was not long in getting a real beauty, and very grand it looks in its glass case.

A Mr. Byres Leake got during the last days of April and on eighteen days' fishing in May 1,370 trout, averaging about 70 *per diem*; on three successive days he caught 122, 107, and 100 fish. Mr. W. L. Boase and party arrived at Inverewe on the 1st of June and fished thirty-eight days. They caught 2,384 trout, weighing 900½ pounds, and let go between 400 and 500 which were under half a pound. I remember that one day Mr. Boase, who was himself an old man, and a friend of his, a Mr. Lindsay, who was an octogenarian, were fishing on one of our lesser lochs, near the Fionn Loch, in quite a small boat, when both of them hooked a trout at the same moment. The two fish were safely secured, and a pretty pair they were, of 5 pounds and 8 pounds. On landing, the two fish were laid side by side on a slab of rock and photographed. On the same small loch I have known of an 11-pound ferox being caught with a small trout fly. Another day a son of Mr. Boase was fishing from the bank close to the Fionn Loch Pier with three small flies, when he hooked a big fish which took him over an hour to land. When weighed it turned the scales at 10 pounds. Eight of Mr. Boase's trout were over 4 pounds and weighed as follows: 10 pounds, 10 pounds, 9 pounds, 8 pounds, 7½ pounds, 6½ pounds, 5 pounds, and 4½ pounds.

But perhaps the best record of all was that made by Mr. F. C. McGrady, and I give an exact copy of his own account of his fishing on the next page.

		Trout.	Weight in Pounds.			Trout.	Weight in Pounds.
May	30	24	$8\frac{1}{2}$	July	1	68	23
,,	31	77	28	,,	2	8	$3\frac{1}{2}$
June	1	72	$31\frac{1}{2}$	,,	3	95	47
,,	3	60	21	,,	4	68	25
,,	4	74	28	,,	5	67	26
,,	5	23	$8\frac{1}{2}$	,,	6	41	$22\frac{1}{2}$
,,	6	134	48	,,	8	63	23
,,	7	180	62	,,	9	116	41
,,	8	189	$74\frac{3}{4}$	,,	10	76	27
,,	10	187	$63\frac{1}{2}$	,,	11	51	$19\frac{1}{2}$
,,	11	119	42	,,	12	31	25
,,	12	97	35	,,	13	18	10
,,	13	32	9	,,	15	71	27
,,	14	96	50	,,	17	20	$6\frac{1}{4}$
,,	15	160	70	,,	18	60	$22\frac{1}{2}$
,,	17	222	74	,,	19	71	24
,,	18	108	$45\frac{1}{2}$	,,	20	38	15
,,	19	85	$31\frac{1}{2}$	,,	22	25	$29\frac{1}{2}$
,,	20	154	$47\frac{1}{2}$	,,	23	40	$10\frac{1}{2}$
,,	22	55	20	,,	24	15	6
,,	24	133	46	,,	25	55	$23\frac{1}{2}$
,,	26	31	22	,,	26	48	20
,,	27	71	$24\frac{1}{2}$				
,,	28	83	$29\frac{1}{2}$				
,,	29	14	13			3,625	1,410

NOTE OF HEAVY TROUT

		Trout.	Weight in Pounds.			Trout.	Weight in Pounds.
June	14	1	$5\frac{1}{2}$	July	6	1	3
,,	14	1	6	,,	12	1	$6\frac{3}{4}$
,,	17	1	4	,,	12	1	3
,,	26	1	$7\frac{1}{2}$	,,	15	1	3
,,	29	1	$3\frac{1}{2}$	,,	22	1	$8\frac{1}{4}$
July	3	2	3 each	,,	22	1	7
,,	3	1	$7\frac{1}{2}$	,,	22	1	$3\frac{1}{2}$

All small trout (under 6 inches) were thrown back.

CHAPTER XII

Now I want to say something about my grandfather, Sir Hector Mackenzie, the fourth baronet, generally spoken of among Highlanders as *An tighearna Storach* (the buck-toothed laird). Of him my uncle writes:

"I always think of my father as well on in life, perhaps because we never saw him excited about anything, but always going about quietly, as if thinking deeply. If a dog pointed at a covey, he of course shot a bird with each barrel, but he never showed a trace of anxiety as to whether we picked them up or not, or where the other birds went. He was as quiet and composed as if it were none of his business, but only ours. I never heard of his having gone deer-stalking or taken part in any exciting work, but, though so quiet, he was always ready for a 'twa-handed crack,' and was bright and cheery about past, present and future. He enjoyed his meals and was a good hand at breakfast, being especially fond of smoked salmon and venison collops, at which none alive could match Kate Archy. If a dish met him with pepper in it, which he detested, he would quietly give it up, saying, perhaps, 'I wish pepper was a guinea an ounce,' or 'The Lord sent us meat; we know where the cooks come from.' On the sideboard there always stood before breakfast a bottle of whisky, smuggled of course, with plenty of camomile flowers, bitter orange-peel, and juniper berries in it—'bitters' we called it—and of this he had a wee glass always before we sat down to breakfast, as a fine stomachic.

"It is impossible to imagine him mixed up with any jolly, rackety ploy, but I can see him now plainly standing on the edge of a drain for hours, directing every spadeful of earth thrown out or stone put in—for tiles were long after his day. He always held in his hand his double Joe Manton with flint-locks, in case of some vermin showing itself or a hare asking for a sudden shot; and as he was never in a hurry to fire and never fired till the animal was covered by the gun-button, the distance at which his gun killed seemed incredulous. At other times he would be busy directing the gardener about some plant, or would sit at his desk going over his rental ledgers, or listening to some complaint from a tenant. About Martinmas-time he would ride off to Gairloch from Conon on his pony to collect rents, with saddle-bags behind him, but no valet, groom, factor, or clerk to help, and before Mackintosh's waterproof days, with no better waterproof cloak than a camlet. What a blessing it would be to landlord and tenant were all lairds now as well acquainted with their tenants and their circumstances as he was! He was the only son of his mother, and, I may add, the only child, and was left an orphan when a mere infant. His Uncle Mackenzie of Millbank, near Dingwall, had charge of him, and he seems to have grown up anyhow, till he fell into the hands of a tutor—the only one he ever had—the Rev. Mr. Robertson (afterwards Dr.), Minister of Eddleston in Peeblesshire. I have no doubt this gentleman cared for him as well as he could, else my father would never have chosen Robertson's son, the third successive member of the family to be Minister of Eddleston, to be tutor to us five boys.

"I think my father was born about 1758. He was short in height, only about 5 feet 5 inches, but in breadth and strength few of any height could match him. His juniper walking-stick, now beside me, is only 2 feet 6 inches long. It is said that some celebrated athlete, hearing of his great strength, contrived to meet him and shake hands with him. My father had heard of the boaster, and on their meeting gave him such a wild squeeze that he just howled to be let go, and took care never to try another. I don't believe any person ever saw my father visibly out of temper or in a hurry. My mother and he spoke Gaelic as freely as English— a great tie between them and their people. I never heard of his wearing a kilt or tartan in any shape. Tweeds were unknown seventy years ago, and I remember him always in iron-grey shooting-jackets, lighter trousers, gaiters and shoes, his waistcoat loose enough to hold easily his large leather snuff-box, divided in the centre, one end full of Fribourg and Pontees' 'Yellow Irish Blackguard,' which he used himself, and the other containing 'Black

Rappie' for friends who preferred that more filthy powder. Whether or not it was owing to my father always using 'Irish Blackguard,' no one ever could tell that he was a snuffer, or saw a spot on his always displayed shirt-breast ruffles. As a great favour I was sometimes allowed by the maids in the laundry to plait the ruffles with an old blunt pen-knife aided by my thumb, and in return for this favour I suppose we ceased sometimes to plague and worry the maids on all suitable or unsuitable occasions.

"For full-dress, he wore a blue swallow-tail with gilt buttons, a buff or white waistcoat, and black trousers with grey-marble silk stockings. He wore no shirt collars, but round his neck was any number of unstarched, soft white muslin neckerchiefs rolled round and round till I suppose he could have endured no more, without losing all power of turning his head. There was a wee knot on the last roll in front, and below that a grand display of my plaited shirt-ruffles sticking through his waistcoat (I admit I never got much praise from the laundry-maids for my starching abilities). His shoes were suited to gouty feet, although he suffered that misery more in his knuckles than his feet. I have even seen him with nankeen trousers during our old-fashioned summers, to which I have alluded before. I don't believe he ever owned a dressing-gown or a pair of cosy slippers. At least, I have seen him shaving with nothing on him but a day shirt, and that in winter. He despised cosiness, but liked to lie on a sofa in the afternoon or evening after a long day occupied in superintending farm work. I seem to see him now on the sofa in the parlour at Tigh Dige, reading newspapers with his head towards the fire and light, and when one was thoroughly read he nipped a bit out of it to prevent a second reading. Except for small mutton-chop whiskers, he was always clean shaven, and never used warm water or any such fine nonsense. His income was about £3,000 a year. The shootings were not let in his time, in the Highlands at least. Landlords then were not so often hard up as now, when with three times their income there is homœopathic hospitality very different indeed from the lavishness in his house. All is now stored up for cutting a splash in London or abroad, just as a couple of big game battues in the year replace the continuous moderate shooting throughout the season which people formerly offered their friends. He was only once in London and on his return showed the Gairloch people how the skin had been worn off his forefinger and thumb by constantly forking out money.

" 'Father,' Frank would say, 'they tell me there is an officer come to-day to the inn at Ceann-t-saile.' 'Frank, run and find out his name,' was the reply. 'Give him my compliments, and say I hope he will come up at once with his things and remain here till he is obliged to leave.' The idea of a gentleman—ladies in those days never inspected our country—being allowed to remain at an inn was contrary to all rules of Highland hospitality and thought disgraceful. The entertained were not always angels unawares, but one day there arrived Major Colby, of the Engineers, who, with a sergeant and some privates, had been sent to the north-west as pioneers of the Government plans for the Ordnance Survey of Britain, a great work, hardly completed yet, though I must be writing of about the year 1816. My father caught many a fish on his hospitality hook, but never one like Colby, a highly educated man of science, from astronomy all the way downwards, full of every kind of information, and most able and glad to pass it on to others. He had been all through the wars with Buonaparte, yet was always ready to come shooting or fishing in burn, loch, or sea with us if his men were carrying on routine work which only needed his presence occasionally. He was with us nearly the whole summer, and I remember what high spirits he was in one day when one of his people won a prize by throwing the sun's rays from a concave mirror from, I think, the top of Slioch to the Clova Hills in Kincardineshire through some glen or other, thus enabling these spots to be fixed accurately for mapping. He was much interested by our dear Uncle Kenneth's account of the war with Hyder Ali and the siege and taking of Seringapatam, at which Uncle Kenneth was present. He retired afterwards to Kerrysdale, and seemed to be more peaceful and happy than anyone I ever knew.

"My father never went out to kill a heavy bag. Such things were never boasted of in those times as now, when a man who shoots, say, one hundred brace in a day is looked up to as quite a hero. Except to vary the house diet and to give some game to a tenant, killing grouse was mere waste, there being no way to dispose of it, no steamers, no railways, no wheels to Gairloch to send the game broadcast all over the kingdom. There was then as much game as could be expected when the gamekeeper was merely a game-killer and never dreamt of trapping vermin. My father shot any kind of vermin that happened to come in his way or hunted them with the dogs. When he went to shoot some grouse we small boys always begged to be allowed to carry the dead. One day I remember so well his astonishing us. From a small bit of water and reeds behind Badachro up got five mallard in front of us; his first barrel brought down two, and after a long wait for the second shot, away it went, and brought down the other three. The cool old hand did not pull trigger till the ducks crossed each other's flight, as ducks often do. A hasty gunner would have fired at once and bagged probably only one. Those were the days of flint-locks. What trouble I have had on a wet day trying to keep the powder in the outside pan dry, or hammering a blunt flint or enquiring for a new one! When I fired I really had to keep the gun for a time pointed at the mark till the explosion took place, whereas now the whole is off like greased lightning. My father always carried his gun on his left arm behind his back, and when a bird or a hare got up unexpectedly before him he took things so coolly that I have seen him use up a pinch of snuff he had between his right thumb and forefinger ere 'Manton' went up to his shoulder and he touched its trigger; but 'Joe' could not scatter his shot, and if the gun were held straight no bird or beast was safe in front of my father at eighty yards' distance.

"Our dinner hour at Tigh Dige was 5 p.m. Beyond washing face and hands, there was no dressing for dinner, as there was always some evening ploy unless it was very wet; indeed, people soon became careless about rain in the warm west, and semi-amphibious. At 9 p.m. a tray with curiously contrived dishes was brought in, four forming the outer ring on the tray and one on a raised stand in the centre. Potatoes and minced collops, rumbled eggs, some cutlets and patisserie, etc., exhausted the housekeeper's ideas of variety in the supper dishes. The meal was soon over, and when the tray had been removed a rummer tumbler, hot-water jug, milk-jug, sugar-bowl, and whisky-bottle, with sufficient wine-glasses, were placed on the table. My father put just one glass of 'mountain dew' into the rummer, then sugar, and then one toddy ladleful of milk. Though the 'dew' would be coarse and fiery, its toddy was made essentially mild as cream; only I nowadays would advise drinking the milk without the 'dew.'

"My father was a great planter of trees, and all the big hard-wood trees scattered about the Baile Mor policies were planted by him. Wire fences were unborn in his day, and enclosing by paling every tree he took a fancy to plant here and there would have been impossible, so he adopted a most simple and effectual protection to his young trees wherever planted. He had a nursery whence hard-wood trees about eight to ten feet high were always ready to be transplanted into carefully prepared pits. In Gairloch in pre-sheep days thousands of wild roses grew everywhere, often eight to ten feet high. For every hard-wood tree transplanted a wild rose with many stems was carefully taken up and planted in the same pit. The rose stems were fastened to the hard-wood tree by wire ties, the result being that the most itchy cattle beast would go a mile for a scratch rather than touch a tree so thorn-protected. Every tree thus planted by my wise father was perfectly safe from injury by cattle, the briers living many years—indeed, almost for ever.

"My father had a poor opinion of those landed proprietors who, though quite aware that their heirs' bread depended on their managing land and tenants successfully, gave them no chance of acquiring much information on the land that was to be their own some day. So, instead of giving his eldest son Frank an allowance of, say, £500 a year, which he could draw from the bank and use in capering about the world idle and useless until his father died, or in going into the Army to learn how easily life is wasted, he gave him a slice of the estate to manage for himself under his father's eye. This portion, if properly cared for, would produce £500 a year, and the son could stay at home with his father and mother and help in many ways where needed. Part of Frank's farms were Bogdoin and Tenahaun of Conon and the Isle of Ewe in Gairloch. There was plenty to do in these then wildernesses, and Frank put them into a very different condition from what he found them in, before his father's death. He managed his property wisely and profitably, and my father's expectations were entirely fulfilled. No young northern proprietor that I ever heard of gave his mind so entirely to agriculture as Frank did all his life.

"My memory shows me my father after breakfast standing on the edge of a drain he had lined out in a field of the home farm, directing the men carefully, with 'Joe Manton' in his left hand. Many a small crofter would come and ask advice on rural matters, and my father would answer as carefully as if the £5 croft was a £200 farm. He would then move from the drain to some other improvement in progress, stopping a partridge or a hare if it unwisely crossed his road, or a grey crow or magpie which foolishly, unaware that 'Joe' killed at eighty yards, had the impertinence to set up their chat within what they believed was a safe distance. The boys were perhaps at lessons, and their mother deep in household matters with the housekeeper or cook at Conon. She might have arranged to meet father at a certain hour to inspect the flax crop, and see whether it was ready to pull, or, if pulled, had been long enough in the retting (rotting) pool, and was fit to take out for drying and scutching. When ready it was spun by the maids, and old Junor, the sheet and tablecloth weaver, finished it off for the well-stocked napery press.

"Only the other day I was using a towel of Junor's make, still quite sound, marked 'C.M.K., 1806,' by my dear mother when I was three years old. It was part of the present to my wife on her marriage visit to Conon in 1826, which all young daughters-in-law in those days expected to get from their mothers-in-law. It is painful to contrast the placidly peaceful, happy life of my parents then with the rush and splash and constant feverish excitement all round us now in the same ranks of society. How eager is the pursuit of fancied happiness, which people imagine cannot be found in the peaceful life their wiser parents lived. One is reminded of the contrast between the light of a good steady lamp and the blaze and rush of a rocket, which too often ends in an explosion and sends the ancestral acres and home to smithereens! Then the wreckage is gathered up by wiser, quiet-going people, as we have seen in too many northern homes which are now occupied by people quite unknown in my young days."

To show the enthusiasm of the people in past days for their lairds I must tell the following story. Very soon after my father's death, my uncle, as factor for the estate, had occasion to come up to Gairloch, and took along with him my two half-brothers, aged twelve and ten. The Tigh Dige and the sporting rights of the whole Gairloch property had been let to an Irishman, Sir St. George Gore, for £300 a year on a lease, so my uncle and the boys put up at the small Ceann-t-saile Inn. When the crofters heard this they were frantic at the idea of *an t'oidhre agus an tanaistar* (the heir and the next in succession) not putting up in the ancestral home, and a mob of them came and surrounded the Tigh Dige, and threatened the Irishman that, if he did not at once invite my uncle and the boys to come and stay with him, he would find himself with a rope and stone round his neck at the bottom of Loch Maree! My uncle had the greatest difficulty in pacifying the people, and had to apologise most profusely to Sir St. George Gore, who was terrified and very nearly started shooting into the crowd. Before long, Sir St. George having proved himself a very unsatisfactory tenant, my uncle gave him notice to quit. This surprised him very much, as he knew he had a pretty long lease of the place, and was quite unaware that, in the case of an entailed property, by Scots law any lease of a mansion-house comes to an end on the death of the proprietor, so that the heir of entail can at once take possession of his home,

The Gairloch people were indeed devoted to their proprietor in those days. How often has my mother described them to me, and how often did she extol their very great merits! Still, when she and my uncle were ruling these five hundred to six hundred families of crofters it was an extra hard time for them, for first of all there was the potato blight—and want generally brings out the bad and not the good qualities of a people; then there was the great upheaval caused by the trustees deciding to do away with the runrig system and dividing all the arable land into crofts of about four acres. They forced the people to pull down their old insanitary houses, where the cattle were under the same roof as human beings, and where the fires were on the floor in the centre of the dwelling-room, with only a hole in the roof to let the smoke out, and made them build new and rather better houses on their crofts, the proprietor providing the timber. My mother told me many a time that, with very few exceptions, the one desire of the whole population seemed to be to learn how they could please the young laird, and how they could best fulfil the wishes of those who were managing this huge estate for him to the best of their abilities.

There is no doubt that the people of the west coast went through periods of terrible hunger in what we now speak of as "the good old times," especially before the introduction of the potato. How they lived in pre-potato days is a mystery. But even prior to the destruction caused by the potato blight, when the potatoes usually grew so well, there was hardly a year in which my grandfather and my father did not import cargoes of oatmeal to keep the people alive, and those cargoes were seldom, if ever, paid for by their poor recipients. One has only to look at the sites of the shielings even some miles from the sea, where great heaps of shells tell their tale. Shell-fish boiled in milk was a great stand-by in those days. I sometimes wonder that they did not carry the milk downhill to the coast, rather than carry the shell-fish up to the hills.

I remember my old faithful servant, George Maclennan, telling me a story which shows how scarce anything in the form of bread was even in comparatively modern times. George's father was the postman at one time who carried the Lews and Poolewe mails through Creag Thairbh to Brahan Castle and Dingwall, fully sixty miles, and a good part of his salary consisted of bolls of oatmeal. Consequently his house often had meal in it when the neighbours' houses were empty. George as a boy was for some reason wandering over the wild moors up on the Fionn Loch side when he met a very old man, whom even I can remember, who was there with his cows at the shieling near the Airidh

Mollach. The old man seemed very faint, and he admitted to the boy that he had not tasted anything in the form of bread for some days, living entirely on milk and the trout he was able to catch with his rod. George had a good supply of oatcake in his pocket, and he gave it to the old man, who was more than grateful.

Shell-fish must have been good strong food if there was something to take along with it, for I was always told that the finest and strongest family of young men ever known at Poolewe— Gillean an Alanaich (the Lads of Allan)—were a family who above all other families in the place were brought up on Maorach a Chladaich (the shell-fish of the shore). But there were shell-fish and shell-fish, and long ago, after sheep had been for some time on what are now my lands, a change was made by the then proprietor, Sir George Mackenzie of Coul, and the place was let to a lot of crofters from Melvaig, a township right out on the point of the Rudha Reidh. Well, as there were no stretches of sand and shingle out on this wild promontory and only rocks and precipices, the shell-fish they had been accustomed to eat was the limpet and that white whelk whose English name I do not know, but which is known in Gaelic as Gille Fionn (the white lad). So when they shifted their abode to the head of Loch Ewe and had to live on oysters and mussels and cockles, they thought the change of diet did not altogether suit them, and, like the Israelites of old, they pined for the shell-pots of Melvaig. I was quite lately at the Rudha Reidh Lighthouse and passed through the sites of the old Melvaig shielings, where masses of limpet and whelk shells were still to be seen all around.

Here is another story of hard times. A very old friend of mine, who was always known at Poolewe as Mackenzie of Cliff House, told me that a great-uncle of his who had a farm at Kenlochewe suffered so badly one spring that he lost all his cattle, with the exception of one black heifer; the meal was done, and starvation stared him in the face. Early in May the heifer calved, and he and his wife put up a kind of bothy in Coire mhic Fhearchar between Meall a Ghiubhais and Beinn Eidh, in the very heart of what is now the Kenlochewe deer-forest, and there they lived on the milk of the heifer and venison. A deer would be killed from time to time, but not very often, as they were scarce in those days, and the venison would be hung up in the spray of a great waterfall, which entirely prevented any blue flies getting at it. Thus they spent five or six months, the happiest, they always declared, they ever spent in their lives, till the corn and potatoes ripened down in the glen in October, when they returned to their home in Kenlochewe.

I once asked an old man, Ali Dubh, who used to work for me, and who as a boy was often with grandparents living in one of the inland crofter townships of the parish of Gairloch, whether they did not sometimes suffer great hardships and hunger. His answer was as follows: "Oh, sometimes we had plenty. I remember one year when there was a terrible snow-storm early in the winter before Martinmas, and all the tenants' stock of goats were smothered at Meallan nan Gabhar. That year we had salted goat and smoked goat hams right on till near Whit-Sunday." "And what about the following years?" I asked him. "Oh, indeed, it was many a long year before the tenants had meat, as it took so long to get up a stock of goats again."

CHAPTER XIII

AGRICULTURE

PEOPLE have an idea that agriculture was very far behind in the old days of the runrig system. That this system was as bad a one as could be there is no denying. There was no incentive to improve your rig or patch, for what you had this year one of your neighbours probably had next year. There were continual quarrels over the distribution of the allotments, and then the whole ground was remeasured with, as my uncle described it, "miles of string," and lots were cast as to who were to get the various bits of ground. I may mention that the trustees left one big township—namely, Inverasdale—under the old system, and before three years had run the crofters unanimously begged to get separate crofts like the rest. I know a chauffeur from a township in Torridon where the runrig system still prevails, and he told me his ground was in thirty-six different patches, none of them contiguous.

In spite of all this, and though the only implements of husbandry were the *caschrom* and *croman* (the old prehistoric Norwegian hand plough and a kind of homemade Highland hoe), I, who am more or less of a farmer myself, am prepared to prove that far more crop was raised out of the soil then than there is now. I remember having it constantly dinned into my ears when I was young that when the people were educated (and not till then) the land would be properly cultivated, and that then every croft would become perfect like a garden. But, alas! it has turned out the very contrary. The modern crofter has nearly given up the use of all hand implements of culture, and trusts to hiring a pair of more or less starved ponies and often a very inefficient plough and harrows. They get the ground scratched over in some kind of way, but much of it only to a depth of a very few inches, all head rigs and difficult stony bits being left untouched. As there is great difficulty in getting horses and ploughs, the crops are almost always so late in being sown that the equinoctial gales are upon them before they ripen; this means disaster and a ruinous harvest nearly every year, owing to the floods and storms.

I maintain that education has done nothing for agriculture among the crofters on the west coast as far as I can see. Though the people are certainly improving their dwellings, I seldom, if ever, see them use the pick, the spade, and the crowbar, which are so essential for trenching and draining and getting rid of boulders. In fact, many of the crofts are going back, instead of being improved and turned into gardens, as they might be with fixity of tenure and fair rents to encourage their owners. In the old *caschrom* days every inch of the ground was cultivated even among boulders, where the best soil is often to be found and which no plough can go near.

And how the women used to work among the potatoes, weeding them by hand so carefully, putting all the chickweed and spurry into creels, carrying it to the nearest burn, and there washing it to give to the cattle for supper, much to the benefit of the milk-supply! Also, how beautifully they earthed up their potatoes with the *cromanan*, whereas now the weeds are often allowed to get to a great height before a horse with a scuffler can be hired or borrowed, for very few four-acre crofts can support a pony besides the cows.

I can remember a good many crofters who were keen cultivators and prided themselves on the number of bolls of meal they could produce from their crofts. Nowadays hardly a boll of meal is made on any croft, and the mills are mostly derelict and falling to pieces, as neither the man nor the woman will bother themselves to thresh the sheaves before giving them to the cows. Many of the girls dislike milking a cow, and they will not accept willingly of service where a cow is kept, though they do not object to having cream in their tea if they can get it without trouble to themselves! I am afraid that education, when it takes the shape of drawing, French, and music, has made the present generation of girls very unsuitable as wives for young west-coast crofters.

Before the crofters' arable land was turned into four-acre crofts,

and the runrig system was done away with, every family in the
west went with their cattle for two or three of the summer
months to the shieling. In the Lews they still continue this custom.
But when the great change was made one of the new ideas for the
betterment of the smaller tenants was that they should give up
their migrations to the shieling, and consume the grass of their
distant hill pastures by grazing them with sheep, instead of with
cattle.

Before the potato blight in the early forties, it was fairly easy
to raise food anywhere on the coast, where sea-ware was procur-
able. Though most of the ground consisted of poor peaty soil
among stones and rocks, sea-ware with its potash would generally
force a crop—often a bumper crop—of potatoes out of almost any
soil, even though wet and boggy, if it was made into what were
known as "lazy beds," such as are so common to-day in the West
of Ireland. Though the good effects of the sea-ware were not very
permanent, the land thus planted with potatoes would give at
least one heavy following crop of oats the next year. There was
also a considerable amount of cultivation inland, there being in
the parish of Gairloch a good number of what are called in Gaelic
Bailtean Monaidh (inland townships). These townships were too
far from the coast for sea-ware to be transported on men's and
women's backs, the only method of transit in the days when there
were no roads and consequently no carts in the district. So what
the inland crofters did was this. They chose fairly smooth pieces
of sloping ground, which had to be as dry as possible naturally,
as they knew nothing about artificial draining, and they would
then surround them with a low dyke of stones and turf, just
sufficiently high to keep the cows from getting over. In some cases
they used movable wicker-hurdles, where birch and hazel were
handy, and into one of the enclosures the cattle were driven after
being milked in the evening, to pass the night, for perhaps a
fortnight or three weeks, until the wise men of the community
considered they had sufficiently manured that particular plot.
Then the cows were made to pass their nights on another *achadh*
or enclosure. In the following spring these manured *achaidhnan*
(fields) were very laboriously turned over by the men with the

caschrom, and a more or less good crop of the small and hardy aboriginal black oats was reaped, and later on ground into meal by the *Bra* or *quern*. Sometimes they would take a second or even a third crop of oats out of the *achadh*, or vary the crop, especially if the soil were hard and stony, with one of grey field peas, which, when ground and mixed with barley meal, made most nourishing bread in the form of scones baked on a girdle over a peat fire. Many a time have I eaten them as a boy.

When the *achadh* was completely exhausted, the dyke was allowed to tumble down, and the field to go wild again under weeds (the sowing of grass seeds was quite unknown then) till it had time to recover itself, in a kind of way. Then, the dyke having been repaired, the same process of manuring the ground with the cattle was gone through over again! Most people would imagine that the time allowed for the cattle to lie on these enclosures for the purpose of enriching them would be about the same, whether early or late in the season, but the crofter knew better what was necessary from years of experience. The old men used to tell me, when I was a boy, that twenty cows on an enclosure in June when the grass was young and in full force did as much enriching in a week as they would do in a fortnight in August or September, when the hill grasses or bents were going back and turning brown. This folding of the cattle at night, though necessary for the production of grain, was not at all good for the cows from a milking point of view. These bits of cultivation were generally high above sea-level and in open, exposed places, and as there are pretty frequently on this north-west coast, even in the height of summer, wild, cold nights with wind and rain storms, the cows often suffered from the exposure and from not being free to go and choose for themselves warm and sheltered spots in which to make their beds.

The old inhabitants of these inland townships had also a way of growing potatoes as well as oats on the cultivated patches away up in the glens, where no sea-ware could be procured, and where it was impossible to carry the manure from their byres and stables in the township, because it was all required for the cropping of what was then known as the "infield" land round their houses.

One way of growing potatoes up in the wilds was by substituting bracken for sea-ware, and making "lazy beds" of it where the soil was fairly deep and moist. The bracken was cut with the sickle in July when at its richest, and the ground given a thick coating of it; ditches were then opened about six feet apart and the soil, from the ditches put on the bracken so that it had a covering of six or eight inches of earth on it. Thus it was left for some nine months to decay, till the spring came round again, when holes were bored in the beds with a "dibble" and the seed potatoes dropped into them. In this case also the sheep and the goats helped in the growing of the potatoes!

In those olden times there were but few sheep kept, and they were all of the *Seana chaoirich bheaga* (little old sheep) breed, with pink noses and very fine wool, quite different from the modern black-faced sheep, much less hardy, and accustomed to be more or less housed at night. They were far less numerous than the goats, and when the people migrated to the shielings they took their sheep and goats with them. These had to be carefully herded by the children all day, to keep the lambs and kids from being carried off by the eagles and foxes. At night at the shielings the sheep and the goats were driven into bothies and bedded with bracken or moss, and when these bothies were cleaned out in the spring they contained a large accumulation of excellent manure for the potatoes. I well remember an old man telling me that when out with the cattle he used in dry summers to set fire to old, useless turf dykes and use the peat ashes for his "outfield" potatoes, and that sometimes he grew better potatoes thus away up in the hills than he could grow at his home in the glen below. But who could be got to do this sort of land cultivation nowadays? It is therefore useless to talk of cultivating these green spots among the hills, which were only forced to produce what would now be considered very poor crops of corn! At that time there was no alternative but either to do this or starve. There is, I think, a very mistaken idea afloat that these Highlanders of the olden times were a lazy lot, instead of which they were, in my opinion, just the very contrary. I know as a fact that the fathers of several of the old Poolewe men I knew so well as a lad used to go in their small fourteen-foot boats in stormy weather in March and April to cut tangle on the coast of the Rudha Reidh promontory, ten miles out to sea from their homes, for manure for their potatoes. They then carried this fearfully heavy wet mass on their backs in creels for a good two miles up a steep hill from the sea-pool of the Ewe, to some cultivable spots on the moor above the present Tollie farm, which still glisten like emeralds among the surrounding heather. I am glad to say they were sometimes well rewarded by Providence, as I have heard that they not infrequently brought home a creel full of potatoes in autumn for every creel of sea-ware they had carried up in the spring, so effective is sea-ware on new land! And the women of those days—how they slaved carrying the peats or kneeling down to cut short grass for hay with small sickles. When collecting shell-fish for food and bait for the lines, they had to stand out in the sea above their knees, and they were continually rounding up the goats barefooted among the most dangerous precipices, in order to get them in at night and thus be able to milk them and make cheese for winter consumption! How different, alas! are the men and the women of the present day, when it is thought a hardship if the women have to make porridge for breakfast or oat-cakes for dinner, because the baker failed to call at the door with his van, of often very bad loaf bread!

CHAPTER XIV

CHURCH AND STATE

THE Disruption in the Church of Scotland took place about the time when I was born, and I never worshipped in the old Parish Church of Gairloch, as our family entered the Free Church. No wonder the people rebelled when worthless men were appointed to big parishes by lay patrons, quite regardless of their being suitable or unsuitable. This was the case at Gairloch when an old tutor, who had hardly a word of Gaelic, tried to make up for his want of the language by the roaring and bawling he kept up in the pulpit while attempting to read a Gaelic sermon translated from English by some schoolmaster! On one occasion when my grandfather and his party were in church, our Mackenzie cousin, who was tenant of Shieldaig, and his family were among the congregation, and were, as usual, invited up to the Tigh Dige to luncheon. Among the Shieldaig party was a small boy of four or five summers who had been brought to church for the first time in his life. My grandfather, wishing to say something to the little chap, asked him what he saw in church, and his reply was much to the point: "I saa a man baaling, baaling in a box, and no a man would let him oot."

I think I must give my uncle's description of the Communion gathering in his time. Those gatherings were much the same in my young days, and I regularly attended with my mother in the famous Leabaidh na ba baine (Bed of the White Cow), where Fingal's white cow calved.

"My father and mother always communicated in Gairloch and Ferintosh, going through the whole five days' ceremonies, for they were unwilling to appear in opposition even to unreasonable customs so long as these were harmless. Owing to want of roads, wheels, or steam, the Gairloch Communion used to be held only once in three years. Consequently it became a very great holy fair. I never remember it but in midsummer in fine weather. For days before the Fast Days every spare hole and corner was got ready for the mob of people that came from the neighbouring parishes, some fifty or sixty miles distant. This was considered a pleasant walk, not by the communicants merely, but by crowds who came, not to communicate, but to see the people and to hear the many clergymen.

"In Gairloch every hole or corner with a roof over it was got ready by strewing it with straw for the visitors' beds during the six nights of their stay. Undressing during that time was never dreamt of by the crowd, and washing was impossible! Our barns and stables were all scrubbed out and ready for visitors, and for days before the feast there was much killing and cooking of cattle, sheep, and salmon, for all the hungry visitors who were expected. Such really hard labour for the house servants all through the five days would, if I were to detail it truly, hardly be believed as occurring in a Christian land in connection with religion. It was simply fearful. On Sunday, as soon as breakfast was over, every hand set to work preparing for the grand, popular, open-house cold luncheon, to which all 'the upper crust' and the clergy were invited. When I remember the condition of the Tigh Dige lower regions in those days, before, during, and after the Sacrament, and the cruel hard labour involved in feeding everybody, I should thank God that I was then merely looking on with amazement, and glad it occurred only every third year.

"Yet I was something more than an onlooker, for I had to form part of the wonderful out-of-door congregation that assembled daily in that most charming Leabaidh na ba baine! The bed is close to the Parish Church, being an exact oval in shape, lined with the finest short grass, and able to hold, it is said, three thousand people. In the bottom of the deep oval hollow at one end was the clergyman's preaching-box, giving him shelter from the sun and rain. Wind could not blow there, and even a weak voice would float over the whole hollow clearly. In front of the pulpit the Communion-tables extended to the farther end of the bed, the soil was pure drifted sand dating back thousands of years, and so porous, that were rain to fall for a month not a drop would be seen, while the sheep kept the grass as short as a mowing machine could do. I should be surprised indeed if a stranger passing along the road, which merely separates the Leabaidh from the church, on hearing, say, three thousand voices floating up out of this wonderful deep hollow, and chanting beautiful ancient Gaelic psalms, could help being perfectly charmed with the solemn sound and feeling that he had never heard the like before. A little farther on I could have brought the stranger back to earth pretty quickly, for on the side of the road he would find very ordinary tables covered with gingerbread and kebbucks of cheese and goodies, etc., to suit hungry mortals, and well-frequented at the week-day services. It is even reported that for a penny certain outside knaves allowed us urchins to have a shy with a stick at a kind of Aunt Sally on which gingerbread was set up for the knocker-off to pocket, while a miss left the penny a prize in the knave's possession. Who knows if this gambling was known to the saints in the Leabaidh?

"I frequently observed great politeness from the young men to the girls, and often I saw a lassie, semi-fainting owing to the heat, much gratified by her beau presenting her with his shoe full of water from the well above the burying-ground! The people got strong advice from the preachers, the Rev. Kennedy, of Killearnan, being a great favourite. One who was present at a Communion where he was helping told me that, after the fencing of the tables to prevent the young and timid from communicating, when all were seated he suddenly shouted, 'I see Satan seated on some of your backs,' whereupon several screamed and more than one fainted and had to be removed. None of your milk and water preachers! The sensational is alone of use."

Even I can remember not so many years ago being present at an Aultbea Communion where a Free Church minister, when fencing the tables, forbade anyone communicating who was "a frequenter of concerts or dances"! It was said in Gaelic, and this is an exact translation of his words, which show how very rigid and narrow is the creed of the Free Church, and also of the Free Presbyterians, even at the present day.

Few in the south could believe their narrowness also as regards the keeping of the Sabbath.

How well do I remember as a young lad, when living at Inveran Lodge on the Ewe, our Free Church minister, whom we liked very much and whose manse was at Aultbea, coming every alternate Sunday to preach in the little old meeting-house at Poolewe. We loved having him to dine and sleep at Inveran, and I know he enjoyed being with us; but as he was very *laidir* (violent) in the pulpit, he naturally perspired very freely, and required a change of underclothing if he passed the night with us. Well, he could do this only if there had been a chance during the preceding week of getting the small brown-paper parcel containing a shirt, etc., conveyed to Poolewe; for though he was driven to church in his own dog-cart, nothing would induce him to carry the smallest parcel in his trap on the Sunday.

At the yearly Communion-time at Aultbea how hospitable the minister and his wife were, and how the luncheon-table in the manse groaned with the very best of everything eatable and drinkable! How they used to implore of us not to think of drinking water, because it had necessarily to be brought from the spring on Saturday and consequently would be flat, but to stick to port and the sherry wine (as they called it); and if water must be taken, to put plenty of whisky in it to counteract its flatness and make it more wholesome! It would have been an unpardonable sin to go to the spring, which was quite near the manse, for a jug of fresh water; anyone guilty of doing so would render himself liable to undergo Church discipline and censure from the Kirk Session.

How well I remember also hearing of the case of a big boat returning from the Caithness herring fishing, which was long delayed on its voyage by storms and adverse winds, and managed to get to Loch Ewe only on a Sunday forenoon shortly before church-time. The owner of the boat was an elder in the Free Church, and very much respected, but even he could hardly solve that most difficult question of the moment—which would be the greater sin, *viz.*, to shave off some of the ten days' growth of hair on their faces to make themselves look respectable, or to keep away from church? At length it was decided that, shaving on

Sunday being a quite unpardonable sin, it would be less wicked, perhaps (just for once in a way), to stay away from church!

My uncle, who had quite a model farm on Isle Ewe, with a byre of thirty pedigree Ayrshire cows, required turnips to be barrowed to them twice a day, but on Sunday the cattleman could not think of using a barrow, as it was on a wheel; so, in his best Sunday suit, he carried in all the muddy turnips for the cows in armfuls, and though a martyr to turnips in this world, he looked to being recompensed accordingly in the world to come! I also well remember how my dear mother, when we lived at Gairloch, always went to her school at Strath, about two miles away, to teach her Sunday class. She might start going there by daylight, but in winter it would be pitch dark before her return. My mother had a favourite old servant who always accompanied her, and who also taught a class. Now, it was necessary to have a small hand-lantern for coming home, and this old Peggy was quite willing to carry when lighted, but nothing would induce her to carry it unlighted, so the lantern had to find its way down to the school some day during the week, otherwise there would be no lantern to light them on their way on Sunday night.

What a pity that such superstition should have been fostered and encouraged in the Highlands by the clergy. If the ministers would preach less about predestination and abstruse dogmas of that kind, and would sometimes take as their text that "a merciful man is merciful to his beast," and persuade their people to clean out their byres and stables on Sunday, they would be doing far more good in my opinion.

Before the manse was built at Gairloch (and I may perhaps mention that the famous geologist, Hugh Miller, was one of the masons who helped to build it as a young apprentice), Cliff House at Poolewe, which my uncle described as Poolewe Inn, a mere dirty smokehole reeking of whisky, was the parish manse, and the incumbent at one time was a good man, but not a very brilliant one. He possessed as his glebe nearly all the arable land on the south side of the Ewe. The minister also had a summer shieling for his cows at the back of the hill, where now stands the derelict mill of Boor. When the minister's corn was ripe every male and female in the neighbourhood was pressed into his service with sickle in hand, and to cheer up his squad of perhaps not very willing workers he always had a piper to play to them. Before leaving his gang of harvesters to go back to the manse for his dinner, he used to walk forward a good bit in front of his reapers, and plant his walking-stick in the corn, and call out to the squad: "Now, good folks, I shall expect you to get the reaping done as far as my stick by the time I return from my dinner, so do your best."

No sooner was the minister out of sight round the corner than someone ran forward, removed the stick, and planted it a good bit behind instead of in front of them. Then the whole gang would start dancing, and would dance furiously till the time drew near for the minister's return. In this way they imposed on the stupid old minister, who on his return would say: "Well done, my squad. You have not only reached my stick, but have got a good bit beyond it."

On one occasion his reverence thought he would like to pass the night at the shieling, where two young girls were in charge of his cows. The shieling consisted of two very small bothies, one of which contained the wooden dishes with the milk, and the other had just room in it for the two girls to pass the night side by side on a bed of heather with a plaid over them. The girls were in the habit of finding just sufficient room close behind their heads for the big wooden receptacle which held all the week's supply of cream, so that it might ripen sooner from the warmth of their bodies, and turn more quickly into butter in the churn. That night they had to pass in the open; in fact, they had to sit up all night with the cows, but they were determined to have their revenge. Peeping into the bothy about four in the morning, when they felt sure the minister would be sound asleep, they noticed that he had hung up his red wig, which, according to the fashion of the times, was large with longish curls, on a peg in the wall just above the receptacle containing the week's cream. So they got a long stick and managed to dislodge the wig from its peg and to drop it into the cream. In the morning the wig could not be found, and the girls suggested it must have been carried off by the fairies, as they were always particularly troublesome about that shieling. But at last the wig was discovered, and the upshot was that the minister never bothered them at the shieling any more.

I am now going to relate the stories of three funerals which took place about a hundred years ago. The first two were conducted in the old, old way, and the wrong way—namely, with whisky flowing like water. The third funeral was without whisky, and was, I think, a pattern funeral, taking into consideration the long distance to the place of interment, and the fact that no wheels could be used for want of roads.

A laird of Dundonnell (which is the southern portion of the parish of Loch Broom) died in Edinburgh, and his remains were brought by sea to Inverness, and from there on wheels as far as Garve, where the road ended. At that spot it was met one evening by the whole of the adult male population of the Dundonnell estate. They were to start carrying the corpse early the following morning. There was no place where even a twentieth part of this crowd could sleep, so they all sat up through the whole of the night drinking themselves drunk, as there was any amount of drink provided for them, though probably but little food! Early in the morning a start was made by the rough track—the Diridh Mor—which led to Dundonnell, some thirty-five miles away. The crowd of semi-drunken men had marched several miles of the way, when one of the mourners, who was rather more sober than the rest, suddenly recollected that they had no coffin with them, they having left it behind them at Garve, and so back they all had to trudge to fetch their beloved laird.

Now for one of our jovial funerals. My uncle writes: "The wettest I ever remember was the Chisholm's, the brother of our good old 'Aunty General.' My father went off early to reach Erchless Castle in time, alone in our yellow coach, with Rory Ross driving and Sandy Mathieson, our butler, on the box beside him. About 8 p.m. of a fine summer evening we boys were play-ing about the Conon front door when we heard the carriage coming, but, to our great amazement, on the box beside Rory sat our father, dressed in full mourning, though we had never heard of or seen him on the box before! The inside seemed packed full of people, whose identity was soon revealed to us at the front door. Out came Mathieson, and then, helped by my father, two seemingly dead mortals were dragged out of the carriage and laid down at the stair-foot, to be promptly rolled up in coverlets and carried upstairs to the double-bedded room. There was an amount of silent secrecy about the business that quite sobered our spirits, which were usually raised to a very high pitch when drunkies met us. I suppose our father considered both cases very serious, and felt their only chance of surviving was to take them home with Mathieson planted between them inside the carriage to keep up their heads and prevent their being suffocated.

"When Mathieson had got the clothes off the poor fools and bedded them, we were allowed to come into the room and got a lesson on the evil of 'moderate drinking,' and I shall never forget their fearful purple faces and stertorous breathing. We then learnt that they were two great friends of ours, the famous Dr. W. of Dingwall and one nicknamed 'Sandy Port,' the British Linen Company banker (then the only bank in Inverness)—a very noted judge of port wine and a great drinker thereof. In about twenty-four hours they recovered sufficiently to have wheels to take them home quietly without tuck of drum.

"Afterwards I learnt from some who were present that after the funeral a grand dinner was eaten in a granary. My father, I think, was in the chair, and the drinking was something quite extra, and as one by one of the diners stepped away quite tight, the others sat up and closed ranks, and peepers in at the end door of the granary, seeing empty seats and heaps of full bottles, quietly became part of the mourning drinkers. In time so many intruded that Mackenzie of Ord and Mackenzie of Allangrange got their blood up, and, each seizing a wooden chair, belaboured the thieves so vigorously—both were extra able young fellows then—that they rushed to the granary door, and, there being no railing to the stair leading up to it, the chairmen belaboured them over the stair-top till they lay in a heap reaching right up to it from the ground, to the uproarious delight of all the mourners. We learnt that the intruders poured over the stair-head, say nine or ten feet above the ground, like turnips being emptied out of a cart. Then the two chairmen returned to the merry party inside, locking the granary door for peace.

"At that funeral every farmer that could muster a horse and saddle within, say, ten to twelve miles attended, and, as stalls for horses in Beauly could then easily be counted, the horses were picketed in rows side by side. The country was more populous then than now, when so many proprietors have cleared away their people to make room for big farms; so, as every crofter felt bound to attend the funeral, the crowd was by the thousand. In those times it was common for the farmers and crofters to tan their own leather, and then make their own shoes, but the leather was not always A1, and the sight of such crowds of horses, each with a saddle whose flaps would make first-rate shoe soles, produced such a thirst for leather that it is asserted that no rider brought home with him that night any flaps to his saddle; indeed, the scallywags seldom had such a good chance for shoe soles!"

I quote again from my uncle: "In April, 1830, Frank and his wife (Sir Francis and Lady Mackenzie), who were both devoted to Gairloch, settled to go there for her confinement, and as these things had given her no trouble previously, and as I, a doctor, was at hand should any help be needed, she and Frank had no fear of danger. But a week before the time when I was told to be at hand, as I was riding along the rough track by Loch Maree to Tigh Dige, I met Kennedy, the gardener, riding with such a dreadful face of woe that I hardly needed to ask for Kythe. Alas! she had gone to heaven the previous day. A dear little girl had come ten days too soon. Then, as Frank was quite unable even to think of any arrangements, I fixed the invitations for friends to meet us at Conon and go thence to Beauly to a very different funeral compared with the one I have already noted. As we had no wheel roads nearer than Kenlochewe, I decided on carrying the body shoulder high from Gairloch to Beauly, willing hands being more than plenty. I sent out word all over the parish for men between twenty and thirty to attend at the Tigh Dige on Monday evening ready to help us to Conon next morning, and I had quite a thousand from whom to choose the five hundred

I wanted, those who were not chosen being anything but pleased.

"So I picked out four companies of one hundred and twenty-five strong men, made them choose their four captains, and explained clearly to them all the arrangements. I was to walk at the coffin foot and Frank at the head all the way to Beauly, resting the first night at Kenlochewe and the next night at Conon, say twenty-four miles the first day and forty the second; the third day we were to reach Beauly and return to Conon, say nine miles. I sized the companies equally, the men in one company being all above six feet, and the others down to five feet nine or so. I had a bier made so that its side-rails should lie easily on the bearers' shoulders, allowing them to slip in and out of harness without any trouble or shaking of the coffin. We started with eight men of No. 1 company at the rear going to work, four on each side; the captain observed the proper time to make them fall out, when the eight next in front of them took their place, and so on till all the one hundred and twenty-five had taken their turn. Before all the men in No. 1 company were used up, the second company had divided, and the fresh bearers were all in front ready to begin their supplies of eight, the first company filing back to be the rear company. Thus all had exactly their right share of the duty.

"At first there was not that precision that was so surprising afterwards, but, once started, had the men been drilled at the Guards Barracks in London, it would have been impossible for them to have gone through their willing task more perfectly and solemnly. Not one word was audible among the company on duty, or, indeed, in the other three; every sound was uttered *sotto voce* in the true spirit of mourning, and I am sure every man of them felt highly honoured by the service entrusted to him. All of us being good walkers, we covered, once we fairly started, about four miles an hour. With the help of Rory Mackenzie, the grieve at Conon, and James Kennedy, gardener and forester at Gairloch, we had prepared plenty of food for the five hundred before we started; the food was carried in creels on led horses for each halt on the way. We had plenty of straw or hay for beds at night, and charming weather all the way.

"Our first halt was at Slatadale, on Loch Maree, where a regular flotilla of boats, drawn to the loch by men from the sea at Poolewe, was waiting for us. They landed us all safely, like an army of dumb people, at Taagan, whence we marched again to the inn at Kenlochewe, where we fed and went to rest for an early start next morning. The captains had their men trained so quickly that really, had I been blind, I could hardly have known when a new company went on duty. Not one word was spoken, but all changed places at a wave of the hand; there was nothing to tell of the change but the tramp, tramp of the new company stepping out on each side of me to reach the front. I have never been, and never will be again, at such a wonderful scene; I have never heard of the like, and were I to live a thousand years I never could forget it. Had the five hundred dreaded being put to death if heard to speak one word, they could not have been more silent. Many years after I had the great pleasure of reading the beautiful lines on the 'Burial of Moses':

" 'That was the greatest funeral that ever passed on earth,
    When no man heard the tramping, or saw the train go forth,
    Noiselessly as the springtime her crown of verdure weaves,
    And all the trees on all the hills paint their myriad leaves;
    So without sound of music, or voice of them that wept,
    Silently down from the mountain's crown the great procession swept.'

"I doubt if ever a more silent, solemn procession than ours was seen or heard of, and, though it was nearly fifty years ago, I never can think of that wonderfully solemn scene with dry eyes. On the second day, some distance east of Achnasheen, we halted to give the men a little rest and some food. And as I spread them out on the sloping grassy braes above the road and saw food handed round by the captains, it was difficult not to think of the Redeemer when He miraculously fed the thousands who came to Him in a wilderness probably not very unlike the bleak Achnasheen moor. Before we moved away again every man had added a stone to the cairn on the spot where the coffin had rested. Is it not there to this day? Among those five hundred surely there were some not faultless in head or heart, yet sure I am that had more than a word of kindly thanks been offered to any one for his loss of a week's work and about one hundred and thirty miles of most fatiguing walking, it would have fared ill with the offerer. Every man was there with his heart aching sadly for us. All were substantially and well dressed in their sailor homespun blue clothes, such as they may be seen wearing going to or returning from the herring-fishing. They were all dressed alike and quite sufficiently sombre for mourners; not a rag of moleskin or a patched knee or elbow was visible; all were in their Sunday-best clothes.

"Our next halt was at the west entrance to Tarvie Wood, opposite to Roagie Island, where another cairn still tells where the coffin rested while the bearers had some more food. There Tulloch met us with his detachment from Loch Broom, about thirty in number, and had he not just sold the Gruinord property he could and would have met us with a regiment like our own, but I fear our men would not willingly have given up their places. Indeed, I had an unpleasant time getting them to allow the Conon tenants to carry the body from Conon to the Highfield march towards Beauly. So our next halt was at the door of Conon, once dearly loved by our charge, and all of us were glad that we had got over so much of our undertaking so wisely and well. We rested till next day at one o'clock, when what some would think a more impressive procession accompanied us, in a crowd of carriages and riders, to Beauly. We had a very long day's walk at not under three and a half to four miles an hour between Kenlochewe and Conon, and though all our men were trained to boating and not to steady walking, not one fell out of our ranks all the way; but a crowd of them lay down on the Conon lawn the moment we halted, and some were hardly able to move to the straw-bedded Conon granaries, where plenty of the best food gave them fresh strength for their last march.

"After the luncheon in Conon House, and after thanking our sympathising visitors, I marshalled our men and we walked off, the six-foot company leading, just as we had left Tigh Dige and Kenlochewe, the carriages and riders following. At the lodge gate the Conon tenants and hundreds of others disorganised us, as they wished to carry the coffin, and had our Gairloch men had but the least drop of whisky there would have been a serious fight. However, I compromised matters by getting them to let the Conon people carry the body to the Highfield march, and then we resumed our arrangement of the two previous days till we entered the Beauly Priory, where we found old John Fraser, the Conon gardener, our sexton when needed, with the grave all ready. After a Burial Service, we gently laid all that was earthly of dear, dear Kythe to rest in the grave till the Resurrection."

I should like to finish this chapter with a description of a contested Parliamentary election in the county, which, of course, included the Lews. I was but a boy of six at the time, and my mother took a keen interest and part in the contest.

The Gairlochs had always been strong Conservatives, and had invariably voted for old Mackenzie of Applecross, who had, I think, been M.P. for the county for many years. Now, my mother did not happen to like old Applecross; and besides, she was of a Quaker family herself, and, like most of her people, a strong Whig; so she set herself heart and soul to help the opposing Liberal candidate, Sir James Matheson, who had just before this come back as a very rich man from China, and had bought the Lews from the Seaforth Mackenzies. My mother got, I believe, every voter on the Gairloch estate to vote for Sir James, and Sir James's majority in the county exactly equalled the number of the Gairloch voters. Lady Matheson and he never forgot the good turn my mother had done them, and, from the time I was a boy of ten till I was a middle-aged man with a nearly grown-up daughter, I was always looked upon (as dear Lady Matheson expressed it) as *enfant de la maison*, and welcome to stay at the castle as long as I liked.

Before saying more about this election I must tell a story of another Ross-shire election, which, though it was much farther back in the century, concerned the same old Applecross. In those far-back days, it appears, votes could be handed to the candidate in the form of letters or mandates. Well, there was an enterprising man called Macdonald of Lochinver, and he had noticed on the Applecross property a beautiful native Scots fir wood in Glenshieldaig, on Loch Torridon, which he wanted to buy and ship away south. Now, he was canny, and, as he knew there was a county election coming on, it struck him votes would be more acceptable to Fear na Comaraich (as the laird of Applecross is called in Gaelic) than cash, so he asked him if he would sell the wood for the Stornoway votes. Applecross agreed, Macdonald sailed away in his yacht, the *Rover's Bride*, for Stornoway, and by threats, and bribery, and cajolery of every kind, he evidently got every vote in Stornoway, and, recrossing the Minch with all the paper votes in his pocket, he handed them to the laird a few days before the election. He then immediately started cutting down the wood. This is the story as it was told to me, and I believe it to be true.

I have heard also that the same Macdonald once got a wood for nothing by a trick. It was a natural fir forest opposite Ullapool, on the Dundonnell side of Loch Broom, belonging to the wife of the minister of Loch Broom. The bargain was made, and what did Macdonald do but go to the manse with payment on a Sunday. The minister refused to accept money on the Sabbath, and thus it is said Macdonald got the wood and never paid anything for it!

How well I remember the fight between Sir James and Applecross! We were living at the time in Pool House, at the head of Loch Ewe, and Sir James actually sent a steamer (one of the first, if not the very first to enter the loch) with my mother and all the voters in the parish of Gairloch to the poll at Ullapool. I was one of the party, and also my dear old uncle, Captain Kenneth of Kerrysdale, attended by a faithful daughter. The Captain was then nearly eighty years my senior. We got back to our homes that night. Still more wonderful, the same steamer took a number of us over the following day to Stornoway with the latest news of the poll, and back in the evening. I doubt whether there were many living in those days who accomplished such a feat as to go from the mainland to the Lews and return the same day.

I remember the great castle was hardly finished then, and the Mathesons were not yet resident there, but my mother was presented by the castle gardener with a bouquet of scarlet geraniums and bits of yellow calceolaria. My astonishment at the latter's resemblance to little slippers was great, for I had never seen a calceolaria in my life. My uncle mentions having seen his first fuchsia when he was a lad at Brahan Castle in the last Lord Seaforth's days.

CHAPTER XV

SMUGGLING AND SHEEP-STEALING

A BOOK dealing with the Highlands could not be considered complete if it omitted to tell something about the drinking habits and about smuggling in the old days. So I quote once more from my uncle:

"I never saw or heard of champagne, hock, claret, etc., on our table, only madeira, sherry, and port of the best quality that could be procured. In my father's day, and long after, doctors and every other person were satisfied that health depended greatly on the quantity of 'good' liquor a person swallowed daily. I have seen, though not in our home, men of note glad of the help of the wall on entering the drawing-room after dinner, until a chair or a sofa came within reach.

"I heard him say that once, going unexpectedly to Gairloch without sending notice beforehand, he was surprised by the want of the usual joy on his appearing, and was sure something was wrong. It turned out that a vessel loaded with brandy, claret, etc., had been chased into the bay by a revenue cutter, and willing hands had carried the cargo into Tigh Dige, into which my father had to enter by a ladder through a window. The revenue folk never dreamed of looking for the casks in Tigh Dige.

"Once, when there on my Edinburgh holiday, the *Rover's Bride* anchored in the bay, and the skipper, James Macdonald, as popular a man as ever stood in leather and a distant connection of ours, was of course nailed for dinner. He was bound for Skye, and hearing I was longing for a chance of getting there to visit our friends, the Mackinnons of Corry, Mrs. Mackinnon being sister to Aunty Kerrysdale, James offered me a passage. When on board next day he asked me to guess his cargo. I said 'Salt for herrings,' but his reply was: 'Tubs of brandy! I'm straight from Bordeaux, and the cruiser is not afloat that can lay salt on the *Bride* if there is an air of wind.'

"Even so late as then, say 1820, one would go a long way

before one met a person who shrank from smuggling. My father never tasted any but smuggled whisky, and when every mortal that called for him—they were legion daily—had a dram instantly poured into him, the ankers of whisky emptied yearly must have been numerous indeed. I don't believe my mother or he ever dreamed that smuggling was a crime. Ere I was twenty he had paid £1,000 for the 'superiority' of Platcock, at Fortrose, to make me a commissioner of supply and consequently a Justice of the Peace and one of the about thirty or forty electors of the county of Ross; and before it had occurred to me that smuggling was really a serious breach of the law, I had from the bench fined many a poor smuggler as the law directs. Then I began to see that the 'receiver'—myself, for instance, as I drank only 'mountain dew' then—was worse than the smuggler. So ended all my connection with smuggling except in my capacity as magistrate, to the grief of at least one of my old friends and visitors, the Dean of Ross and Argyle, who scoffed at my resolution and looked sorrowfully back on the happy times when he was young and his father distilled every Saturday what was needed for the following week. He was of the same mind as a grocer in Church Street, Inverness, who, though licensed to sell only what was drunk off the premises, notoriously supplied his customers in the back shop. Our pastor, Donald Fraser, censuring this breach of the law, was told, 'But I never approved of that law!' which was an end to the argument. He and the Dean agreed entirely that the law was iniquitous and should be broken.

"Laws against smuggling are generally disliked. People who if you dropped a shilling would run a mile after you with it, not even expecting thanks, will cheerfully break the law against smuggling. When I was young everyone I met from my father downwards, even our clergy, either made, bought, sold, or drank cheerfully, smuggled liquor. Excisemen were planted in central stations as a terror to evildoers, but they seemed to stay for life in the same localities, and report said they and the regular smugglers of liquor were bosom friends, and that they even had their ears and eyes shut by blackmail pensions from the smugglers. Now and again they paraded in the newspapers a 'seizure of whisky,' to look as if they were wide awake; wicked folks hinted that the anker of whisky was discovered and seized when it was hidden in the gaugers' peat stack! This saved the gauger much trouble searching moors and woods for bothies and liquor. I was assured that one of our old gaugers, when pensioned off, retired rich enough to buy a street in a southern town, and I believe the story was quite true. Indeed, in my young days few in the parish were more popular than the resident gauger. Alas! when the wicked Commissioners of Excise went in for 'riding officers' and a squad of horrid coastguard sailors with long, iron-pointed walking-sticks for poking about wherever earth seemed to have been lately disturbed, it ended all peace and comfort in smuggling, for these rascals ransacked every unenclosed bit of country within their limits each month; accordingly, the gauger soon began to be the most detested of men.

"In the good old times, when we were going to shoot, my mother often called Hector Cameron, our dear shooting help, gave him a tin can, and desired him to bring it back with barm— i.e., yeast. It never occurred to her that we might fail to meet with a bothy where brewing was carried on ere we came home. I have been in several during an ordinary day's walk in moor or wood, and of course had a mug of sweet 'wort' or a drop of dew and drank to the brewer's good luck. In those days we baked at home, and as barm from the recognised beer-makers was generally bitter from the hops used, and my mother and we children could not eat bitter bread, what could the dear soul do but prefer barm from the smugglers? On the watershed between Strath Bran and Fan-nich, in sight almost of the road in Strath Bran, between Ding-wall and Lochcarron, and on the hill road from Strath Bran to Lechky, within a few yards of its many passengers, I have been in a bothy with regularly built, low stone walls, watertight heather thatch, iron pipes leading cold spring water to the still-rooms, and such an array of casks, tubs, etc., as told that gaugers never troubled their owners. They sometimes troubled malt barns, or rather caves. Once when shooting I fell through the cunningly concealed roof of such a cave into a heap of malt, within fifty yards of the present high-road above Riverford.

"On an occasion in the Dingwall court a criminal came before us Justices accused by two cutter-men of being caught making malt. On the way to Wyvis by a country road, the cutter police-men observed a grain or two of barley, then some more, and a length a continuous stream of grain, which had evidently dropped from a hole in a sack carried in a cart or on a horse. In due time the grains ceased opposite to a steep heather-clad hillock close to the road. A poke from their wicked iron-pointed sticks showed that the heather belonged to a pile of blocks of turf nicely arranged, and when these were pulled down, lo and behold! there was the door to a hillock cave in which malt was being nicely made. In the absence of the maltster one of the cutter-men got into the cave, while his comrade built up the turf neatly again as if no one had touched it, and then hid himself behind a heather knoll ready to pounce out when required.

"Soon after this the maltster came up the road, stopped at the hillock, pulled down the turf and got in, all but his feet. In a second these were flourishing in the air, while fearful shouts came from the cave, and in a minute out came the maltster, coatless, and away he ran down the road like mad, while his opponent emerged from the cave with the coat in his hand. He and his comrade ran after the maltster, and caught him in his house. One can easily imagine the maltster's thoughts when, sure that all was safe as usual, he was grappled by two hands the moment his head was in the cave. He admitted he *knew* it must be Satan who seized him. It is very seldom the Bench is so convulsed with laughter as it was when listening to this smuggling story.

"Many years after, when I was factor for Gairloch, I had to support the anti-smugglers, and I warned the crofters that anyone convicted of smuggling would be evicted; for, irrespective of law-breaking, no person who works in a smuggling bothy is ever a well-doing, rent-paying tenant. One day the riding officer and his two helps came to complain that Norman Mackenzie, a Dia-baig tenant, had been caught brewing 'dew,' and after beating him and his two men badly had escaped and absconded, and that as I could, of course, lay hands on him, I must, as a Justice of the Peace, do so, and commit him to Dingwall, eighty miles off! I could only promise to do what I could, and, getting word to Norman, who was about the smartest and best young crofter on the estate, I had an interview with him. His excuse was that he was going to be married, and that he could not ask his friends to drink the horrid Parliament whisky. So he was making some proper stuff for them merely for his marriage. He could not imagine that this was a reasonable cause for eviction.

"Alas! in spite of my desire to protect Norman, I could not help telling him he must go to Dingwall and give himself up to the Sheriff, our law agent going with him and explaining matters. So he was landed in the gaol, and in a day or two I had a letter from our agent saying Norman was fined £30 or thirty days in gaol, and that he feared Norman would 'go out of his mind' with the public disgrace of the thing. But, like many well-doing crofters, Norman had a poke of money in my hands in case of a rainy day, people like him dreading their friends knowing they were 'men of money,' which would leave them no rest till it was all borrowed from them; so I wrote to our agent telling him, if he got Norman's consent, to pay the fine and put to my debit his £30 fine, then loose him, and let him go home. But the few days in the far too cosy gaol had quite dispelled Norman's sense of degradation, so he declined to pay the fine, and at the end of the month he came home, if a sadder and wiser man, at any rate not a poorer one!

"Why does any accident happening to a gauger give general pleasure—far more so than an accident to a policeman? I have heard of a Strathglass gauger being quietly murdered. It was known he would on such a day and hour be riding to where he knew a bothy was in full work. One part of the road wound round a corner where a step missed would probably land horse and rider one hundred feet below in a horrid rocky ravine. As he came round the corner a woman rose up from the side of the road and suddenly threw her gown over her head in an apparently innocent fashion to shelter herself from the wind; the horse instantly lurched over into the ravine, and both it and its rider soon died from the accident (?) to the sorrow (?) of the smugglers.

"Sometimes the Dingwall Sheriff was not so ready to imprison law-breakers as he was in Norman's case. One day when I was factor for Gairloch a boat's crew from Craig brought before me at Tigh Dige one of their neighbours who had been caught red-handed killing their sheep. They had heard of a sermon to be preached at Shieldaig, of Applecross, on a week-day, and, there being only four tenants at Craig township, were surprised when the fourth refused to take the fourth oar and go with them on the ground that he was not well. When they reached Shieldaig they found the preacher had not come, so they turned home, and were there too early for 'number four,' whom they found, though he had told them in the morning he was poorly, coming down the hill by the peat path with a creel on his back, which, of course, could not contain peats, as that drudgery was left to the inferior animals, the women. The three were soon alongside of their friend, and, lifting some heather from the top of the creel, there they found a sheep-skin belonging to one of the anxious enquirers, and below it the sheep cut up for the salt cask. Then they made him take them to where he had left the head, etc. They had often missed sheep before, and, seeing wool so over-plentiful with number four, were satisfied he was too fond of mutton!

"A Sassenach may doubt our west-coast crofters being able to catch sheep by running them down on the open moor or hill, but it is constantly done when they need wool and have no sheep-dog, and at night sheep are quite easily handled when sleeping. So next morning the criminal, with his head low enough, was brought before me; and, not having in these degenerate times the power of pit and gallows at my command, I had after examination to issue a warrant sending him to Dingwall gaol for trial. He made no defence, but when I asked what possessed him to kill the sheep he replied, 'The devil!' The end of the story is that he was home in a few days, the Sheriff, without any enquiry, beyond the statement in the committal warrant, informing me that the Lord Advocate did not think it a case for prosecution! So all I could do was to eject him, and I learned he was welcomed on the neigh-bouring Torridon estate, where no doubt he found the mutton as good as at Craig!

"A somewhat similar case occurred to our stalker, Watson. At

Badachro my father had long ago given a site for a house as a feu. A mutton-lover had been ejected from Aultbea, and got a room belonging to the feu. Watson had a tame ewe always feeding near his house, well-marked by half her face being black. She was 'there yesterday, gone to-day.' He was sure his neighbour had taken it. The neighbour and his wife and family always looked well-fed, though no person knew where their food came from. One day one of their children, five years old, was inveigled into Watson's to get 'a piece.' Asked how they were getting on the child answered, 'Very well.' 'What had they for dinner yesterday?' 'Mutton and broth.' 'Did they eat all the mutton?' 'No; the rest of it was salted.' 'What did they do with the skin?' 'It's below the bed.' Instead of getting a search-warrant, Watson waited till he saw me a week after, and by then nothing was found.

"About that time a great flood had changed the course of the Kenlochewe River. On the bank stood the bothy of a strongly suspected mutton-lover, a pauper with a wife and well-fed children, he himself being sickly and on the poor roll. His sole occupation lay in keeping two collies, and they provided a constant supply of puppies, which he carried about and used to sell, 'for the amusement of the children,' to the poorest crofters, for the more prosperous ones rarely have dogs. Now, his bothy, before the rain changed the gravelly course of the river, stood on the bank of a deep black pool. This pool soon lost all its water, and was then exposed as the cemetery for innumerable bones of sheep, which had undoubtedly been thrown in there from the bothy, where the mutton had been consumed, though never bought for the family supply.

"I had been joking once with Rory Oag about his never improving his stock, as all others did, by buying new rams. He decided to follow my advice, and actually bought a good ram and sent him off to the hill among the ewes. A few days after, longing for a look of him, he took a walk on the moor, where his dog directed his notice to—his new ram's head! A mutton-lover had caught and killed it, and carried off the body, but had left the huge horned head as being too heavy for its value in broth! The thief was evidently sorry to see such an unusually fat sheep on

Rory's moor, and probably 'borrowed' him the very night he was turned loose. Rory never threw his money away again to improve his stock. In cases so strongly suspicious as these I have mentioned, I always saved Sheriff, Lord Advocate, etc., all trouble, by merely evicting paupers and crofters who had no visible means of support to make them fat and rosy, at the request in private of all their suffering neighbours.

"Sheep-stealing on a different and large scale was then general all over the north. Ere I became tenant of Wyvis, a Mr. Mitchell had it stocked with black-faced wedders. He lived in the south generally. Stock going south from Ross-shire must cross the Caledonian Canal bridges. One day Gillespie, tenant of Ardachy, being at the Fort Augustus bridge, came upon some hundreds of black-faced dinmonts driven by two ordinary shepherds. Sheep have marks on the face or ears made by their owners to prevent theft or the loss of stragglers. Many sharp sheep-farmers know the marks of each farm, and Ardachy at once knew these were Wyvis dinmonts. So he said to the driver, 'Where are you going with Mr. Mitchell's dinmonts?' and was answered, 'To the south.' Months afterwards, happening to meet Mitchell, he said: 'So you're changing your stock on Wyvis.' 'Indeed I am not,' was Mitchell's reply. 'Then go and count your dinmonts,' said Ardachy, 'and you'll be surprised.' And so Mitchell was, for they were nearly all gone!

"I had a flock of four hundred to five hundred dinmonts (cheviots) on one part of Wyvis, herded by George Hope. They were always on the same ground, and were all safe one Saturday afternoon, but not a tail was to be seen on the following Monday morning. Hope spent days travelling all round the country looking for them before I heard of the theft. By that time they were 'over the hills and far away.' We traced them across the canal bridges and into Morayshire but not a hoof ever returned to Wyvis. The great sheep-farmer, Walter Scott, told me he gave up sheep-farming in the Lews, as he could not count on having less than five hundred or six hundred 'missing' sheep every year."

CHAPTER XVI

LOCAL SUPERSTITIONS

How well do I remember our country when all the lunatics were at large. There were no asylums, and there was no cure except the great and only possible one of Loch Maree. The cure was still in vogue in my time. The patient was brought to the loch and put into a boat, which made at once for the Holy Island (Eilean Maree). Then a long rope was tied round the unlucky person's waist, and he or she was suddenly dropped into the water and dragged behind the boat three times round the island, taking the *car deasal* (the way of the sun) being a very important part of the cure! The crew rowed for all they were worth, and if the patient was still alive and capable of swallowing anything he was landed on the island, and as if he had not got already more than sufficient water inside him, he was made to swallow a lot more from Naomh Maolruaidh's (Saint Malrubas) Holy Well. The awful shock and the fear of having it repeated did, I believe, occasionally subdue some of the most violent cases, but it was a cruel ordeal, and quite an example of "kill or cure."

We had two mad Marys always going about Gairloch—Mairi Chreagan (Mary of the Rock) and Mairi Sganan. Each one thought the other very mad and herself quite sane, and whenever they met they fought like wild cats. Then we had Eachainn Crom (Bent Hector) and the Oinseach bheag (the little she-idiot), and all sorts and sizes of lunatics, some of whom were often quite amusing. Our favourite was Iain Bait (Drowned John) from Loch Broom. He was more often called Bàthadh (drowning). He was a singer, and could go on singing Gaelic songs for ever at the top of his voice. On one occasion he fell into the Ullapool River when it was in flood, and commenced yelling out "*Bàthadh, bàthadh, a Dhia gle mise*" ("Drowning, drowning! O God, save me!"); but when he got hold of some heather or a bush on the bank of the river and felt himself a little safer he called out, "*Ah! fhaodadh noch ruigeadh tu a leas"* ("Oh! perhaps now Thou need not take the trouble"). He was quite sharp in some ways. On one occasion when the Ullapool people had offended him he avenged himself very cleverly. Seeing a long line with many hundreds of hooks baited with fresh herring lying in some outhouse ready to be set in the sea the following day, he waited till everyone was in bed and asleep and then set it right along the village front. As Ullapool indulged largely in ducks in those days, and as ducks, unlike hens, are night-feeders, the long line was doing its work all night, and endless operations, many of which proved fatal, had to be performed in the morning on the ducks.

There was also a famous mad Skye woman who used to go round the country, called Nic Cumaraid. She was accompanied by a big drove of pigs. She always slept outside in the heather, and the pigs lay close up round her and kept her warm, but I only used to hear of her and never actually saw her.

Fearachar a Ghunna (Farquhar of the Gun) was a very well known character all over the eastern side of the county. He always carried an old blunderbuss of a gun with him, and collected every conceivable horror, such as old bones and skins and filthy rags. He lived in a bothy on the Redcastle glebe, and as the smell from Farquhar's accumulations became quite unbearable, the minister applied to the Sheriff to have Farquhar ejected from his hovel. It seems the minister had been long in Canada, and came to Redcastle only when he got the call to the parish. On being examined by the Sheriff, Farquhar suggested that the minister must have a peculiarly sensitive nose when he was able to smell the stipend of Redcastle all the way from America!

My uncle gives the following instances of the manner in which dangerous lunatics were treated in pre-asylum days, the misery the unfortunates suffered, and the scandal that occurred from having even harmless lunatics running all over the country. He says:

"When I was a boy I went for a short time to school at Tain, and the home of a dangerous lunatic was then the upper cell in Tain Gaol, a square tower in the centre of the town having at its base the Town Cross, on the steps of which the fishwives used to sit and display their wares to purchasers. Some friend had given

Donald, the lunatic, a strong cord with an iron hook at its end. It used to be thought fun to call on Donald Heuk (Hook), as we named him, to let down his hooked cord, which we fastened to anything movable, from a penny roll to a peat, and on our crying 'Heuk, Donald!' up went the prize instantly to the iron cage at the top of the tower. Donald used to shoot down many queer things from his cell on to the people passing through the street; for though he could not see the cross or things around it, he had a clear view of the street. Wicked boys were sometimes accused of getting Donald to lower his cord and hook on the coming of the fishwives, and as soon as the creels were uncovered the hook was through a haddock's or cod's gills or a skate's mouth, and 'Heuk, Donald!' saw the prize in a minute flying up to the top of the gaol. It is said that on one unlucky day when the hook was down a boy put it through the back of a fishwife's petticoats, and on his calling out 'Heuk, Donald!' up in the air sailed a most unusual kind of fish. The poor fishwife kicked and screamed furiously, till, the hold giving way, she came to the ground like a shot, and got badly hurt. After this Donald's hook was instantly taken away.

"The Inverness Court House, where the Judges sat, was a mere box in size and attached to the present town steeple, which was part of the gaol. Such places as the gaols and asylums then in Britain would not be credited now but by those who had seen or been in them. Our northern dangerous lunatics were locked up in our gaols, a most unenviable berth, as I can vouch from personal inspection. We had no asylums then in the north, where we were overrun with lunatics. One of that tribe, who was harmless except that he believed he was a calf, went about driving people nearly mad by imitating the cry of a calf from morning till night with the lungs of a bull, till at last he had to be caged in the gaol, where he sang out unceasingly 'Baa-a-o-u! Baa-a-o-u!' The town folks got used to this noise, but once when our father took us over to a Circuit Court, the Court had hardly begun ere the Judge asked what unearthly noise was that. He could hear nothing for it, and ordered the noise to be removed. We happened, luckily, to be on the loose, and soon twigged there was fun ahead, for there were the gaoler and the town officers in full rig dragging 'Baa-a-o-u' down the gaol stairs and off to the old bridge that was washed away in the 1848 flood. The ingenious builders had contrived to build a wee cell in the spring of one of its arches, with a foot square iron grated hole for air and light. On shovelling away the road gravel above, an iron-plated padlocked door appeared in a few minutes. The door was thrown open, 'Baa-a-o-u' was rammed by force into the cell, and the door relocked and gravelled over. Everything was just the same as before, except for the incessant 'Baa-a-o-u-ing' issuing from the grated cell window. The sound gave far more pleasure to us boys, I really believe, than a band of music would have done, and I have no doubt that 'Baa-a-o-u' remained in that cosy cell till the judges left Inverness.

"Before asylum times one of the many wandering lunatics belonging to the district used to prowl about Dingwall groaning, a martyr to toothache. Good-natured Dr. Wishart persuaded Jock to come to his surgery in town, though he himself lived at his farm of Uplands, near Tulloch, and offered to cure Jock's malady. So Jock was brought to the surgery and persuaded to show the wicked tooth. In a second it was extracted, but the doctor, nippers and tooth in hand and hatless, had only just time to spring into the street. He fled along it, pursued by Jock, uttering loud threats to take the doctor's life, till some friend put out a foot and upset Jock and let Dr. Wishart disappear.

"Jock's appetite was quite abnormal. In those happy times no door was ever locked at night, front or back, in summer or winter, for at Conon every soul in the district was bound to sleep between 10 p.m. and 6 a.m. unless sick. Jock, however, was one of those who was bound by no rules. His dress was a very short kilt, and he had bare legs and feet summer and winter, so he made little noise on his travels. The Conon pantry was close to the backdoor, and on getting up one morning the house-keeper was shocked to find her pantry door open and a cold pudding she had put away the previous night gone, dish and all. The mystery as to who could have stolen it was explained by the clean dish being found next day in one of the recesses of Conon Bridge, with the words 'The pudding was goot' chalked by Jock above it, for ere his reason fled poor Jock had been at school. He would gladly fill his huge stomach with anything he could cram into it. I admit that one advantage of the new county police over our old rural constables, who, being only paid by the job, cost a mere fraction of the thousands now paid to the semi-military gentlemen that parade the public roads in fine weather, is that tinkers and others are not allowed to leave their dead horses at the roadsides, to the joy of all dogs and the horror of travellers. In Jock's day we managed matters after the manner of the ancients, to his great delight, as he was devoted to high horse venison. He was sure to be found near every dead horse till its bones had been picked clean by him and the doggies, who, aware of Jock's unfair competition with them for horse-flesh, never could see him without an uproar and a try at his bare legs; and but for his great skill in pelting them with stones they would have made Jock give up eating their beloved banquet. I was once assured by a looker-on that as he was passing by a dead horse at the roadside he saw Jock's bare legs in the air, their owner's head and shoulders out of sight feasting on some titbits far up inside the horse's ribs. I quite believe this disgusting story, which probably helped to promote the building of our present asylum palaces and the gathering into them of all poor insane Jocks and Jimmies."

In the 'sixties I had an old acquaintance of the name of Colin Munro, who was a very well educated man and had practised as a solicitor for many years in our county town of Dingwall. Somehow or other he came into money, and invested it in a very large sheep farm near me, called Innis an Iasgaich (Fisher Field). He had not taken up his abode there very long, and had got a nice byre of cattle, when suddenly the cows went all wrong, and instead of milk all that could be drawn out of their udders was a horrid mixture of blood and pus.

His servants declared some old woman had bewitched the cows, and that the only way to counteract the harm done was to get a still more powerful witch from a distance, who would undo what the local witch had done. So they told Colin Munro the name of a competent woman, who lived in the township of Achadh Ghluinachan, in the big strath of Loch Broom. To please and pacify his servants, and as there was no veterinary surgeon to be had in those days, he sent a messenger for the *cailleach* (old woman), and in due course she arrived.

Colin Munro sat up all that night (there was really no night, as it was June) so that he might watch the movements of the witch. About three in the morning he saw her sneak out of the house and make for the hill, instead of going to the byre, as he supposed she would have done. So he followed, stalking her very carefully, as if she had been an old hind, and watched her from some little distance. The first thing she did was to light a small fire. Then he saw her hunting about for *lusan* (herbs or plants) and putting them on the fire until the smoke rose up heavenwards. After a bit she returned, and Colin ordered the milkmaids to go and try the cows in his presence, which they did, and, wonderful to relate, the milk of every cow was as perfect as it was before they were bewitched. He could not do otherwise than give the *Banabhuidseach* (witch) a handsome present. He never could account for this miraculous cure of the cows.

Again my uncle writes: "Our old keeper Cameron hated the sight of a hare. He looked on it as an unclean, 'no canny' brute, only fit for mad people to eat, as witches frequently turned themselves into hares especially when they were employed stopping the milk of cows. Indeed, little more than twenty years ago the Tarradale game-keeper, hearing me scoffing about witches, asked me in private if I really believed they did not exist. 'Well,' says he 'that's extraordinary. Everyone round here knows' that Jock Maclean's wife is a witch. My own cow had her milk stopped last winter. One morning at dawn I went to the byre, and on opening the door out sprang a hare and ran through my legs, and away straight down to Jock Maclean's door, which she entered, that being, of course, her home.' Mackenzie, the keeper, was a well-educated man, more intelligent than most of his position, but a firm believer in witchcraft."

I shall add another superstition, very prevalent in the east country, against pulling down an old house and building a new one.

This did not meet me at Gairloch, but it did at Redcastle, on the east coast. When dividing a field into crofts there, I told the crofter he would need to build the house on his own ground, as his present house was on somebody else's. There was so much shrugging of shoulders and humming and hawing about it that a neighbour whispered to me, "It's about the black cock." "The black cock?" said I; "what had it to do with his house?" But seeing that there was something secret about it, I waited a little, and learnt that some years ago one of Colin Macdonald's sons took the "falling sickness"—i.e., epilepsy—the only cure for which, according to the old belief, is burying a jet black cock alive in a grave dug in the clay floor of the family kitchen. I believe the very centre is the proper place. While the cock is undisturbed the epilepsy keeps away, but if it is dug up, as it probably would be if the house were removed, woe to the family of the disturber from the evil spirit of epilepsy!

The people on the west coast used firmly to believe that events which were going to happen were often foretold by supernatural sounds and sights.

On our purchasing Inverewe and deciding to make our home on the neck of the Plocaird, I began to make enquiries as to what special use had been made of that promontory in the old days, when the Mackenzies of Lochend, who were offshoots of our family, owned the place. I was told by the old people round about us, whose parents at least had lived in those days, that the Plocaird was where Fear cheannloch (the man or laird of Lochend) kept his cows at night, for at that time most of the cattle in the Highlands had no roofs to shelter them summer or winter. There still remained the old dyke from sea to sea across the neck of the peninsula for keeping in the cows, and there was one bright green little oasis among the heather where had stood the bothy of the herd, Domhnall Aireach (Donald the Cowman). Into this green spot I at once dibbled a lot of the good old single *Narcissus Scoticus*, which I had got from my great-uncle at Kerrysdale. How they still bloom there every spring, though I planted them nearly sixty years ago.

Among the old stories in connection with the Plocaird and its

185

sole inhabitant, Domhnall Aireach, I was told that the old herd and his wife used to be much troubled by certain uncanny sounds and apparitions, and that the place was said by them to be haunted. The sounds they were said to hear were just as if there had been a blacksmith's forge on the shore below their bothy, and there appeared at night to be a continuous hammering of iron and steel going on. Moreover, every now and then, in the gloaming, a couple of *coin mhora bhreaca* (big spotty dogs) tied together would rush past their door!

Some years after our house was finished we decided to build an addition to it, and instead of quarrying the stones for it in a distant quarry, as had been done before, we thought we could get the material we required by breaking up some big boulders of good quality just below the site of the old herd's bothy. So for many weeks there was a continuous din of iron and steel, and of hammers and crowbars and jumpers boring into and breaking up these boulders. At the same time I had started a big kennel of black-and-white setters about half a mile away, and these fifteen or twenty dogs were let out on couples for exercise on the shore twice a day.

Now, the dogs knew quite well that since the Plocaird point had been enclosed and planted there were more hares and grouse, etc., in it than anywhere else near at hand, so whenever the keeper's attention was taken off them for a moment a couple of the older and more cunning ones would give him the slip, and make tracks for the Plocaird, and in their regular course would rush past the very site of Domhnall Aireach's bothy on their couples. Does it not seem, therefore, that these events which were to take place, and did actually happen, had been supernaturally heard and seen by old Donald and his wife more than a hundred years beforehand?

The best-known Gairloch fairy of modern times went by the name of the Gille Dubh of Loch a Druing. How often did I hear of him when I was a boy! His haunts were in the birch-woods that still cluster round the southern end of that loch and extend up the sides of the high ridge to the west. There are grassy glades, dense thickets, and rocky fastnesses in these woods that look just the very place for fairies. Loch a Druing is on the north point, about two miles from the present Rudha Reidh lighthouse. The Gille Dubh was so named from the black colour of his hair. His dress, if dress it could be called, was merely leaves of trees and green moss. He was seen by very many people and on many occasions during a period of more than forty years in the latter half of the eighteenth century. He was, in fact, well known to the people, and was generally regarded as a beneficent fairy. He never spoke to anyone except to a little girl named Jessie Macrae, whose home was at Loch a Druing. She was lost in the woods one summer night. The Gille Dubh came to her, treated her with great kindness, and took her safely home again next morning. When Jessie grew up she became the wife of John Mackenzie, tenant of Loch a Druing farm, and grandfather of the famous John Mackenzie who collected and edited the *Beauties of Gaelic Poetry*.

It was after this that Sir Hector Mackenzie of Gairloch invited Sir George Mackenzie of Coul, Mackenzie of Dundonnell, Mackenzie of Letterewe, and Mackenzie of Kernsary, to join him in an expedition to repress the Gille Dubh. These five lairds repaired to Loch a Druing armed with guns, with which they hoped to shoot the fairy. Most of them wore the Highland dress, with dirks at their side. They were hospitably entertained by John Mackenzie, the tenant. An ample supper was served in the house. It included both beef and mutton, and they had to use their dirks for knives and forks, as such things were very uncommon in Gairloch in those days. They spent the night at Loch a Druing, and slept in John Mackenzie's barn, where couches of heather were prepared for them. They went all through the woods, but they saw nothing of the Gille Dubh!

The existence of water-kelpies in Gairloch, if perhaps not universally credited in the present generation, was accepted as an undoubted fact in the last. The story of the celebrated water-kelpie—it was sometimes spoken of as the Each Uisge, and at other times as the Tarbh Oire—of the Greenstone Point is very well known in Gairloch. The proceedings for the extermination of this wonderful creature formed a welcome topic even for the *Punch* of the period. The creature is spoken of by the natives sometimes as "The Beast." He lives, or did live in the 'fifties, in the depth of a loch, called after him Loch na Beiste, or Loch of the Beast, which is about half-way between Udrigil House and the village of Mellan Udrigil.

Mr. Bankes, the then proprietor of the estate on which this loch is situated, was pressed by his tenants to take measures to put an end to the beast, and at length was prevailed upon to take action. Sandy Macleod, an elder of the Free Church, was returning to Mellan Udrigil from the Aultbea church on Sunday in company with two other persons, one of whom was a sister (still living at Mellan Udrigil in 1886) of the well-known John Mackenzie of the *Beauties*, when they actually saw the "Beast" itself. It looked something like a big boat with its keel turned up. Kenneth Cameron, also an elder of the Free Church, saw it another day and a niece of his told a friend of mine she had often heard her mother speak of having seen the Beast. Mr. Bankes had a yacht named the *Iris*, and in her he brought from Liverpool a huge pump and a large number of cast-iron pipes.

For a long time a squad of men worked this pump with two horses, with the object of emptying the loch. The pump was placed on the burn which runs from the loch into the not far distant sea. A deep cut or drain was formed to take the pipes for the purpose of conducting the water away. I have myself more than once seen the pipes stored in a shed at Laide. But, unfortunately, it was forgotten that the burn which came into the loch brought a great deal more water into it than the pump and the pipes carried out; consequently, except in very dry weather, the loch never got any less.

When this plan failed, it was proposed to poison the Beast with lime, and the *Iris* was sent to Broadford in Skye to procure it. Fourteen barrels of hot lime were brought from Skye and taken up to the Loch, along with a small boat or dinghy. None of the ground officers of the estate would go in the boat for fear of the Beast, so Mr. Bankes sent to the *Iris* for some of the sailors, and they went in the boat over every part of the loch, which had only been reduced by six or seven inches after all the labour and money that had been spent on it. These sailors plumbed the loch with the oars of the boat, and in no part did it exceed a fathom in depth, except in one hole, which at the deepest was but two and a half fathoms. Into this hole they emptied the fourteen barrels of hot lime.

It is needless to say that the Beast was not discovered, nor has it been further disturbed up to the present time. There are rumours that the Beast was seen in 1884 in another loch on the Greenstone Point. There was one curious fact about this kelpie hunt—*viz.*, that the eccentric English laird who started it was *cam* (one-eyed), the tinker who soldered the pipes together was *cam*, so was the old horse which worked the pumps, and it was altogether such a *gnothach cam* (one-eyed business) that people began to wonder whether, if the Each Uisge were ever captured, it might not prove to be *cam* also.

So angry was the laird at his failure to capture the kelpie that he was determined to avenge himself on something or someone; and at last he decided to wreak his vengeance on the unfortunate crofters whose townships were in the vicinity of the loch. Unlike the kelpie they, poor wretches, could not escape him, so he fined them all round a pound a head, which in those days, when money was so scarce, meant a great deal to them.

CHAPTER XVII

THE FAMOUS GAIRLOCH PIPERS

In 1609 an ancestor of mine, who was also one of the most famous of the Gairloch lairds, John Roy Mackenzie, paid a visit to the laird of Reay in Sutherland. I believe the laird of Reay (Lord Reay) was his stepfather. On John Roy's return from his visit to Tongue House, Mackay accompanied him as far as the Meikle Ferry, on the Kyle of Sutherland. On their arrival at the ferry it seems there was another gentleman crossing, accompanied by a groom, who attempted to prevent anyone entering the boat but his master and his party. Mackay had his piper with him, a young, handsome lad of only seventeen summers. A scuffle ensued between the piper and the groom, the former drew his dirk, and with one blow cut the groom's hand off at the wrist.

The laird of Reay at once said to his piper: "Rory, I cannot keep you with me any longer; you must at once fly the country and save your life." John Roy said: "Will you come with me to Gairloch, Rory?" And the piper was only too glad to accept the offer.

As they were parting, the laird of Reay said to his stepson: "Now, as you are getting my piper, you must send me in exchange a good deer-stalker." On his return home the latter at once sent Hugh Mackenzie, whose descendants still live in the Reay country. To this day it is remembered how and in what capacity their ancestor came from Gairloch.

I may mention that, besides the piper, John Roy took two good deer-hounds back with him from Sutherland, and even their names are not yet forgotten—"Cu dubh" and "Faoileag" ("Black Hound" and "Seagull").

Rory, the young piper, who was also a Mackay and was born about 1592, was soon after followed by an older brother, called Donald. It was Donald who was in attendance as piper on the twelve sons of John Roy, when Kenneth, Lord of Kintail, met them at Torridon, where John Roy so nearly met with his death.

Rory was piper in succession to four of the Gairloch Lairds—namely, John Roy, Alasdair Breac (who was a head taller than any of John Roy's eleven other sons), Kenneth, the sixth laird, and his son Alexander. Rory's home was at Talladale, on the mainland, while his first two masters, John Roy and Alasdair Breac, resided mostly in their island homes on Eilean Ruairidh Beag and Eilean Suthainn, in Loch Maree, opposite Talladale, which were, I suppose, considered safer at any rate for the ladies and the children, in those wild times. The last two chiefs, however, whom Rory served, lived in the original Tigh Dige or Stank [1] House of Gairloch, which had the moat round it and the drawbridge. Rory did not marry till he was sixty years old. He had just the one son, the celebrated blind piper, and during the latter part of his life he lived in the Baile Mor of Gairloch, so as to be near his masters in the Stank House. Rory died about 1689, in extreme old age, being, like his son, almost a centenarian. He was buried in the Gairloch churchyard. He is said to have been a remarkably handsome and powerful Highlander. He literally *played* an important part in the many fights which took place during the earlier part of his career.

John Mackay, the only son of Rory, was born at Talladale in 1656. He was not blind from birth, as has been erroneously stated, but was deprived of his sight by smallpox when about seven years old. He was known as Iain Dall (Blind John) or an Piobaire Dall (the Blind Piper). After mastering the first principles of pipe music under his father's tuition, he was sent to the celebrated Macrimmon in Skye to finish his musical education. He remained seven years with Macrimmon, and then returned to his native parish, where he assisted his father in the office of piper to the laird of Gairloch.

After his father's death he became piper to Sir Kenneth Mackenzie, the first baronet of Gairloch, and after Sir Kenneth's death to his son, Sir Alexander, the second baronet and ninth laird of Gairloch. He combined the office of bard with that of piper.

[1] Stank = moat.

Iain Dall retired when in advanced years, and Sir Alexander allowed him a good pension. Like his father, he married late in life. He had but two children—Angus, who succeeded him, and a daughter. After he was superannuated, he passed his remaining years in visiting gentlemen's houses, where he was always a welcome guest. Like his father, he lived to a great age. He died in 1754, aged ninety-eight, and was buried in the same grave as his father in the Gairloch churchyard. He composed twenty-four pibrochs, besides numberless strathspeys, reels, and jigs, the most celebrated of which are called *Cailleach a Mhuillear* and *Cailleach Liath Rasaidh.*

When he was with Macrimmon there were no fewer than eleven other apprentices studying with the master piper, but Iain Dall outstripped them all, and thus gained for himself the envy and ill-will of the others. On one occasion, as Iain and another apprentice were playing the same tune alternately, Macrimmon asked the other lad why he did not play like Iain Dall. The lad replied, "By St. Mary, I'd do so if my fingers had not been after the skate," alluding to the sticky state of his fingers after having eaten some of that fish on which Macrimmon had fed them at dinner. And this has become a proverbial taunt which northern pipers to this day hurl at their inferior brethren from the south.

One of the Macrimmons, known by the nickname of Padruig Caogach, composed the first part of a tune called *Am port Leathach* (the half tune), but was quite unable to finish it. The imperfect tune became very popular, and, as it was at the end of two years still unfinished, Iain Dall set to work and completed it. He called it *Lasan Phadruig Chaogach*, or "The Wrath of Padruig Caogach,". thus, whilst disowning any share in the merit of the composition, anticipating the result which would follow.

Patrick was furiously incensed, and bribed the other apprentices, who were doubtless themselves also inflamed by jealousy, to put an end to Iain Dall's life. This they attempted while walking with him at Dun Bhorreraig, where they threw the young blind piper over a precipice. Iain Dall fell eight yards, but alighted on the soles of his feet and suffered no material injury. The place is still called Leum an Doill (the Leap of the Blind).

The completion of Macrimmon's tune brought great fame to Iain Dall, and gave rise to the well-known Gaelic proverb which, being translated, says: "The apprentice outwits the master." Iain Dall made a number of celebrated Gaelic songs and poems. One of them, called *Coire an easain*, was composed on the death of Mackay, Lord Reay. It is said not to be surpassed in the Gaelic language. Another fine poem of his was in the praise of Lady Janet Mackenzie of Scatwell on her becoming the wife of Sir Alexander, the ninth laird of Gairloch. His fame as a bard and poet seems to have almost equalled his reputation as a piper. Several of his songs and poems appear in that excellent collection *The Beauties of Gaelic Poetry*.

Angus, the only son of Iain Dall, succeeded his illustrious father as piper to the lairds of Gairloch. He was born about 1725. He was piper to Sir Alexander Mackenzie, tenth laird of Gairloch, and when Sir Alexander visited France as a young man he left Angus in Edinburgh for tuition. We know little of him beyond that he was a handsome man, and that he at least equalled his ancestors in musical attainments. He attended a competition in pipe music whilst in Edinburgh. The other competing pipers, jealous of his superior talents, made a plot to destroy his chance. The day before the competition they got possession of his pipes and pierced the bag in several places, so that when he began to practise he could not keep the wind in the pipes. But Angus had a fair friend named Mary. To her he went in his trouble. She found for him a sheep-skin, from which, undressed as it was, he formed a new bag for his beloved pipes, and with this crude bag he succeeded next day in carrying off the coveted prize. He composed the well-known pibroch called *Moladh Mairi*, or "The Praise of Mary," in honour of his kind helper. Angus lived also to a good old age, and was succeeded by his son John.

John Mackay, grandson of the blind piper, was born about 1753, and became, on his father's death, family piper to my grandfather, Sir Hector Mackenzie of Gairloch. As a young man he went to the Reay country, the native land of his great-grandfather Rory, and there received tuition on the little pipes which are often used for dance music. He lived in the latter part of his career at Slatadale, where he married and had a numerous family, for whose advancement he emigrated to America with all his children except one daughter. She had previously married, but her father was so anxious that she should emigrate, with the rest of the family that she had to hide herself the night before they left Gairloch, in order to avoid being compelled to accompany them. John Mackay was a splendid piper, and when he went to America Sir Hector said he would never care to hear pipe music again, and he never kept another piper. John prospered in America, and died at Picton about 1835. One of his sons, who was Stipendiary Magistrate in Nova Scotia, died in the autumn of 1884. The daughter who remained in Gairloch was married to a Maclean, and their son, John Maclean of Strath, called in Gaelic Iain Buidhe Taillear, has supplied much of the information here given regarding his ancestors, the hereditary pipers of the Gairloch family.

It is a singular fact that the four long-lived Mackays were pipers to the lairds of Gairloch during almost exactly two centuries, during which there were eight lairds of Gairloch in regular succession from father to son, but only the four pipers.

CHAPTER XVIII

In the year 1862 my mother bought for me the two adjoining estates of Inverewe and Kernsary, on the west coast of Ross-shire.

Kernsary lay inland, but Inverewe had a good many miles of coast-line, and, after taking about two years to settle where we should make our home, we finally pitched upon the neck of a barren peninsula as the site of the house. The peninsula was a high, rocky bluff, jutting out into the sea.

The rest of what are in Scotland usually called "the policies" (*i.e.*, the enclosed grounds round about the mansion) consisted mostly of steep braes facing south and west, with the exception of a narrow strip of land down by the shore—the only bit where the coast-line was not rocky—and this strip, which was an old sea-beach, was turned into the garden. I may say the peninsula, whose Gaelic name, Am Ploc ard (the High Lump), so aptly describes it, consisted of a mass of Torridon red sandstone.

This promontory, where the rock was not actually a bare slab, was mostly covered with short heather and still shorter crowberry, and the only soil on it was some black peat, varying from an inch to two or three feet in depth. There had been more peat originally in some of the hollows, but it had been dug out for fuel by the crofters who had occupied the place forty years before my time. There was nothing approaching good soil on any part of the peninsula, hardly even any gravel or sand; but in a few places the rotten rock and the peat had somehow got jumbled up together, and when we came across some of this we thought it grand stuff in comparison with the rest. There was just perhaps one redeeming point about what otherwise looked so hopeless a situation for planting—*viz.*, that the rock was not altogether solid.

We had to excavate a great deal of the rock behind the site of the house before we could begin to build, and we noticed that the deeper we blasted into it the softer it became, and that there were even running through it veins of a pink kind of clay. The exposure of the Ploc ard was awful, catching, as it did, nearly every gale that blew. With the exception of the thin low line of the north end of Lewis, forty miles off, there was nothing between its top and Labrador; and it was continually being soused with salt spray. The braes above the site of the house were somewhat better, but even they were swept by the south-westerly gales, which are so constant and so severe in these parts.

Now I think I ought to explain that, with the exception of two tiny bushes of dwarf willow about three feet high, there was nothing in the shape of a tree or shrub anywhere within sight. One of these little willow-bushes I have carefully preserved as a curiosity, and on the site where the other was I lately planted an azalea, which will, I think, soon look down on its neighbour, the poor little aboriginal willow.

I started work in the early spring of 1864 by running a fence across the neck of the peninsula from sea to sea, to keep out the sheep. I was very young then (not being of age when the place was bought), and perfectly ignorant of everything connected with forestry and gardening, having never had any permanent home, and having been brought up a great deal on the Continent; but I had all my life longed to begin gardening and planting, and had, I fully believe, inherited a love for trees and flowers from my father and grandfather.

My mother undertook the whole trouble of house-building, and I set myself to the rest of the work with a determination to succeed if possible. Oh that I had only known then what I know now, and could have started with my present experience of over forty years! For example, I had never heard of the dwarf *Pinus montana*. Had I known its merits then, as I know them now, I would have begun by planting a thick belting of it among the rocks round my peninsula, just above high-water mark, to break the violent squalls carrying the salt spindrift which is so inimical to all vegetation.

I did not know that there was little use in planting *Pinus austriaca*, mountain ash, service, or even birches, in the middle of a wood, as, though they look nice for some years, they eventually get smothered by the faster-growing trees, and one has the trouble of cutting most of them out. If I were beginning again I would commence, as I have already said, with a row of the Tyrolese *Pinus montana* above high-water mark, then put *Pinus Austriaca* behind it, and for the third row I would plant that admirable tree *Pinus Laricio*. This triple row of pines would form my fortification against the ocean blast, and, behind the protection thus afforded, I would start putting in my ordinary forest trees—Scots pines, silver firs, sycamores, oaks, beeches, etc.

If I were asked what tree I have the highest opinion of for hardiness and rapidity of growth on bad soil and on exposed sites, I would certainly award the first prize to the Corsican pine. I have seen them in their own island on mountains 9,000 feet above sea-level, with nothing between them and Spain or Algeria, growing to an enormous size—some of those I measured there spread twenty feet in circumference—and here, at the same age, they make nearly double the amount of timber compared with Scots fir, and are proof against cattle, sheep, deer, and rabbits, which no other tree is that I know of. They told me in the ship-building yards at Savona that old Laricio timber was as good as the best Baltic redwood.

I am ashamed to confess, but it can no longer be hidden, that, among trees, many of the foreigners are far and away hardier and better doers than our natives. The Scots fir (as bred nowadays) is often a dreadfully delicate tree when exposed to Atlantic gales. It was not so in the good old times, as one finds the enormous remains of *Pinus sylvestris* forests right out on the tops of the most exposed headlands of our west coast. My brother, the late Sir Kenneth Mackenzie of Gairloch, gave me one hundred plants of the right breed from his old native fir-wood of Glasleitir, on the shores of Loch Maree, which, like the rest of that good old stock at Coulan, in Glen Torridon, or in those grand glens of Locheil, are as different in growth and constitution from what are too often sold nowadays as Scots firs as Scots kale is from cauliflower. I have seen the seedlings side by side in the seed-beds in my brother's Gairloch nursery, and in the months of March and April the seedlings from the bought seeds were of a rusty red, as if scorched by fire, whereas the home-bred ones were of a glossy dark green.

For four or five years my poor peninsula looked miserable, and all who had prophesied evil of it—and they were many—said, "I told you so." But at last from the drawing-room windows we could see some bright green specks appearing above the heather. These were the Austrians and the few home-bred Scots firs which had been dotted about in the places of honour near the house. About the fifth or sixth year everything began to shoot ahead; even the little hard-wood trees, which until then had grown downwards, started upwards, many of them fresh from the root. Now came the real pleasure of watching the fruit of all our labour and anxiety.

The young trees had fewer enemies then than they would have nowadays. Grouse strutted about among them, wondering what their moor was coming to, but did no harm. Black game highly approved of the improvements, and by carefully picking all the leading buds out of the little Scots firs did their level best to make them like the bushy *Pinus montana*. Brown hares and blue hares cut some of the fat young shoots of the Austrian pines and oaks; but, on the whole, my young trees fared well in comparison with the way young plantations here would fare now from the rabbit plague, and the roe, and the red deer.

I planted very few of the rarer trees to begin with. Wellingtonias were then the rage, and I felt bound to invest in four of them, and planted them in the best sites I could find near the house. I tried to make pits for them. I took out the little peat there was, but how well I remember the clicks the spades gave when we came to the bed-rock! Next morning (the night having been wet) all we had produced were four small ponds, and I had to get an old man to bring me creels of rather better soil for them on his back from a distance. I have just measured my Wellingtonias. In the forty-three years of their existence they have made some sixty-six feet of growth, and measure about eight feet round the trunk six feet from the ground, and their strong leaders show they are still going ahead. So much for the old man and his creels of soil.

Silver firs in the hollows have done well, and some of them also are sixty to seventy feet high. One thing has surprised me very much—*viz.*, that oaks, of which I planted but few, thinking it was the last place where oaks would thrive, are very nearly level with the firs, larches, and beeches.

It was only after the plantation on the peninsula had been growing fifteen or twenty years, and was making good shelter, that I began cutting out some of the commoner stuff, especially my enemies the "shop" Scots firs, as I call them, which continued more or less to get blasted by the gales of the ocean. Then it was I began planting all sorts of things in the cleared spaces—Douglas firs, *Abies Albertiana*, copper beeches, sweet and horse chestnuts, *Abies nobilis*, *A. Pinsapo*, *A. lasiocarpa* and *A. Nordmanniana*, *Cupressus macrocarpa* and *C. Lawsoniana*, *Thuja gigantea*, bird-cherries, scarlet oaks, etc., and now these trees appear almost as if they had formed part of the original plantation. I am still proceeding in this style, and have dotted about a lot of Eucalypti, tree rhododendrons, Arbutus, Griselinias, Cordylines, and clumps of bamboos and Phormiums which are giving a charming finish to the outskirts of my plantation.

Even the eucalypti I find much hardier than that bad breed of Scots fir; no wind, snow, or frost seems to hurt them here; and, in case it may interest my readers, I shall name those I find thoroughly hardy—*Eucalyptus coccifera*, *E. Gunnii*, *E. whittingehamensis*, *E. cordata*, *E. coriacea*, *E. urnigera*, and one or two others; but I warn all against trying *Eucalyptus globosa*—the very species that most people persist in planting.

I ought, perhaps, to mention what does not do quite so well with me—*viz.*, the common Norway spruce. They will grow in low-lying hollows at the rate of nearly three feet a year, but as soon as they get to about thirty feet in height they look (as my forester very aptly describes them) like red-brick chimneys among the other trees, and even if not directly exposed to the ocean gales they get red and blasted. I tried also a few *Pinus Strobus* in the peninsula, but they quite failed. I much regret not having experimented on either *Pinus Cembra* or *Pinus insignis*. I know the first named would succeed, and, as the Monterey cypress (*Cupressus macrocarpa*) does so very well, I should have the best of hopes of the Monterey pine also, because they both come, I am told, from the same locality in California.

My latest craze is cutting out spaces, enclosing them with six-foot fences (deer, roe, and rabbit proof), and planting them with nearly every rare exotic tree and shrub which I hear succeeds in Devon, Cornwall, and the West of Ireland. I think I may venture to say that I have been fairly successful, and nothing would give me greater pleasure than to have a visit of inspection from some of the members of the Royal Horticultural Society. I fear I must confess to feelings of exultation when I visit that charming collection in the temperate house of Kew, and assure myself that I can grow a great many of its contents better in the open air, in the far north, than they can be grown at Kew under glass.

What a proud and happy day it was for me, about fourteen years ago, when Mr. Bean of Kew honoured me with a visit, and I had the pleasure of showing him my Tricuspidarias, Embothriums, and Eucryphias, my small trees of *Abutilon vitifolium*, my palms, loquats, Drimys, Sikkim rhododendrons, my giant Olearias, Senecios, Veronicas, Leptospernums, my Metrosideros and Mitrarias, etc. I have, too, some of the less common varieties. One of them is a nice specimen of *Podocarpus Totara*, from which the Maoris used to make their war canoes holding one hundred men, and I have *Dicksonia antarctica*, raised from spores ripened in Arran. My *Cordyline australis* are all from seed ripened at Scourie, in the north of Sutherland. The *Billardiera longifolia*, from Tasmania, with its wonderful blue berries, is a most striking climber. *Acacia dealbata*, the Antarctic beech, *Betula Maximowiczii* from Japan (with leaves as big as those of the lime), the New Zealand Rata, and *Buddleia Colvillei* from the Himalayas, are all flourishing, thanks to the Gulf Stream and lots of peat and shelter. There are (as I suppose must be the case everywhere) a very few plants which are not happy here, and they are varieties which I dare say most people would have thought would revel in this soil and climate—*viz.*, the Wistarias, Camellias, Kalmias, Euonymus, Tamarix, and Cyclamens. I hope to master even these in course of time. One thing I wonder at is why so many of my exotics seed themselves far more freely than any natives, except perhaps birch, and gorse, and broom, though I ought perhaps to mention that neither gorse nor broom is indigenous to this particular district. The strangers which seed so freely are Rhododendrons, *Cotoneaster Simonsii, Berberis Darwinii, Veronica salicifolia, Olearia macrodonta, Diplopappus chrysophyllus*, and *Leycesteria formosa*.

And now I venture to say something about the garden—the "kitchen garden," as my English friends always take care to call it. As is often the case with us Highlanders, I possess only the one garden for fruit, flowers, and vegetables, and, as I have already stated, it was mostly made out of an old sea-beach, which most people would say does not sound hopeful. Even now, in spite of a wall and a good sea-bank, the Atlantic threatens occasionally to walk in at its lower doors, and the great northern divers, who float about lazily just outside, appear quite fascinated by the brilliant colours inside, when the lower doors are left open for their benefit.

The soil of this old sea-beach was a four-foot mixture of about three-parts pebbles and one part of rather nice blackish earth. The millions of pebbles had to be got rid of. So in deep trenching it, digging forks were mostly used, every workman had a girl or boy opposite him, and the process of hand-picking much resembled the gathering of a very heavy crop of potatoes in a field. The cost of the work was great, as thousands upon thousands of barrow-loads of small stones had to be wheeled into the sea, and the place of the pebbles made up with endless cartloads of peaty stuff from old turf dykes, red soil carted from long distances, and a kind of blue clay marl from below the sea, full of decayed oyster-shells and crabs and other good things, hauled up at very low tides. There is also a terrace the whole length of the garden cut out of the face of a steep brae, which was just above the old beach. It had to be carved out of the solid gravel and covered with soil brought from afar. The cutting at the top was fully twelve feet deep, and against it a retaining wall was built, which I covered with fan and cordon trained fruit-trees.

When the cutting was first made we found a number of large holes or burrows going deep into the hillside. These, we were convinced by the various signs we found, must have been inhabited in prehistoric times by a colony of badgers, and no sooner was the light let into these galleries than up came a thick crop of raspberry seedlings, as far in as the light could penetrate. It appeared evident that the badgers, like bears, had been keen on fruit, and had made their dessert off wild raspberries, and that the eating and digestion of the fruit had not prevented the seeds from germinating. This is the case nowadays with the seeds of *Berberis Darwinii*, which the birds swallow and then distribute all over the place. There were no signs of any wild raspberries about here at that time, but the sight of them encouraged me greatly, and I thought that where wild rasps, as we call them, once grew, tame rasps could be made to grow. My expectations in this respect have been fully justified. I think I may say that my garden, which took me three or four years to make, has most thoroughly rewarded me for all the trouble and expense incurred.

In good years, as many of my friends can testify, I grew Bon Chrétien pears on standards which are as luscious as any that could be bought in Covent Garden Market. Curiously, they were always better on the standards than on the walls. Alas! last year, which was the very worst year I have experienced since my garden was made, they were, as my gardener expressed it, not equal to a good swede turnip. I have had excellent Doyenne de Comice pears and Cox's Orange Pippin apples on my walls, and masses of plums of all sorts both on the walls and on standards. There is one thing I may mention, which I hardly suppose even my friends in the south can boast of—*viz.*, that I have never yet, in over forty years, failed to have a crop of apples, and, I might almost add, pears and plums as well, though the quality varies a good deal. Really our difficulty is that we have not force sufficient to get them thinned, so thickly do they set, a fact which I suppose must be credited to our good Gulf Stream.

Now I turn to the flowers, and I think almost anything that will grow in Britain will grow with me. I was once in a garden in a warm corner of the Isle of Wight in June, when my hostess and I came upon the gardener carrying big plants of Agapanthus in tubs from under glass to be placed out of doors. His remark as we passed him was, "I think, my lady, we may venture them out now," and I could not refrain from answering the old man back: "If not, then I do not think much of your climate, for in the far North of Scotland we never house them, nor even protect them in winter." I have had great clumps of Agapanthus in the open for thirty years and more, and the white, as well as the blue variety, flowers magnificently every year.

Ixias are as hardy a perennial here as daffodils. *Crocosmia imperialis* runs about my shrubbery borders and comes up with its glorious orange blooms in October in all kinds of unexpected places, just like twitch grass; *Alstrœmeria psittacina*, *Scilla peruviana*, *Crinum capense*, the Antholyzas, and several Watsonias (including even the lovely white *Watsonia Ardernei*), are quite hardy, and *Habranthus pratensis* also blooms every year; and as for lilies, I have had *Lilium giganteum* ten feet high and with nineteen blooms on it.

We never lift our scarlet lobelias, nor our blue *Salvia patens* (except when shifting them), and the dahlias are often quite happy left out all winter. I have never happened to come across *Schizostylis coccinea* anywhere else equal to what I grow here in November; one can see its masses of dazzling scarlet on my terrace from a boat sailing about in the bay.

Tigridias live out all the year. Some seasons they even seed themselves profusely, and I have seen the seedlings coming up thick in the gravel walks. In a good July I have seen the tea-roses on my lower terrace wall almost as good as on the Riviera, but the hybrid perpetuals do decidedly less well here, I think, than they do, for instance, in Hertfordshire, and florists' Anemones and Ranunculus and also the Moutan Pæony have so far nearly defied me. On some of my lower walls I grow the Correas, and *C. alba* blooms the whole winter through and is most charming. Callistemons (scarlet bottle-brush) flower, and *Cassia corymbosa*, *Habrothamnus elegans*, and Romneya, seem quite happy; *Akebia quinata*, Lapageria, and *Mandevilla suaveolens* are growing, but have not yet bloomed with me.

Just one more remark, and that is about our rainfall. This is supposed to be a very wet part of the country, but, according to my gardener, who keeps his rain-gauge very carefully, we had under 55 inches in 1907, whereas there are places in Britain where the fall is 130 and even 140 inches.[1]

[1] The average annual rainfall for our district from 1901 to 1933 was 57 inches. The driest year was 1933 with 45 inches and the wettest 1903 with 68 inches.—EDITOR.

CHAPTER XIX

THE INVEREWE POLICIES (2)

by the Editor, M. T. SAWYER

SINCE my father's death, three years after this book was originally published, a quarter of a century has passed, and so many things have happened in the garden which I inherited from him that it may be of interest to add some further notes on the subject. During that time I have tried as best I could to cherish his wonderful collection and to augment it in the way I feel he would have done had he been alive.

One of the most striking things about the garden and a great source of encouragement and inspiration to me, has been the steadily increasing number of people who visit Inverewe. In spite of our remoteness and the shortage of petrol, they still manage to come, and in the summer of 1948 there were over 700 visitors.

It always gives me an inward pleasure that my father and I should have been able to give such enjoyment to people. What better memorial could a man leave behind than this little oasis of peace and interest, snuggling down between the Atlantic and bare rocky hills?

Walking round with some New Zealand officers in 1945, I noticed their amazement at seeing Tree Ferns (*Dicksonia antarctica*) 11 feet high, and Club Palms (*Cordyline*) 20 feet high, so reminiscent of their homeland. And they were equally admiring of the Griselinias and Olearias, which they said they had never seen so large at home.

As he stood above the Water Garden, one of the officers suddenly stopped and remarked, "Say, chum, that makes one feel homesick," and, pointing to a sheet of cream waving plumes of the Pampas Grass (*Arundo conspicua*), he turned to me and said, "Down there is what the Maoris call 'Toetoe.'" Then, taking out his knife, he shaped carefully a huge leaf of New Zealand Flax

(*Phormium tenax*) and threw it right over the ponds and bamboos until it nearly reached the sea, far away below.

In the same way, Australians, visiting at the end of the war, were much attracted by *Clianthus puniceus*, which is so like the Glory Pea of their continent; scarlet Bottle Brush (*Metrosideros*) and, above all, the different Eucalyptus trees. Some of these trees are over 90 feet high, and they begged branches to dry and burn in the way they do at home. "Say," they asked, "why is the little Koala bear not here?"

South Africans, too, have marvelled at the *Phygelius capensis* and *Schizostylis coccinea* (Kaffir lily), which are quite as prosperous here as along the banks of streams in their native Natal; or as scarlet, flame, mauve and white Watsonias, *Agapanthus* and *Dierama pulcherrima* at the Cape.

In this corner of Western Ross so many New Zealand, Chilean and Australian plants are quite happy. *Calceolaria violacea*, a delicate little mauve-flowered shrub from Chile, has been flourishing for many years. And again it seems strange that *Dianella tasmanica*, with its beautiful turquoise blue berries, should thrive and increase as much as Couch Grass in a climate of mist and rain and in a soil of peat; or that one of the most exquisite plants here, the giant Forget-me-not (*Myosotidium nobile*), should prosper so far from its native home in the Chatham Islands, off the east coast of New Zealand. I was given two diminutive plants some fifteen years ago, and for a long time they only just existed. Then one day I happened to read an article in *The Times* by a sailor who had recently landed in the Chatham Islands. He related how he had been amazed to find plants growing on the shores all amongst rotten seaweed and carcases of sharks, with large, vivid green rhubarb-like leaves and huge heads of brilliant blue Forget-me-not flowers. I realised that this must be none other than *Myosotidium nobile*, and I quickly bedded my small plants with seaweed off the adjacent shore; but I had no dead sharks. The ebb, however, leaves herring fry behind and so I collected pails-full and gave the plants an ample top dressing. I now have large beds which are a great sight when in full flower. The plants even seed themselves quite naturally.

In the previous chapter my father cites about ten shrubs which seeded themselves. A great many more do now, all amongst the Heather and Bracken. Some of the wild species of Rhododendrons which seed freely here are: *decorum, ambiguum, arboreum, Griffithianum, barbatum, campylocarpum, cinnabarinum, eximium, Falconeri, fictolacteum, sino-grande, sutchuenense, Thomsoni, neriiflorum, yunnanense* and *niveum*. Further shrubs which seed easily are: *Myrtus Luma*, several kinds of Eucalyptus, Griselinia, *Drimys, Plagianthus Lyalli, Pernettya*, several kinds of *Olearia, Pittosporum, Eucryphia glutinosa* and *Tricuspidaria lanceolata* (sometimes called *Crinodendron Hookerianum*), originally discovered one hundred years ago on the island of Chiloe off Chile and resplendent in May and June with its rose-crimson lanterns. Amongst these shrubs some have achieved unusually large dimensions, *Eucryphia* being 27 feet high and covering 84 feet, with *Tricuspidaria* 26 feet high and covering 93 feet. The Tree Ferns (*Dicksonia antarctica*), so admired by the New Zealanders, are good seeders too, although many of the young ones succumbed during the frost of 1947.

During the past eighteen years Camellias have done well here and bloom freely. They seem to do best in rather open, exposed places and are very partial to a good top dressing of old manure in winter. That great gardening authority, Lord Aberconway, motored many miles about fifteen years ago to see one *Magnolia stellata*. It was 26 feet high and spread to a circumference of 69 feet. He said that, as far as he knew, it was the largest existing specimen; and it is much larger now.

There are several other Magnolias, but they never bloomed very freely until I began to give them all the wood ash I could secure. There was no more trouble once the potash deficiency had been made good. The huge *Magnolia Campbellii* celebrated its thirtieth birthday six years back by displaying one immense bloom right on the top. The next year it produced eleven blooms; then it had none and in the fourth year it bore thirty or forty. They made a grand show on its leafless boughs against a blue March sky.

Whether any other treatment would have been as effective I do not know, but in a recent autumn I buried a huge wildcat, which had removed a hen and her seven well-grown chickens in one night, under a *Buddleia asiatica* which had ceased to bloom altogether and was three parts dead. The effect was electric and the following year it bore a profusion of blooms and has never looked back since.

The Fir and Larch trees serve as useful hosts to shrubs which climb up their trunks and branches: *Billardiera longiflora*, with its sapphire berries, *Berberidopsis corallina*, *Clematis Armandii*, *Lonicera Heckrotti* and *heterophylla* and *Passiflora coerulea*. One *Hydrangea petiolaris* has climbed 50 feet up a larch tree and is a wonderful sight when in flower.

Hydrangeas ramp here in all shades as they are growing in peat full of iron. One gets that intense prussian blue and then in November and December they gradually turn the most beautiful ultramarine. A point of interest is that, after the Hydrangeas have absorbed the iron in the peat, usually a matter of eight or nine years, they slowly assume a paler and paler shade until fresh peat is given to them.

Palms, the Chusan *Trachycarpus Fortunei*, seem to do well, some being 15 feet high. Round one was a large clump of *Philesia buxifolia*. Some years ago it took root in the hairy trunk of the palm, and is now 6 feet up; its huge rose, wavy trumpets looking beautiful hanging down the palm trunk. I have tried *Phœnix canariensis* but so far have failed.

Droughts, as can be imagined, are seldom much worry to us, but we do sometimes have terrible gales and, in spite of the Gulf Stream, very occasional strong frosts. In 1946–1947, the worst winter I have known, we had upwards of 25° and some of the very old, big *Olearia semidentata* were killed, as were some of the *Clianthus*. What struck me as so extraordinary in that winter was the way the Ling heather of the hills and moors was withered, while *Erica mediterranea, arborea* and *australis* never looked better.

Another strange thing was that in places *Rhododendron ponticum* was killed and hybrids blackened, whilst *Rhododendron fragrantissimum, Dalhousiae* and *Rhododendron zeylanicum* from Ceylon, came out unscathed. It should be mentioned that this hardiness of the species and vulnerability of the hybrids was not in any way due to protection or exposure, because the damaged and un-damaged shrubs were to be found close together. In the previous chapter it will be remembered my father also noticed the same symptoms as between foreign and native trees.

I have often pondered over the effects of that severe frost and wondered why Heather and Brooms were badly hit, leaving the more delicate, imported shrubs untouched. I think perhaps the reason was that the hardest frosts in February and March were preceded by a milder spell than is usual in January, and it may well have been that the sap failed to rise so quickly at that time in the imported shrubs as it did in the others. Hence, when the frost arrived, it took a heavier toll of the second category than of the first.

Another effect of the frost was the damage inflicted by voles, which gnawed and ring-barked some *Syringa* (Lilacs) 2 feet up and a *Cordyline*. But in my larder I had some deer fat, no longer suitable for cooking purposes, so I smeared it thickly round the ringed trunks of the lilac trees. That was three years ago, and, although the trees seemed to have had their supplies of sap completely severed by the voles, they are now recovering and look like blooming once again.

I have only been able to give a few brief notes on the garden in this chapter, but I hope one day it may be possible to publish a fuller description of the trees, shrubs and plants which favour our temperate climate, nearly in latitude 58°. Their existence here would not be possible without the loving care bestowed on them by my gardeners, and I think it fitting to close the chapter with a word about four of these friends.

Old Donald Grant, who was with my father for nearly sixty years, is now dead. There is a stone to his memory in our "Peace Plot," which was planted just after the first world war. Robert Campbell, who had charge of the kitchen garden, is also dead. We were indeed lucky in the choice of their successors. Kenneth John Urquhart and Murdo Cameron have spent over forty years with us and have as great an interest in the trees and shrubs as I have myself. Murdo is a son of Alexander Cameron, the Tour-naig Bard, who was our Sheep Manager for over thirty years.

CHAPTER XX

VANISHING BIRDS

THIS is a sad subject to take up, but, alas! I fear it cannot be disputed that birds of many, if not of most, kinds are far less numerous now on the west coast of Ross-shire than they were fifty or sixty years ago.

Let me start with the game birds. The Black Grouse is a bird of the past as far as this part of the country is concerned. Even on my small property I used to kill from twenty to thirty brace of Black Game in a season. In 1915, as far as I know, only one pair remained, but the old Grey-hen was shot by accident, and the cock, which was a very old acquaintance, disappeared. When I bought this estate there had been no cultivation of the arable land for some fifty years at least, and there was not a vestige of wood on the 12,000 acres, except one small patch of low, scrubby birch. Now all the arable land is cultivated, and there are a number of plantations dotted over the property of from fifty to three or four years' growth, which anyone would have thought ought to have encouraged Black Game, but even in parts of Argyll, which a few years ago was swarming with them, they are now comparatively few. I know of one place in that country where, in 1914, 250 Black-cock were killed, and in 1916 the total bag of Black Game was one Black-cock. Along the shores of Loch Maree my mother once counted sixty Black-cock on the stooks of a very small field, and the old farmer, to whom the patch of oats belonged, told her he had counted one hundred the previous evening. The keeper on that beat told me quite lately that along the whole loch-side, a stretch of country of from twelve to fourteen miles, he knows of only one Black-cock.

When I was a small boy in the 'fifties I used to follow the head-keeper, whose duty it was to provide game for the larder; on the low ground round the head of Loch Gairloch the bags used to consist of Black Game, Partridges, and Brown Hares; now there is not a single head of Black Game, nor a Partridge, nor even a Brown Hare to be found. From Cape Wrath, I may say, to the Clyde the Partridges are extinct, or very nearly so. They used to be fairly plentiful up and down this west coast, and quite good in many parts of Skye and Argyll, and even here, with only little bits of arable land, I have killed as many as fifty brace in a season in the 'sixties and 'seventies. No one can account for their disappearance, and though they have been reintroduced on various occasions, the restocking has been of no avail.

Though Red Grouse have not done very well on this coast for the last few years, there are still enough on some parts to replenish it if we could get a few good breeding seasons. Both north and south of us, however, I hear very ominous reports of districts where big bags were once made—in some cases about nine hundred brace used to be the bag—but where now there are practically none. Similar reports come from some of the inland portions of Inverness-shire and from many of the islands, from Islay right up to the Lews, where it is feared Grouse-shooting will soon be a thing of the past.

I have a record of all the game killed on a property on the west coast from 1866 to 1916. In the 'seventies (1872) 1,939 Grouse were shot, and 1,244 and 1,356 were killed in 1890 and 1891. Since then they have gone down and down till they got to 98, 90, 85, 62, and only 31 in 1914. The Black Game on the same estate used to average about 80, but now they run from 1 to 3 on an average for a season. The Ptarmigan used to be from 59, 47, and 55 each year, and after coming down as low as 4 they seem quite to have disappeared. From many other hills that used to hold them, our own hill of about 2,600 feet included, the White Grouse has completely vanished.

The Grey Lag Goose, which we formerly considered a nuisance, especially when flocks of them devoured our young oats in spring, used to hatch out their broods in the islands of many of our lochs. They too have left us, and are not likely ever to return. We are now surprised if we see half a dozen Wild Ducks floating about on the loch opposite our windows, where formerly there used to be eighty to one hundred waiting for dusk in order to start feeding on the stubbles and potato-fields. Snipe, Golden Plover, Green Plover, Greenshank, Dunlin, and Whimbrel are on the verge of extinction. I saw only one Whimbrel in May, 1918, and they used to be in flocks resting on our shores at the migration-time. The Golden Plover has entirely changed its habits, and has become migratory. A very few come in March to breed, but instead of passing the winter in hundreds on our low grounds along the coast, and during frost and snow swarming down to our shores at ebb-tide, they now completely desert this country in September.

I have known 350 Snipe shot in a season on a neighbouring shooting only a few years ago. They bred also in considerable numbers on my own ground, and gave me a lot of sport. Now there is hardly a snipe to be seen anywhere. The Rock Pigeons, which used to provide such good practice for our guns, have also pretty well disappeared. The Great Northern Diver is becoming quite scarce, whereas it used to be common. The Redthroat is also extinct here, and the Blackthroats have ceased breeding on many a loch where they used to nest every year regularly and without fail; but there are still a few pairs about.

The rapid decrease of the Lesser Black-backed Gull is one of the most striking instances of a bird disappearing. They were wont to breed in their thousands in the islands of Loch Maree, and their eggs were quite a source of food-supply in the hungry months of May and June; now there are hardly any, and they get fewer and fewer every year, in spite of the islands being now watched and preserved. The Storm Petrel, which used to breed in large numbers in a small island in this parish, now no longer does so, and I never see a Common Guillemot on the sea, though there are still plenty of Razorbills, Puffins, and Black Guillemots about.

No Nightjars have been seen for years here, though they used in former times to fly about the gardens and nest close to my house. The Wheatear, which was formerly the commonest of all small birds on our moors, is now quite rare. The House Martin deserted us thirty or forty years ago. Prior to that they came in swarms, not only nesting under the eaves of many of the bigger houses, but also in thousands in the precipitous Tolly rock on Loch Maree. The Rooks, which used almost to darken the sky with their multitudes, and the Jackdaws are gone, for which, however, we are truly thankful.

In 1918 we had about the heaviest crop of rowanberries I have ever seen, and they remained on the trees in scarlet masses right through November and long after every leaf had fallen. In former years huge flocks of Fieldfares and Redwings came from Norway at the end of October and very quickly finished them off; this year all I saw was a tiny flock of Redwings, about a score all told, which, with the few Blackbirds, Song Thrushes, and Missel Thrushes (also in very reduced numbers), were quite unable to make any impression on the berries, which were nearly all wasted. In summer I did not see a single Ring Ouzel, neither breeding among our rocks nor later on descending with their broods to feed on our cherries and geans. Can anyone explain what has caused so many of our birds to disappear?

I have seen the following uncommon birds in the parish of Gairloch during my lifetime—*viz.*, Quail, Turtle Dove, Kingfisher, Golden Oriole, Hoopoe, Rose-coloured Pastor, Chough, Crossbill, Great Grey Shrike, Bohemian Waxwing, and Pied Flycatcher.

CHAPTER XXI

PEAT[1]

HAVING been honoured by a request from the Secretary of the Inverness Scientific Society and Field Club to write a paper, I rather reluctantly agreed, doubting my capability of producing with my pen anything sufficiently interesting to make it worth listening to; and now that I have written on "Peat," I feel as one who is not an authority on the subject, but rather as one in search of knowledge. Still, I hope that I may be the feeble means of rousing someone else more capable than myself to take up and go fully into the subject on which I write. I have often wondered why so very much energy has been expended in writing and theorising on the fundamental gneiss and the Torridon red, whereas no one seems to take any notice of the thick black layer which usually covers both these ancient rocks in this part of the country.

The American tourists profess to be always interested in what they amusingly term "the elegant ruins of the old country." Now, though my peat is undoubtedly a ruin, and a very old one, I fear I cannot exactly lay claim to its being very elegant (being certainly more useful than ornamental), but I do think it deserves to be classed among the most interesting natural phenomena of our land. Not only is the actual peat itself interesting, but still more interesting are the many objects found preserved in it. What excitement there is when in Egypt or at Pompeii there are found grains of wheat in a mummy, or well-preserved figs or walnuts are taken from under twenty feet of volcanic ash! Why should I, in my humble way, not be quite as much elated when, from the bottom of one of my bogs, I take out handfuls of hazel-nuts as perfect as the day they dropped off the trees; or, still more wonderful, when I find the peat full of countless green beetle wings, still glittering in their pristine metallic lustre, which may have

[1] A paper read at a meeting of the Inverness Scientific Society and Field Club in 1908.

been buried in these black, airtight silos before Pompeii was thought of?

To mark the manner in which the climate of our earth has changed at different periods must always be an interesting subject to the student of Nature, ancient or modern. I cannot help thinking that, if the lower strata of some of our very deepest peat-bogs were carefully examined, with the help of the microscope, etc., the botanist and entomologist would derive information which would give us some approximate idea of their age, and prove that a somewhat different vegetation covered the earth when the peat began to form, and that our country was then the abode of plants and insects (if not of still higher forms of animal life) which are either very rare or quite extinct with us now.

One bird has become extinct even in my day—*viz.*, the great auk; and what were indigenous plants are becoming extinct from various causes, chiefly, I fancy, climate. I know as a fact that, in my grandfather's time, the woods of this country were full of *Epipactis ensifolia*, a lovely white orchidaceous plant, which is so rare now that I have only twice in my lifetime seen one here though I have found them in abundance in the woods of the Pyrenees. Why has it died out? Surely it is that the climate has changed, and that it liked the hot summers of the last century, when my grandfather regularly feasted at Gairloch on ripe strawberries and cherries on the King's birthday, the 4th of June; whereas now, if he were alive, and still thought strawberries and cherries necessary for the proper keeping of the festival, he would require to shift the day to the 4th of July at least.

The green beetle wings in the peat appear to be those of the rose-beetle, which is now rather a rare insect with us, but which, judging by their débris in the peat, must have swarmed at one time, like the locusts in Egypt in the days of the plagues. Nowadays one comes across a few of them only in sunny places facing the south, but these remains have been found in dark, dank hollows, looking due north. Perhaps in the good old beetle days the climate was so hot that they chose the shade in preference.

Now as to when the peat began to form. It is evidently a postglacial deposit, because, when out deer-stalking, I notice beds of it lying on the top of ice-polished slabs of gneiss. Geologists can give us no idea of the age of the rocks, though they can tell us that some rocks are young in comparison to others. I wonder whether they can make any guess at the date when the snow and glaciers began to recede uphill from high-water mark? To look at some of the ground in the Torridon and Gairloch deer-forests, one would say that the final disappearance of the glaciers from some of their high corries could not be such a very old story, as in some places neither peat nor even plants have as yet managed to cover the slabs of glaciated rock, which have still nothing on them but carried stones and boulders of every shape and size, just as they were dropped on the slabs when the ice departed. One cannot help wondering what the climate was like when the ice began to disappear; if it was like the climate of Switzerland in the present day—hot and dry in summer, and cold and dry in winter—it would not encourage a growth of peat. If, on the contrary, it was cool and wet, it would encourage a growth of the sphagnum mosses, which I look on as the main creators of peat.

If the peat commenced to grow immediately on the departure of the ice, it would be most likely that the low grounds were then covered with Arctic plants, such as *Azalea procumbens*, *Betula nana*, *Saxifraga oppositifolia*, which our present climate has banished to the highest tops. Now, how interesting it would be if, when microscopically examined, traces of the Azalea, for instance, with its hard, twisted roots and stems, were found at the bottom of the peat-bogs at the sea-level. Last year I found quantities of yellow seeds at the base of a nine-foot cutting in the solid peat. So I sent some of them, all washed and clean, to the late Professor Dickson of Edinburgh. He showed them to my friend Mr. Lindsay, the curator of the Edinburgh Royal Botanic Gardens, and said he had come to the conclusion that some hoax had been played upon me, and that the seeds were modern and not ancient. He was then just starting on a tour to Norway, and on his return, sad to say, Professor Dickson died, and I never heard any more of my seeds. But I determined not to give up my interest in them, so the other day I began looking for the seeds again, and found them in quantities in the lowest part of the peat, where it rested on the subsoil. I had other bogs examined, and there they were also found among the compressed brown sphagnum below a great depth of solid black peat. So I sent them, this time unwashed, to my friend Mr. Lindsay, who in his reply said that at first he was in doubt as to whether they were whin or broom seeds, but on comparing them with modern seeds of both these shrubs, he had come to the conclusion that they were whin seeds. Notwithstanding my having perfect faith in Mr. Lindsay (as a botanist), I cannot take in the idea that these seeds are whin. Neither the whin nor the broom is a native plant here. One hundred years ago the only broom plants in the district were a few sown round the garden of my far-back predecessors in this place—the Mackenzies of Lochend of that day—and the first whins that ever grew anywhere near here were produced from seed sown by a certain Rev. Mr. Macrae, a minister on the Poolewe glebe, and some sown also by a member of the Letterewe family at Udrigil. It is certain it was not an indigenous plant here in modern times, whatever it might have been in the beetle days, and there can be no doubt that the shrubs or plants which produced these seeds lived contemporaneously with the beetles.

We now find hazel, birch, alder, and willow in the most perfect state at the bottom of the bogs, with the silvery bark on the former kinds as perfect as when they were growing, but no one has found the gnarled, twisted stems of the whin or broom in any bog in this country. A most intelligent man, who has taken a very lively interest in these seeds, has put forward the theory that they may have been the seeds of the buck or bog bean which grew at one time on the bottom of shallow lochs which have since filled up; but Mr. Lindsay is not of this opinion.

There is, I think, an impression abroad that peat is a very modern growth and is quickly formed. I think this idea is quite erroneous. That it is very modern compared with our rocks is certain, but, still, I hold to the belief that our peat is a very old formation, though still growing slowly. Can anyone tell when was the Bronze Age up here? We found a perfect bronze spearhead in one of the peat-bogs, pretty near the surface, with a deer's antler lying close to it; and, to show what a preservative peat is, part of the wooden shaft of the spear was still to the fore when the spear-head was found. Now, in the days of the primitive man who owned this spear this peat-bog must have been very much what it is now, otherwise the spear would not have been so near the surface.

There was also a very valuable find of bronze antiquities in this neighbourhood a few years ago. On going to examine the place, I found that the peat was not three feet deep, showing that it had not grown much since the day when the owner had buried his treasures, as it would not be likely that he would have hidden them in a place having less than a couple of feet of peat at least. Close to my house there is a bog in a hollow, enclosed all round with a rim of rock, and on trying to drain it we found it impossible to do so without cutting the rock. We probed the peat and found it fourteen feet thick.

Usually the trees found under the peat have their roots fixed in the subsoil and their stumps are close to the bottom; but this is not always the case, for near the surface of this bog we found several immense stumps, and, on attempting to count the rings on one of the roots which we sawed off, we arrived at the conclusion that the tree was about four hundred years old when it ceased to live. Now, it is about four hundred years since my ancestors came from Kintail and took possession of Gairloch by a *coup de main*, and we know that at that time (and probably long before then) these shores had a resident population. It is therefore unlikely that these trees would have been allowed to remain standing so close to the seashore at the head of Loch Ewe for very long after the place became inhabited. Supposing these trees, then, to have been dead some five hundred years, and that they were four hundred years old when destroyed, that takes us nearly one thousand years back. Query, then how old is the lower layer of peat in the bog which lies fourteen feet below the stumps?

I have heard of a bog at Kenlochewe which was drained and improved, and in it were two distinct sets of fir roots, one above the other, with a considerable layer of peat between them. Nearly all the bog stumps in this country have marks of fire on them and charcoal about them. Now, it would seem that in this case two successive forests sprung up, grew to maturity, and were destroyed, and that between each crop of fir there had been a sufficient interregnum for the peat to form and to cover up and preserve each set of roots. It would be what the lawyers would call "a nice question" as to how many centuries the remains of the two forests and the layers of peat represent.

One must not, however, judge altogether of the age of peat by its depth. The best peat I have ever seen for burning purposes was only one foot in depth below the top sod, and had grown on blue clay, so that, as we cut the fuel, the lowest end of each peat had the clay attached to it, and turned into red bricks in the fire. These peats were nearly equal to coal, and were evidently like the Irishman's pig, very little and very old, which is much more of a merit in peat than in pigs.

I might go rambling on with my peat stories—about peat at the bottom of lochs, and submarine peat-bogs which I have seen at low spring-tides, which, I am ashamed to say, I have never thoroughly examined, and which must, at least, have the merit of being really very old; but instead of commencing anew I will stop.

Since writing the above I have been in the Lews, and I have seen there peat such as I never imagined could be found anywhere in Great Britain. On the mainland of Ross-shire it is uncommon to find peat six or eight feet deep, but between Skigersta and North Tolsta the peat for miles is from sixteen to twenty-six feet in depth.

Can any of my readers help me to fathom some of the many mysteries that lie at the bottom of our peat-bogs and lochs, which have always interested me so much? What puzzles me perhaps most of all are the stems of birch and hazel which I find six and eight feet below the surface, with the bark (especially of the former) as smooth and glistening as if the trees had been cut only the previous day; indeed, the bark of the bog birches is generally much whiter than that of the more or less stunted modern birches of this west coast, which is a purple-grey tint and quite different from the white stems of the birches along the shores of Loch Ness

—in fact, they are as snowy white as the bark of those that grow to-day in Sweden and Russia!

I quite well know what most people will say—*viz.*, that the peat is a great preservative, and that, as in the case of ensilage in a silo, decomposition has been arrested by the exclusion of atmospheric air. But I would first of all ask my readers how the birch-trees got into the bottom of these bogs. I suppose they would answer that peat grows, and that it grew round these birches and hazels, and thus preserved them, quite forgetting that peat will not grow except where it is wet, and that neither birch nor hazel will grow if the ground is at all wet. They also have, perhaps, very little idea of the delicacy of the thin, white, outer skin of the birch bark. Perhaps they imagine that if they cut down a birch or hazel tree, and laid it on the top of a peat-bog, it would gradually sink down of its own weight, or that the peat would grow up round it, and that thus the silvery bark would be preserved; but I dare say most people have also very little idea of the slowness of the growth of peat, and I may mention that this white outer skin of birch bark is just like silver paper, and would not remain attached to the stem more than a very few months, and the birch branch or stem laid on the top of the bog would turn into pulp and disappear long before the peat could grow over it to preserve it.

It might be argued that, supposing a birch-wood grew at the very foot of a mountain of, say, 2,000 to 3,000 feet high, and that the mountain was covered most of the way up with a deep bed of peat, and that, owing to an earthquake or some other inexplicable cause, the peat on the hillside began sliding down like a black avalanche and overwhelmed the birch-wood, then one would certainly quite understand the white bark on the birches being preserved. But, unfortunately, this theory is impossible, as deep peat does not form on steep mountains in a sufficient quantity to cause a landslide; and besides, where I came across the white-stemmed birches in the bogs there are no hills high enough or near enough for peat or anything else to have slipped down and covered these thousands of acres of flat moor.

Then, as regards the remains of forests at the bottom of lochs, I happen to own a great many lochs and tarns, and when boating on them, on a calm day with a clear sky, the tree-stumps can be seen side by side, just as they grew before these lochs existed. Now, how were these lochs created to the ruin of thousands of acres of forest? It would be most interesting to examine some of the deeper lochs, with an electric light appliance, to see if there are remains of forests in them as well as in the shallower ones. I dare say some people will imagine that the roots have got washed into the lochs in great floods; well, this might have happened so far as logs or branches are concerned, but the stumps I refer to are all firmly rooted in the bottom, each one just where the original grain of *Pinus sylvestris* seed fell, germinated, and grew up.